Methods in Latin Computational Linguistics

Brill's Studies in Historical Linguistics

Series Editor
Jóhanna Barðdal (*Ghent University*)

Consulting Editor
Spike Gildea (*University of Oregon*)

VOLUME 1

The titles published in this series are listed at *brill.com/bshl*

Methods in Latin Computational Linguistics

By

Barbara McGillivray

BRILL

LEIDEN | BOSTON

Library of Congress Cataloging-in-Publication Data

McGillivray, Barbara, author.
Methods in Latin computational linguistics / by Barbara McGillivray.
pages cm – (Brill's studies in historical linguistics, ISSN 2211-4904 ; v. 1)
Includes bibliographical references and index.
ISBN 978-90-04-26011-5 (hardback : alk. paper) – ISBN 978-90-04-26012-2 (e-book)
1. Latin language–Data processing. 2. Computational linguistics–Methodology. I. Title. II. Series: Brill's studies in historical linguistics ; v. 1.

PA2057.5.M37 2014
006.3'5–dc23

2013045104

This publication has been typeset in the multilingual "Brill" typeface. With over 5,100 characters covering Latin, IPA, Greek, and Cyrillic, this typeface is especially suitable for use in the humanities. For more information, please see www.brill.com/brill-typeface.

ISSN 2211-4904
ISBN 978 90 04 26011 5 (hardback)
ISBN 978 90 04 26012 2 (e-book)

This book is printed on acid-free paper.

Contents

Preface

My PhD in Computational Linguistics at the University of Pisa gave me the chance to work on various exciting research activities on automatic acquisition of verb valency structures and lexical-semantic preferences from Italian and English corpora. Given my background in Classics, I was also happy to participate in a project on extracting valency structure from Latin annotated corpora. It thus felt natural to present these explorations in my PhD dissertation. My main aim was to address Latin linguists interested in verb argument structure, and present them with some case studies highlighting the potential of computational approaches. Already then was it clear that this topic was going to challenge the traditional barriers between Computational Linguistics on the one hand and Latin Linguistics on the other.

While working on turning my dissertation into a monograph, I realized that more emphasis needed to be placed on the methodological issues that arise when applying computational methods to historical language data, and that this was a fascinating topic in itself. Computational Linguistics for historical languages has been receiving increasing attention over the past years in the Computational Linguistics community, and the use of annotated corpora is slowly becoming more and more common among historical linguists. However, so far there has not been a book that specifically addresses these topics.

One of the obstacles to this exchange between fields lies in the technical complexities that computational methods present. I tried to put myself in the place of a historical linguist who has not employed statistical techniques in her work, and, relying on my background in Mathematics, I dedicated two chapters to illustrating the main notions behind the computational and quantitative aspects of the research presented here. In this book I address computational linguists as well, showing them how their field can benefit from an investigation of the challenges presented by historical data.

Writing this book has inspired my view on the exciting change that linguistics is faced with at the present moment, which we are all experiencing as a consequence of the fast technological progress that touches many aspects of our lives. I am very pleased to have contributed to suggesting a way to face this change.

I would like to express all my gratitude to my mother for always believing in the non-canonical choices of my university carrier. Special thanks to Gard, who has enriched these years with inspiring linguistics conversations and incredible support.

List of Abbreviations

Aen.	*Aeneid*
Amph.	*Amphitruo*
Ap.	*Apocalypse*
B. G.	*De Bello Gallico*
CA	Correspondence Analysis
Caes.	Caesar
Cat.	*In Catilinam*
Cic.	Cicero
DG	Dependency Grammar
Georg.	*Georgics*
GLM	Generalized Linear Model
IQR	Interquartile Range
IT	*Index Thomisticus*
IT-TB	*Index Thomisticus* Treebank
LDT	Latin Dependency Treebank
LWN	Latin WordNet
MAD	Median Absolute Deviation
MCA	Multiple Correpondence Analysis
Men.	*Menaechmi*
Met.	*Metamorphoses*
Mostell.	*Mostellaria*
MWN	MultiWordNet
NP	Noun Phrase
Ov.	Ovid
PDT	Prague Dependency Treebank
Petron.	Petronius
Plaut.	Plautus
PoS	Part of Speech
PP	Prepositional Phrase
PV	Prefixed Verb
PWN	Princeton WordNet
Sall.	Sallust
Sat.	*Satyrica*
Sent. P. L.	*Scriptum super Sententiis Magistri Petri Lombardi*
SP	Selectional Preference
Th.	Thomas Aquinas
Verg.	Vergil

Vulg.	*Vulgate*
WN	WordNet

List of Figures

CHAPTER 1

Historical Languages, Corpora, and Computational Methods

This book explores the challenges of developing the field of Latin Computational Linguistics. My core aim is thus methodological: to show how it is possible to fruitfully combine computational methods with historical language data, particularly synchronic and diachronic data from the Latin language. This is a challenging task and very little work has been done in this direction so far. One of the reasons is that many still see an opposition between the two fields of Computational Linguistics and Latin Linguistics (and Historical Linguistics in general), which would have diverging aims and consequently different methods. For such a hypothetical opposition to hold, Computational Linguistics and Latin Linguistics should be the results of a categorization of the field of linguistics into complementary subfields, just like, say, synchronic vs. diachronic linguistics, Romance linguistics vs. Germanic linguistics, and so on. However, I believe this not to be the case.

Computational Linguistics aims at designing, implementing, and applying computational models for natural languages. This includes developing computer systems that automatically process languages (from a morphological, syntactic, semantic, or pragmatic point of view), as well as building, enriching, and using corpus data (Corpus Linguistics), and much more. Therefore, Computational Linguistics offers a series of methods that can, at least in principle, be applied to a variety of language data. Data from historical languages, however special, do not constitute a conceptual exception to this, and the innovations and adjustments required in such a transition, as well as its limitations, are the principal topics of this book.

1.1 Challenges of Latin Computational Linguistics

Rather than being two separate categories in a one-dimensional classification of linguistics, Computational Linguistics and linguistics of Latin can thus coexist as the result of a bi-dimensional categorization, where the methods chosen (first dimension) are computational and the language studied (second dimension) is Latin. This holds (at least partially) for other historical languages as well.

 | DOI: 10.1163/9789004260122_002

Why would such a combination be beneficial and why has it not been appropriately investigated before? Why is there not a particular interest in defining, say, Italian Computational Linguistics or Portuguese Computational Linguistics, and why does this book focus on defining Latin Computational Linguistics? The reason is that, when applying computational methods to research on Latin data, a number of questions and challenges arise, which are partially specific to the Latin language, its scholarly community, and the nature of its texts, and partially shared by other historical languages. What are these challenges? In this section I will give a brief overview of the main challenges which will be analytically be dealt with in the rest of the book.

Linguistic features. A large part of Computational Linguistics research has been developed for English, or at least tested on this language. Since English is an inflectionally poor language with a so-called fixed word order, many computational models developed for this language tend to pay little attention to the role played by morphology in a number of linguistic phenomena. Instead, if we try to build a computational resource or model for Latin, the morphological layer of annotation is an essential one. For this reason, it is important to resort to annotation schemas developed for other morphologically rich languages. An example is Czech, for which annotation schemas and treebanks have been created. The decision to follow existing standards developed for Czech was taken by the creators of the three Latin syntactically annotated corpora which will be presented in section 2.3.3.1. In a similar vein, when I designed the corpus-based valency lexicon presented in chapter 3, I recorded linguistic features particularly relevant for further investigations on Latin verbs; for example, the lexicon records the order of verbal arguments and their morphological features through specific patterns. These are important examples of some of the challenges researchers face when building computational resources for Latin.

Research questions, commercial applications, and academic tradition. Computational Linguistics has mostly focussed on current languages. The interest in developing computational resources and methods for the most widespread extant languages is motivated, among other things, by their applications to various areas of society with important commercial uses, such as Language Technology: computational lexicography, machine translation, speech recognition, virtual assistants, and text summarization, to name just a few examples. On the other hand Historical Linguistics has not fully explored computational approaches. The business picture for extinct languages is different from the one for current languages due to the lack of direct commercial interests. Furthermore, the nature of the linguistic investigation for historical languages with a long academic tradition like Latin displays a strong connection with the philological tradition and literary studies, and weaker links with more applied and technological disciplines. This means that the motivation behind Computational Linguistics research is in many cases driven by commercial applications, while research in Latin Linguistics often originates from theoretical questions about linguistic phenomena or their diachronic change. However, Latin (and Historical) Linguistics can benefit hugely from a computationally-oriented innovation in its methods, as I will show in his book.

Less-resourced status and data sparseness. One of the most striking differences between Latin and the modern languages for which a considerable amount of research has been done in the field of Computational Linguistics is the number of corpora, lexicons, and processing tools available. In section 2.1.1 I discuss the idea of basic resource toolkits necessary for the study of languages, as introduced by Krauwer (1998). In the case of Latin, and even more so for other historical languages, we are still quite far from reaching a complete set of resources. This means that, when possible and appropriate, a special effort needs to be invested in building annotated corpora and other resources for historical languages (such as valency lexicons like the one described in chapter 3). This is sometimes achieved by exploiting existing material and by building on research done for other languages. The lack of large computational resources for Latin has also the effect of making some of the existing computational models (which rely on large amounts of data to make statistical generalizations) difficult to apply to this language. As I explain when I explore models for automatically acquiring verbal selectional preferences from corpora in chapter 4, particular care is needed to overcome these hurdles, so as to maximize the reliability of statistical generalizations based on small datasets.

The diachronic dimension. Another essential characteristics of historical corpora is their diachronic nature. With some exceptions (like the *Index Thomisticus* Treebank, based on the works by Thomas Aquinas, see section 2.3.3.1), corpora for historical languages tend to be assembled by combining works written by different authors over different time periods. This is because the aim is often to find patterns of language change, and sometimes also because of the sparsity of the available texts. In both cases, the diachronic nature of the corpora is a complicating factor for which no definitive solution is yet available based on Computational Linguistics research on modern languages, given the typically limited time span covered by contemporary corpora.

Dealing with language data spanning over several centuries leads to a series of challenges when attempting to apply processing tools developed and tested on synchronic data. An example is LatinISE, a 13-million-word Latin corpus which I have built for the Sketch Engine (see section 2.3.2). LatinISE covers a huge time span, ranging from archaic Latin to current documents, and, in its initial development phase, was processed by the same lemmatizer and part-of-speech tagger. Similar experiments have been done on parsing various historical corpora, for which an overview is given in section 2.3.3.2. In spite of all these difficulties, spelling variation and language change present interesting challenges that can shed new light both on the limits and the potential of automatic language processing tools, as well as on the linguistic phenomena *per se*.

Native speakers. Historical languages lack native speakers. This means that the manual creation of so-called gold standard resources is more time-consuming and prone to errors than for modern languages. Gold standards for historical languages are particularly important when testing and evaluating automatic models; for example, programs that automatically give the syntactic analysis of sentences can be trained on analysed data (gold standard) before being run on raw data. Therefore, the availability of large, high-quality gold standards is particularly expensive and slow for historical languages, and represents an area where considerable progress can be made. This emphasises once more the importance of creating and annotating large corpora and language resources for historical languages.

A new view on linguistics. The challenges I have presented so far should not discourage attempts in Latin Computational Linguistics. Instead, they present a crucial chance for Latin linguistic research to move forward, as I show in this book. Computational Linguistics does not only offer a series of tools to analyse languages and provide data ready to be used for studies on linguistic phenomena. Computational Linguistics is also able to reveal new insights into the way language works, for example by confirming or contradicting theoretical intuitions about language. For instance, the so-called 'syntax-semantics interface' assumes that the semantics of verbs partially affects their syntactic behaviour (Levin, 1993). In order to test this hypothesis, computational linguists have carried out several experiments on grouping verbs into sophisticated classes based on their syntactic properties, for example their argument properties (Schulte im Walde, 2003; Lenci et al., 2008). The extent to which verb classes obtained this way share certain semantic properties can help researchers detect the properties that are relevant for verb semantics and how these properties vary across languages. Another example concerns cognitive models of language, which aim at automatically processing language by trying to mirror the way human brain works. Alishahi (2008) proposes a model for the acquisition of argument structure and selectional preferences in children. By simulating cognitive processes, computational models like Alishahi's can provide insights into the mechanisms of human language.

By using corpora as source of evidence for processing language and creating other linguistic resources, Computational Linguistics naturally promotes a *quantitative* view on language data. The traditional, so-called qualitative approach involves a manual inspection and analysis of corpus data or single examples. Quantitative approaches employ statistical techniques to analyse corpus data; I give an example of this in chapter 6 on Latin preverbs. Computational linguists greatly prefer quantitative methods over qualitative ones, because of their flexibility and their ability to handle large amounts of data, as well as their suitability to automatic processing tools. This opens up a whole new series of research questions and answers that would not even be conceivable with a qualitative view alone.

To sum up, Computational Linguistics is not just a series of tools to produce new and richer data available for linguistic analyses; it also implements a new way of looking at language. By introducing this new way to investigate Latin, this book promotes a radical methodological innovation in Latin Linguistics.

A growing interest. Computational Historical Linguistics is receiving increasing attention within the Computational Linguistics community. Several conferences in this field have started to give space to workshops dedicated to the challenges of historical data: for example, the Northern European Association for Language Technology hosted a workshop devoted to Computational Historical Linguistics in 2013.[1] Addressing a larger audience than the Computational Linguistics one, language technology for ancient languages has gained interest in the research community for Cultural Heritage applications, as attested by several initiatives, including the LaTeCH (Language Technology for Cultural Heritage, Social Sciences, and Humanities) workshop organized within several Computational Linguistics and Artificial Intelligence conferences over the past years.[2] On a similar note, research in Digital Humanities adopts Natural Language Processing methods to analyse the growing amount of digital material available in the Humanities. An excellent overview of this field is offered by Piotrowski (2012).

1 http://spraakbanken.gu.se/eng/nodalida-chl-ws-2013.

2 See, for example, http://sighum.science.ru.nl/latech2013/.

Why Latin? Even if most of the aspects mentioned above affect historical languages in general, in this book I will focus on Latin as the test case for my argumentation, and will give attention to the specific features of Latin Computational Linguistics. This choice has a number of reasons. First of all, the amount of textual material available for Latin is large enough to allow some generalizations based on quantitative considerations. Moreover, Latin happens to be in a fortunate position among extinct languages thanks to the availability of a considerable number of texts in electronic format, enriched with morpho-syntactic information. This has allowed me to build on such collections of texts and create new resources. Latin thus offers an ideal testbed for the application of computational methods to extinct languages, which can be extended to other, less-resourced languages. The primary goal of the research material I present here is to support this argumentation.

1.2 Promoting Corpora and Computational Methods

A crucial aspect of a fruitful exchange between the disciplines of Latin Linguistics and Computational Linguistics concerns the way Latin texts are collected, accessed, and investigated for linguistic analyses. So, any attempt into Latin Computational Linguistics is likely to start from corpora.

Linguists can rely on native speakers' intuitions for their studies on extant languages. In the case of historical languages like Latin, access to linguistic judgements by native speakers is impossible; this has justified the recourse to textual evidence throughout the history of Latin Linguistics (and Historical Linguistics and philology in general). Traditionally, linguistic evidence has been collected either by looking directly at editions of original works, or indirectly by referring to resources like dictionaries, thesauri, and lexicons. However, starting from the mid 20th century, linguists have been collecting large amounts of texts in more structured units called *electronic corpora*. Of all languages, Latin played a crucial role at the very beginning of this process, with the development of the first electronic corpus, the *Index Thomisticus* (Busa, 1980). Since then, corpora for a number of languages have come on the scene and have been used as a basis for linguistic investigations.

Several digital editions of texts are nowadays available to the scientific community working on Latin. Examples of such editions are: the Perseus Digital Library (10 million words, Bamman and Crane 2008),[3] the Library of Latin Texts

3 http://www.perseus.tufts.edu.

(Centre Traditio Litterarum Occidentalium 2010, more than 50 million words), and the Bibliotheca Teubneriana Latina (CETEDOC 1999, 10 million words). Such raw text corpora, together with the possibility of inspecting concordances (i.e. word forms in their context, typically displayed as a given number of characters to the left and the right of each target word), provide important information on the distribution of word forms in a text. This allows linguists to do things they have done in the past (like analysing language synchronically and diachronically), but more efficiently, because large text collections available in electronic format can be more easily searched and provide more data than samples collected for individual studies. However, raw text corpora do not allow for more advanced explorations. For example, we cannot automatically search for the contexts of all word forms of a given lemma (such as all inflections of the lemma *puella* 'girl'), syntactic roles (such as all subjects of *fero* 'bring'), or all words semantically related to a given word (such as all synonyms of *domus* 'house'). The solution is to encode this information in the text through *annotation*.

1.2.1 *Corpus Annotation*

Annotation provides each word form in a sentence with one or more labels that mark its attributes; for example, a morpho-syntactic annotation would add a 'genitive' tag to *puellarum* (genitive plural of *puella* 'girl'). Traditionally, in a linguistic study, whenever a scholar refers to the presence or distribution of a word, construction, or attribute in certain texts, the assumption is that she has analysed them, based on certain criteria, in order to obtain evidence for her theoretical statements. Annotated corpora are often public, and manual annotation is performed by expert annotators (in the best cases there is more than one annotator, to ensure more reliable results), within a clearly identified theoretical framework. This allows linguists to perform more accurate analyses based on data which have been independently collected and analysed.

If we want to go beyond collecting evidence for a single, small-scale study, and aim at annotating large corpora, the manual procedure quickly becomes less and less feasible. This is where Computational Linguistics can help. Among other things, Computational Linguistics aims at developing tools that automatically process languages: Natural Language Processing (NLP) tools. These tools can be used to automatically annotate corpora. Automatic annotation can be combined with manual annotation into semi-automatic annotation, so that the automatic output can be further manually checked and corrected. Over the past years, semi-automatically annotated Latin corpora have become available to the scientific community. For what concerns morpho-syntactic annotation, three corpora (treebanks) have appeared: the Latin Dependency

Treebank (LDT, 53,000 words; Bamman and Crane 2006), the *Index Thomisticus* Treebank (IT-TB, 138,000 words; Passarotti 2007b), and the PROIEL Project treebank (90,000 words; Haug and Jøndal 2008).

This book advocates the use of corpora in Latin Linguistics by reporting on research based on Latin treebanks, to show their potential for Historical Linguistics research. On the one hand, treebanks allow Latin linguists to perform analyses they have always performed, but in a more efficient way; on the other hand, treebanks make it possible to perform new analyses and build new and larger resources. For example, the morpho-syntactic annotation of the first two treebanks I mentioned above (LDT and IT-TB) has allowed me to create a fully corpus-based valency lexicon for Latin verbs (chapter 3).

1.2.2 *The Less-Resourced Status of Latin*

The corpus-based valency lexicon presented in chapter 3 is the first computational resource of this kind for Latin. As such, it fills a substantial gap in the state of the art, given the fact that Latin is considered a less-resourced language from a computational point of view; see Passarotti (2010) for an in-depth discussion on this topic. This is particularly striking if we compare the number and size of Latin annotated corpora and resources with those available for extant languages. For example, the English WordNet (Miller et al., 1990)—a lexical-semantic database containing a large part of the English lexicon organized in synonym sets—consists of 155,000 lemmas, more than ten times as many as Latin WordNet (Minozzi, 2009). Further, a syntactically annotated corpus for English, the Penn Treebank (Marcus et al. 1993; 2.9 million words) is several orders of magnitude larger than the Latin treebanks.

As anticipated at the beginning of this chapter, the availability of English resources can be exploited to speed up the process of building new resources for Latin. Moreover, the existing language-independent computational models already developed for modern languages can be adapted to the case of Latin, although this is not at all a straightforward operation, given the linguistic peculiarities of Latin and the special philological and literary interests surrounding Latin data. I have chosen this hybrid approach based on existing models in my research on verbal selectional preferences for Latin, i.e. the kind of lexical preferences verbs have on their arguments (e.g. FOOD for the objects of *eat*), reported on in chapter 4. Because this is among the first models adapted to the automatic acquisition of semantic information from Latin annotated corpora, this work offers a methodological reference for the Computational Linguistics community as well.

1.2.3 *Quantitative Latin Corpus Linguistics*

In this book I will show how Latin corpora can be used not only to build lexical resources like valency lexicons or to acquire semantic information like selectional preferences, but also to carry out studies on a variety of linguistic phenomena, and find new results. Corpora (and especially annotated ones) are extremely valuable as a direct basis for diachronic and synchronic research in Latin Linguistics, since they provide the scientific community with large amounts of texts in a standardized format. This makes it possible to carry out quantitative corpus-based studies that are replicable, adding a high degree of scientific integrity to them. Unfortunately, such quantitative corpus-based studies in Latin Linguistics are still a very rare event.

Even when corpus data are used in mainstream linguistics, they are usually subject to manual inspection and analysis: the researcher typically collects a sample of texts specifically chosen for that research, and analyses them on a case-by-case basis. The only quantitative data provided are sometimes absolute or relative frequencies (i.e. percentages), very rarely tested for significance. Such qualitative approaches do not give the full picture of a phenomenon in a large corpus. This is why quantitative approaches employing statistical techniques are ideal for detecting broad trends in the data; they are also very good for giving an account of corpus size and significance issues, allowing the researchers to quantify the role played by different factors in a complex dataset.

The corpus-based quantitative study on Latin preverbs I describe in chapter 6 will give me the chance to apply a quantitative approach and advanced multivariate statistics techniques to a very interesting topic in Latin morpho-syntax (preverbs), and is the first one that systematically quantifies the interplay of different diachronic, genre, and linguistic factors on this topic.

1.3 Audience

The audience addressed here includes computational linguists and Latin linguists, as well as the small but growing category of Latin computational linguists, of course. The first group will have a chance to be introduced to an overview of the challenges involved in applying Computational Linguistics to the Latin language, and to concrete examples of solutions adopted to face such challenges. These solutions can then be properly considered when approaching other historical and/or less-resourced languages with computational methods.

Latin computational linguists will find a series of research results that are placed at the state of the art of their field: the valency lexicon described in chapter 3, the selectional preference model in chapter 4, and the statistical analysis of chapter 6.

Finally, Latin linguists will benefit from being exposed to three concrete examples of original Computational Linguistics research involving Latin data, as well as a more detailed illustration of the techniques used (chapters 5 and 7). The three pieces of research presented as case studies (valency lexicon, selectional preference model, and investigation on preverbs) aim at showing the methodological contribution of this work. What Latin linguists will not find here is, of course, a traditional study, which falls outside the scope of this book. In other words, they should not expect to find the illustration of a specific linguistic phenomenon, followed by the choice of a theoretical framework, the selection of texts, a report on the manual analysis of these texts, and finally an interpretation of the results based on the manual analysis and aimed at confirming or rejecting the previously chosen theory. The reasons for that lie in the methodological scope of this book, as well as in the new research paradigm I offer here.

1.4 A New Paradigm

In addition to the merits of computational resources and models, and quantitative corpus methods, in this book I would like to stress the benefits of a *collaborative* approach to research. In this approach a researcher builds on resources and models previously created by others by adding new contributions in the form of: new layers of annotation (for example syntactic annotation of an existing morphologically annotated corpus), new resources (such as the valency lexicon I present in chapter 3), or new applications of existing models or techniques (like the selectional preference model applied to Latin data in chapter 4, or the study on preverbs in chapter 6).

If I had followed a traditional paradigm, I would have chosen a set of Latin texts for illustrating a theoretical point, and thus I would have created a small corpus with a possibly idiosyncratic annotation specifically designed for the theoretical framework and the phenomenon under study, and, probably, not directly comparable with other studies. Instead, I chose to start from large (or the largest available), richly annotated corpora that already exist and were built based on a shared set of annotation guidelines under the theoretical framework of Dependency Grammar, which is at the present time the standard framework for treebanks. The contribution of this work lies in the variety of methods I have applied to these corpus data, which range from subcategorization extraction to lexicon building, automatic lexical acquisition, and quantitative corpus research. This way, I aim to show that the field can move forward based on collaborative efforts.

1.5 Corpora and Language

In this book I will refer to two Latin treebanks (the LDT and the IT-TB), containing works by a number of different authors, partially covering the Classical era and the Medieval era. This is the source of linguistic data I used for building a valency lexicon and acquiring verbs' selectional preferences, as well as for carrying out the corpus study on Latin preverbs. It is thus important to define here the scope of this research by discussing my point of view on the relation between corpora and the Latin language.

McEnery and Wilson (2001, 32) define a corpus as “a finite-sized body of machine-readable text, sampled in order to be maximally representative of the language variety under consideration”. From a corpus we naturally expect to be able to generalize the information contained in it to the language as a whole. Consequently, corpus-based studies aim at describing a larger portion of language than that included in the corpora themselves. In statistical terms, this larger portion of language is called a *population*, and a *sample* is the subset of the population providing the data evidence for the analysis.

Two criteria to evaluate the suitability of a corpus (seen as a sample) for a linguistic analysis are its size and its content. First, the number of observations that are in the population, but are not captured by the sampling procedure (usually called ‘unseen events’) decreases as the size of the sample grows. Second, a still popular criterion for a good selection of texts in a corpus is the notion of *representativeness*: ideally, a representative corpus accounts for the whole range of variability in the features of a language. Some scholars have linked the degree to which a corpus is representative of the general variety of a language with it being *balanced* from the point of view of the chronological period of the texts, genre, modality, domain, etc.

In spite of the efforts to build balanced and representative corpora, representativeness is an ideal limit and all corpora show a certain degree of arbitrariness (Lenci et al., 2005, 41). If we see corpora as a sample from a sublanguage, any model of these data will generalize over the whole population through estimates, and will consequently contain some uncertainty. In this perspective, any choice of the linguistic sample is bound to be improvable, thus no choice is perfect. We can then turn the focus from an absolute value of representativeness to a measure quantifiable in statistical terms and hence translate the question of the goodness of the sample into the following:

TABLE 1.1 *Composition of the corpora used in this book by author: dates of birth and death of the author, literary age, genre, and number of word tokens*

Corpus	Author	Time	Age	Genre	Word tokens
Plautus	Plautus	ca. 254–184 BC	early republic	comedy	17,011
LDT	Cicero	106 BC – 43 BC	late republic	rhetoric	6,229
↓	Caesar	100 BC – 44 BC	late republic	historiography	1,488
	Sallust	86–34 BC	late republic	historiography	12,311
	Vergil	70 BC – 19 BC	Augustan	epic	2,613
	Propertius	ca. 50–ca. 15 BC	Augustan	elegy	4,857
	Ovid	43 BC – 17/18 AD	Augustan	epic	4,789
	Petronius	ca. 27–66 AD	imperial	novel	12,474
	Jerome	ca. 347–420 AD	late imperial	religious	8,382
IT	Thomas Aquinas	ca. 1225–1274 AD	medieval	theology	54,878
TOTAL					108,021

How much uncertainty is it possible to remove from the data?

The answer to this question lies in a quantitative approach to Corpus Linguistics, which is one of the goals of this book. As I show in chapter 6, statistical modeling and data exploration techniques such as regression analysis aim at reducing and quantifying the degree of uncertainty present in the data. As a preliminary methodological conclusion, I could say that, in addition to choosing the corpora so that they are as representative as possible of the sublanguage under study, the statistical techniques should be chosen in such a way that uncertainty is maximally reduced in the data and it is as safe as possible to generalize the results to the whole population.

How does all this apply to the corpora I used? Table 1.1 records the composition of the corpora I used in terms of the number of tokens, alongside chronological and genre details.

From this table we can classify the data into six literary periods and eight genres spread over 10 authors. The chronological gaps between Petronius, Jerome, and Thomas are substantial compared with the relative homogeneity observed for the other authors. Moreover, the number of tokens is considerably higher in Thomas than in all the other authors. These observations lead us to conclude that these corpora are not a balanced sample by genre and era. However, the statistical techniques I have chosen are able to accurately assess the impact of this imbalance. In addition, there are further methodological and pragmatic reasons to believe that the choice of the corpora is good, given the practical circumstances of this investigation, as I will discuss now.

1.5.1 *Which Latin?*

I have been discussing the issues related to the features of a good corpus, and how statistics allows us to generalize from a sample to the whole population. The next question concerns defining this population, i.e. *what* a corpus of Latin is supposed to be representative of. Generally speaking, we expect a corpus-based study of Latin to aim at offering a (possibly new) view on a linguistic phenomenon regarding the Latin language in general, or a clearly limited portion of it. In both cases, we need to have an idea of what we mean by the Latin language.

The dichotomies. A number of scholars have acknowledged the difficulty of defining the Latin language. Among these, Poccetti stresses the fact that any account of the history of Latin must deal with its manifold nature and a series of dichotomies: local vs. universal, dead vs. extant, spoken vs. written, vulgar vs. literary (Poccetti et al., 1999, 9–30). Latin can in fact be viewed as the language of a particular city, while at the same time representing a universal heritage, extending its time span long after the end of the Roman empire. In turn, the chronological matter brings with it the question: to what extent can Latin be seen as a dead language? Such a characterization, originated in the area of Renaissance Italian philology, has been emphasized by a long scholastic tradition, which still represents the first filter through which most learners approach the Latin language. This tradition has favoured a normative view on Latin grammar, restricted to a limited time span (the Classical era and its literary sources, Cicero *in primis*), which was considered the qualitative peak defining the identity of Latin (Giacomelli, 1993, 13). On the other hand, Latin has expressed its vital role as a language for international communication throughout the centuries, also thanks to its continuations in the Romance languages and in the technical domain of a number of languages not directly derived from Latin, such as English. Latin texts are still produced, for example, by the Vatican, the Latin version of the online encyclopedia Wikipedia, and certain linguistic circles working on Latin. Finally, the contrast between written Latin transmitted by the available sources and spoken Latin reconstructed from indirect evidence has to do with the fuzzy dichotomy between literary Latin and vulgar Latin, which has led to a number of studies and debates, particularly for the relevance of non-Classical Latin in the investigation on the origin of Romance languages: cf. e.g. Rosén (1999, 15–18).

All these dichotomies are mirrored in the texts that are available for Latin. According to a classification of dead languages based on their sources (Mayrhofer, 1980; Untermann, 1983), Latin is a large-corpus language (*Großcorpus-Sprache*), thanks to the amount of its available texts. In spite of these factors, the corpus of texts available for Latin is extremely heterogeneous, displaying an uneven distribution along various dimensions, including the diachronic one (Poccetti et al. 1999, 28–29; Rosén 1999, 31). For example, the sources for archaic Latin (consisting of a few epigraphs and literary fragments from the 6th century BC) are very sparse and contrast with the number of texts available from the 3rd century BC on.

Spoken Latin. The overall body of Latin texts contributes to giving us a complex picture of this language. The linguistic tradition nonetheless recognizes that this picture is not complete, not only because of the fragmentary character of the texts or the lack of evidence from certain genres, registers and eras, but also because it obviously leaves out all direct accounts of spoken Latin. According to Bloomfield, "writing is not language, but merely a way of recording language by means of visible marks" (Bloomfield, 1933, 21). Therefore, spoken evidence would be the best evidence for all languages, including Latin. However, this is particularly difficult in the case of Latin, given the nature of its sources. The word 'vulgar' is often used to indicate the spoken component of Latin. Our knowledge of spoken or vulgar Latin is mediated by the available written texts. Along with inscriptions and papyri, a list of authors have been proposed as sources for vulgar Latin, including Plautus' plays, Cicero's letters, and *Cena Trimalchionis* by Petronius. Nevertheless, scholars tend to agree that these sources, alongside the literary genre, display different aspects of the vulgar nature of the language, ranging from domain specificity to social class, background, and target audience. We should thus consider these texts as showing some vulgar elements, rather than calling them vulgar *tout court* (Poccetti et al. 1999, 21–27, Rosén 1999, 19).

Spoken Latin is thus largely unknown and unknowable. However, I do not see reasons to dismiss the value of corpus studies as source of insight to a language merely because they rely on literary language. I believe that, no matter how high the value of spoken language is with respect to written language, texts are still the best evidence we can have for studying Latin. This also explains my choice to include Thomas in the corpus. Some might object that Thomas was not a native speaker of Latin. Based on what I said so far, I believe that relying on traces of spoken Latin and texts by native speakers as the only basis for a linguistic analysis would lead to exclude important contributions. This is in line with Croft (2000)'s position, according to which a language is "the population of utterances in a speech community"; an *utterance* is defined as a token, i.e. "a particular, actual occurrence of the product of human behavior in communicative interaction (i.e. a string of sounds), as it is pronounced, grammatically structured, and semantically and pragmatically interpreted in its context" (Croft, 2000, 26). In other words, this approach moves the focus from *who* writes (the individual authors) to *what* is written (the texts), and considers all utterances (even coming from different speech communities) as equally relevant for the study of language. In addition, given the diachronic aim of my case study, the data from Thomas are essential for detecting a linguistic trend in time. Finally, there is a statistical/methodological motivation that led me to this choice. The corpus for Thomas is large compared with the other authors, and I used statistical techniques that account for these size differences. On the other hand, if I had excluded Thomas, I would have had a much smaller corpus, which would have led to more uncertain results and a larger margin of error in the estimates.

1.5.2 *An Operational Definition of Language*

In section 1.5.1 I outlined the problems arising when defining the time span of the Latin language, the extent to which it can be considered a dead language, and our access to its spoken varieties. Given all these difficulties, the best option for defining Latin seems to be to overcome any dichotomy and consider Latin as the outcome of a series of particular historical, geographical and cultural circumstances, necessarily leading to an inhomogeneous linguistic system where elements from different areas and registers met and were only partially transmitted by the sources.

Here I propose a way to define the language variety of Latin which I want to investigate; this definition forms the basis for the use of corpus evidence for the case study on Latin preverbs reported on in chapter 6. I can imagine the corpora I used as a subset of a larger unannotated corpus; this larger corpus can be thought of as the whole Perseus Digital Library (given that the texts of the Latin Dependency Treebank are a subset of this) joined with the *Index Thomisticus* (the texts of the *Index Thomisticus* Treebank are a subset of this). I operationally define the sublanguage studied here to be this larger corpus.

An advantage of this choice resides in its possibilities for future research, which introduce an important methodological innovation of the current work. In fact, through the statistical analyses I reported on in this book it is possible to make predictions to the population by using the corpus sample available. I can hypothesize that the corpus constituting the sublanguage just defined will be annotated in the future, thus providing a basis to test the validity of my predictions. The syntactic annotation can already be approximated by an automatic parsing, which is in fact in progress for the *Index Thomisticus* and parts of the Perseus Digital Library (Bamman and Crane, 2008; Passarotti and Ruffolo, 2009). Hence, in the future it will be possible to evaluate my study by comparing its results and generalizations with the parsed data.

Good corpora. Under which conditions is it safe to assume that the corpora I used are a good sample for the sublanguage of Latin I just defined? The best way to obtain a sample from a population is by *random sampling* (Gorard, 2003; Rasinger, 2008); in random sampling each member of the population has the same chance of being included in the sample. Evert (2006) introduces a new way of looking at random sampling in linguistics. According to Evert, language is not inherently random because language utterances are not random bags of words. Although linguistic samples are not random at the word level, the randomness may be seen at a different level. To illustrate this, Evert (2006, 180) uses the metaphor of language as a large library:

> The selection of a particular corpus as the basis for a study among all the other language fragments that could also have been used is like picking an arbitrary book from one of the shelves in the library. It is this choice which introduces an element of randomness into corpus frequency data; and it is this element of randomness, in turn, that needs to be accounted for by the methods of statistical inference.

Hence, linguistic data do not consist of words that are put together randomly; instead, they are combined based on syntactic rules, conventions, pragmatic considerations, and so on. This causes serious problems for statistical tests that assume randomness. However, if I consider the corpus compilation level, I can be justified in assuming an element of randomness while using those tests, provided that I define the hypothesis and the population with this new perspective in mind. In other words, the conditions under which I can regard my corpora as good samples translate into the following question: is the choice of the texts in the corpora biased somehow? If that is not the case, then the corpora can be considered a random sample at the text level, in the sense specified by Evert. See Jenset (2010, 43–45) for a discussion of these issues in Historical Linguistics.

The corpora I used were in fact not built with the aim of a particular linguistic study in mind. Indeed, the IT-TB was built by collecting the concordances of the lemma *forma* 'form' in the *Index Thomisticus*; consequently, the choice of the IT-TB is not biased by the purpose of studying Latin preverbs, since I can assume that the occurrences of *forma* are randomly distributed with respect to the occurrences of preverbs. For what concerns the LDT, although I might recognize that some well-known authors are included in it, no particular selection criterion appears in the documentation. Finally, for the study on preverbs I also analysed two plays by Plautus. However, it is reasonable to assume that these plays do not contain any kind of biased evidence for Latin preverbs. These considerations allow me to consider the corpora I used as a good sample from the population I have defined, provided that I use appropriate statistical techniques that account for the peculiarities of the texts.

1.6 Outline of the Book

Chapter 3 presents the valency lexicon I extracted from two Latin treebanks. Chapter 4 illustrates a system for acquiring selectional preferences from the two treebanks by using the valency lexicon and Latin WordNet. Chapter 5 covers some technical aspects useful to understand the details of the model for selectional preferences. In addition, it gives a brief introduction to general concepts such as vector spaces and clustering, assuming no advanced background knowledge from the reader.

Chapter 6 illustrates a corpus-based quantitative case study on Latin spatial preverbs which uses the valency lexicon and state-of-the-art statistical techniques. Chapter 7 illustrates the techniques used for the quantitative analysis contained in chapter 6, again without assuming technical knowledge from the reader. The two technical chapters (chapters 5 and 7) display a different style from the main text, because they aim to explain the statistical techniques I used, as well as providing quantitative details, which were left out from the text of their relative chapters (4 and 6), in order to make it flow more smoothly. Therefore, these chapters complement the previous chapters by providing more elements to understand the full span of the argumentation. Finally, chapter 8 provides some conclusions, summarizes the contribution of my work, and suggests future directions of research.

CHAPTER 2

Computational Resources and Tools for Latin

2.1 The Role of Latin

If we go back to the origins of Computational Linguistics and Corpus Linguistics, we find that, among all languages, Latin played a truly crucial role. Latin is in fact the language of the first electronic corpus, the *Index Thomisticus* (IT) (Busa, 1980), whose development started in the late 1940s and continued for half a century. The IT contains Thomas Aquinas' *opera omnia*, or 11 million word tokens, a huge figure for those times and still a considerable one for our times. It was first encoded in punched cards, then on magnetic tapes, and finally in digital format.

In spite of this important precedent, after an early phase computational and corpus research has been focusing on modern languages, especially English. Researchers have worked on both building larger and larger corpora, and developing Natural Language Processing (NLP) tools for automatically annotating them at all levels, from lemmatization and morphological analysis to syntactic, semantic, and pragmatic analysis. Research in developing computational resources and tools for Latin for a long time has not kept up with the advances in the field of Computational Linguistics for modern languages. Several different projects aiming at building computational resources and tools for Latin have only started quite recently, and this chapter aims at giving an overview of their achievements.

2.1.1 *Why Are Computational Resources Needed?*

Krauwer (1998) introduces the idea of a *Basic LAnguage Resource Kit* (BLARK), which he defines as "the minimal set of language resources that is necessary to do any precompetitive research and education at all" (Krauwer, 2003, 4). Such language resources range from spoken and written language corpora, monolingual and bilingual dictionaries, morphological analyzers, parsers, annotation standards and tools for corpus exploration and exploitation. Different languages require different resources and some resources may only be relevant for certain languages.

Ancient languages do not have complete BLARKs. The reasons for this lie in the cost (and challenges) of creating historical corpora and in the lack of investments to implement new and large computational resources for these languages. As Passarotti (2010) observes, of all ancient dead languages, Latin

 | DOI: 10.1163/9789004260122_003

is definitely in a lucky position, because its BLARK is *in fieri* and relatively rich, as the overview in the next sections attests to.

2.2 Corpora and Digital Editions for Latin

The first step towards developing computational resources for Latin consists of collecting the textual material in a format that can be handled by NLP tools. For this, it is necessary to digitize part of the immense amount of Latin texts produced throughout the long history of this language. Those texts were not originally produced digitally, which means that a conversion from paper to electronic format is necessary. This labour-intensive task typically involves manual transcription or Optical Character Recognition (OCR); see Piotrowski (2012, 25–52) for a comprehensive overview of the issues and the techniques used to digitize historical texts. Here, I will briefly review some of the digital editions of Latin works available today.

The first example I will consider in this brief overview is the *Index Thomisticus* (Busa, 1980). It is available online[1] and contains the best critical editions of the *opera omnia* by Thomas Aquinas (118 texts), together with works by other authors related to Thomas (61 texts), for a total of around 11 million words. The online version can be searched by word forms.

Some of Latin digital editions were conceived to be used by philologists and therefore contain rich information on the tradition of the texts. For example, the projects *Musisque deoque* and *Poeti d'Italia in lingua latina tra medioevo e rinascimento*,[2] coordinated by scholars from the Italian universities of Padova, Trieste, Venezia Ca' Foscari, and Verona, collect the digital editions of Latin works by Latin authors from the Classical era and works by Italian authors between Dante Alighieri's birth (1265) and the first half of the sixteenth century. For each work the critical text is provided, including the codicological variants and, if possible, scholia and ancient glosses, as well as the Italian translation. On the website it is possible to search for the passages containing certain words (and all the variants obtained via inflection, compounding and derivation); it is also possible to impose constraints on the search such as the metre or the position in the line.

1 http://www.corpusthomisticum.org/.

2 http://www.mqdq.it/mqdq/home.jsp.

Other projects have chosen a specific edition rather than displaying the complete philological information for their texts. These digital editions are aimed at linguists and literary scholars as well as philologists, and can be searched by advanced search engines. An example is the *Corpus Grammaticorum Latinorum* (CGL), which contains the digitized version of seven volumes by the grammarians of the Late Antiquity in the editions by Heinrich Keil (Leipzig, 1855–1880) or in more recent editions. This corpus is now available online[3] and can be searched by lexical forms.

The last example I will mention is the *Library of Latin Texts* (LLT), jointly produced by the centre Cetedoc (CEntre de Traitement Électronique des DOCuments headed by Paul Tombeur at the Catholic University of Louvain-la-Neuve), by the publisher Brepols, and by the centre CTLO (Centre Traditio Litterarum Occidentalium). The LLT corpus is available on CD-ROM. It is a database which is searchable by lexical forms and chronological eras, and includes the digital editions of Latin texts from the archaic age to the modern age. It contains 6 million words for the Classical era, over 20 million words for the patristic era, and over 600,000 words for the modern era, for a total of more than 50 million words.

2.3 Corpus Annotation and NLP Tools

The texts of the digital editions briefly reviewed in section 2.2 can be browsed and searched through internal search engines. Thanks to such tools, philologists, linguists, and literary scholars can extract the occurrences of single word forms or sequences of word forms, together with their context (concordances) and frequency data on their distribution in the text. However, in order to perform more advanced searches on the texts, it is necessary to add further linguistic information on their words. In other terms, as I anticipated in section 1.2, it is necessary to *annotate* these texts and make them into linguistic corpora.

The annotation layer added to a text determines the range of searches possible on it. For example, a lemmatized and morphologically annotated corpus contains the morphological analysis of all its words, in terms of their lemmas and their morphological features. This allows the user to search not only for the single forms in the text (e.g. all passages containing the form

3 http://htl2.linguist.jussieu.fr:8080/CGL/index.jsp?link=historic.

monui[4] or *puellae*[5]), but also for all occurrences of a given lemma (e.g. all passages where any form of the verb *moneo* is present, or where *puellae* is a singular genitive), or all occurrences of a given part of speech (PoS), e.g. all nouns in the corpus.

2.3.1 *Annotating Morphology*

Morphological features of words can be included either through a manual annotation or through automatic methods. Time and cost savings are certainly among the advantages of automatic annotation. In addition, automatic methods lead to systematic errors which are easier to detect and correct than manual mistakes, which are typically inconsistent. Since Latin corpora manually annotated at the morphological level also contain syntactic annotation, I will review them in section 2.3.3.1, and will focus on automatic methods in sections 2.3.1.1 and 2.3.1.2.

2.3.1.1 PoS-Tagging

PoS-tagging is a term used in Computational Linguistics to indicate the annotation of a corpus with a label (or tag) for each word, indicating its PoS. Given their crucial importance for processing corpora, several PoS-taggers have been developed in Computational Linguistics for modern languages. Rule-based taggers tend to be language-specific. They work based on a set of rules that help the program assign the correct PoS to a word based on the distribution of the parts of speech in a language.

Over the past years, rule-based taggers have been overtaken by so-called statistical taggers, which have many advantages, including a language-independent nature. Statistical taggers are based on machine learning algorithms that go through two main phases: training and testing. During the training phase, the system learns patterns from annotated data; in the testing phase, the system is run on new, unannotated data, and produces a PoS-tagging for each of them.

The availability of training data makes it possible to evaluate statistical taggers. For evaluation purposes, a tagger is run on data for which (usually manual) annotation is available (often called *gold standard*). Then, the results from the tagger are compared with the gold standard and several scores are calculated so as to measure the system's performance. *Precision* is the ratio

4 Present perfect tense, indicative mood, first person singular of the verb *moneo* 'admonish'.

5 Genitive or dative singular or nominative plural of the noun *puella* 'girl'.

between the number of words correctly tagged with one specific tag and the total number of words tagged with that tag; *recall* is the ratio between the number of words correctly tagged with one specific tag and the number of words tagged with that tag in the gold standard.

For an overview of tagging experiments on historical languages, see Piotrowski (2012, 86–96). Here, I will give a couple of examples of parsing experiments on Latin. Passarotti and Dell'Orletta (2010) report on work done to train a PoS-tagger on 61,024 morphologically annotated tokens from the *Index Thomisticus* Treebank data (introduced in section 2.3.3.1), so as to obtain a morpho-syntactic disambiguation of the morphological lemmatization contained in the *Index Thomisticus*. Their preliminary experiments used the Hidden Markov Model-based HunPos tagger (Halácsy et al., 2007) and reached the following performance results: 96.75 % of correctly disambiguated coarse-grained PoS + fine-grained PoS, and 89.90 % when morphological features were also used.

Bamman and Crane (2008) report on experiments on PoS-tagging of Classical Latin with the TreeTagger (Schmid, 1994) trained on a set of 47,000 tokens from LDT. Their accuracy rates in assigning the correct PoS are around 95 %.

LASLA (Laboratoire d'Analyse Statistique des Langues Anciennes, University of Liège, headed by Joseph Denooz) have developed specific tools for morphosyntactic disambiguation and PoS-tagging of their textual database, although they are not publicly available. The LASLA database contains over 1.5 million words and is provided with an online search module.[6] This search engine allows for simple searches by lemma, bibliographic reference, or complete morphological analysis, as well as complex searches.

2.3.1.2 Automatic Morphological Annotation

Several software systems are available for producing a lemmatization and morphological analysis of Latin texts. First, the Morpheus system (Crane, 1991)[7] was developed within the Perseus Digital Library project. The Perseus project was founded in 1987 by the Department of Classics at the Tufts University and is supervised by Gregory Crane; it contains more than 5 million Latin words. Morpheus was first developed for Ancient Greek back in 1985, and a Latin version was created in 1996. Thanks to the analyzer Morpheus, the Perseus Digital Library is searchable by word forms and lemmas.

---

6 http://www.cipl.ulg.ac.be/Lasla/.

7 http://www.Perseus.tufts.edu/hopper/morph.jsp.

CHLT-LEMLAT (Passarotti, 2007a)[8] was realized at the Institute of Computational Linguistics (ILC-CNR) in Pisa by Andrea Bozzi, Marco Passarotti, and Paolo Ruffolo. CHLT-LEMLAT provides all the possible morphological analyses of an input word.

Another morphological analyzer for Latin is Words,[9] designed by William Whitaker. Words is an electronic dictionary for Latin and contains 39,000 lexical entries from different chronological eras. When the user submits an input word, Words responds with its morphological analysis and its English translation.

2.3.2 *A Large Annotated Corpus for Latin*

An interesting application of morphological NLP to Latin data is represented by LatinISE (McGillivray and Kilgarriff, 2013). LatinISE is a 13-million-word corpus of Latin available in Sketch Engine, a corpus query tool widely used in a high number of lexicography and corpus research projects (Kilgarriff et al., 2004).

I created LatinISE by collecting texts from three online digital libraries: LacusCurtius[10] by Bill Thayer, IntraText,[11] and Musique Deoque.[12] These websites contain texts from standard editions which cover a wide range of chronological eras and genres. I converted the texts from HTML format into the verticalized format required by the Sketch Engine. During the conversion, I kept the metadata information already present in the texts in the form of names of authors, titles, books, sections, paragraphs, and lines (for poetry).

For lemmatizing the data, I used the PROIEL Project's morphological analyser developed by Dag Haug's team. For example, consider the following phrase:

(1)	sumant	exordia	fasces
	take:SBJV.PRS.3PL	beginning:ACC.N.PL	fasces:NOM.M.PL
	'let the fasces open the year'		

The corresponding analysis looks like this:

8 http://webilc.ilc.cnr.it/ ruffolo/lemlat/index.html.

9 http://archives.nd.edu/words.html.

10 http://penelope.uchicago.edu/Thayer/I/Roman/home.html.

11 http://www.intratext.com.

12 http://www.mqdq.it.

```
> sumant
sumo<verb><3><pl><present><subjunctive><active>
> exordia
exordium<noun><n><pl><acc>
exordium<noun><n><pl><nom>
exordium<noun><n><pl><voc>
> fasces
no result for fasces
```

The analyser gives all possible analyses for each word form. In order to find the correct one, I needed to disambiguate these analyses in terms of the most likely lemma and PoS for each token in context.

The three Latin treebanks introduced in section 2.3.3 (the *Index Thomisticus* Treebank, the Latin Dependency Treebank, and the PROIEL Project's Latin treebank) provide lemmatized and morpho-syntactically annotated data for a total of over 242,000 tokens. I used those data to train TreeTagger (Schmid, 1995), a statistical part-of-speech tagger developed by Helmut Schmid at the University of Stuttgart. I ran TreeTagger on the output from the morphological analyser, with lemma and PoS, so that TreeTagger could assign the most likely PoS and lemma to each word form.

As an example, consider the following phrase:

(2) praemia si cessant
prize:NOM.N.PL if:CONJ stop:IND.PRS.3PL
'if the prizes are lacking' (*Einsiedeln Eclogues*, 1st century AD)

The corresponding annotated corpus data look like this:

```
<character name="Th">
<line>
praemia N          praemium
si                 C          si
cessant V          cesso
<g/>
,
```

In this example, the first line shows the metadata encoding the name of the character uttering the words, Thamyra; the second line contains a tag indicating the beginning of the poem's line; the third, fourth, and fifth line contain the word form, followed by the PoS tag ('N' for 'noun', 'C' for 'conjunction', and 'V' for 'verb') and the lemma; finally the sixth and seventh lines contain the tag that precedes punctuation marks in the Sketch Engine format and the comma, respectively.

LatinISE is currently in its 1.0 version and further processing is in order to evaluate the results of the automatic lemmatization and PoS-tagging, as well as to add full morphological and syntactic annotation. However, the creation of this corpus shows a concrete example of application of NLP tools to Latin texts and, at the same time, the challenges of creating a large Latin corpus with metadata information. For further details on LatinISE see McGillivray and Kilgarriff (2013).

2.3.3 *Annotating Syntax*

In this section I will survey manually syntactically annotated corpora (called 'treebanks'; section 2.3.3.1) and systems for automatic annotation of syntax (also known as 'parsing'; section 2.3.3.2).

2.3.3.1 Treebanks

A *treebank* is a collection of sentences manually annotated at the syntactic level and represented as syntactic trees. Therefore, treebanks are corpora that can be searched via syntactic criteria; for example, in a treebank it is possible to search all subjects of a given verb, or all verbs that have a pronoun as their direct object. Computational linguists exploit treebanks for developing automatic methods of syntactic annotation, as shown in section 2.3.3.2.

Three treebanks are available for Latin: the *Index Thomisticus* Treebank (IT-TB), the Latin Dependency Treebank (LDT), and the PROIEL Project Treebank. All these treebanks are annotated with a Dependency Grammar approach (see section 3.3 for a description of the annotation scheme). Hence, the annotation provides each word of a sentence with a tag for its syntactic function and a reference to its dependency head.

IT-TB. The IT-TB[13] was created by Marco Passarotti at the Catholic University of the Sacred Heart in Milan (Passarotti, 2007b) within the project 'Lessico Tomistico Biculturale' (LTB). It focusses on texts from the *Index Thomisticus* (see section 2.2) and currently contains over 9,000 morphologically and syntactically annotated sentences (for a total of over 175,000 tokens) extracted from the concordances of the word *forma* in the *Scriptum super Sententiis Magistri Petri Lombardi* by Thomas Aquinas.

---

13 http://itreebank.marginalia.it/.

LDT. The LDT is being developed as part of the Perseus Project (Bamman and Crane, 2007). It shares the same annotation guidelines as the IT-TB and consists of 53,143 tokens, extracted from works contained in the Perseus Digital Library (see section 2.3.1.2). The LDT includes texts by the following authors: Caesar (1,488 tokens), Cicero (6,229), Jerome (8,382), Ovid (4,789), Petronius (12,474), Propertius (4,857), Sallust (12,311), and Vergil (2,613).

PROIEL Project Treebank. The third Latin treebank started as part of the wider project PROIEL (*Pragmatic Resources of Old Indo-European Languages*).[14] This multilingual project, supervised by Dag Haug at Oslo University, has created a parallel corpus of the New Testament in Ancient Greek and of its translations in Latin, Gothic, Armenian, and Old Church Slavonic. It also contains some extensions, covering Caesar's Gallic War, Cicero's Letters to Atticus for Latin and *Peregrinatio Aetheriae* for vulgar Latin. The PROIEL Project parallel treebank is morphologically and syntactically annotated and contains 70,000 words.

CoLaMer. The project CoLaMer, collaboratively developed by the Universities of Köln and Regensburg, has started to develop a fourth Latin treebank on texts of the Merovingian age.

2.3.3.2 Parsing

Parsing is the Computational Linguistics term that indicates automatic syntactic annotation. Similarly to PoS-taggers (see section 2.3.1.1), rule-based parsers exploit work on manually constructed rules. On the other hand, statistical parsers are trained on annotated data from treebanks. For example, a statistical parser trained on the IT-TB will learn the syntactic structures present in that corpus; after training, such a parser can be used to parse new portions of the *Index Thomisticus* or other corpora displaying similar stylistic features. As any other automatic method, parsing involves a margin of error, which must be accounted for when using its output data. Nevertheless, the result of parsing is often used in semi-automatic annotation of corpora, where parsed data are further manually checked and corrected.

A first attempt at parsing Latin is described in Koch (1993), who applied an existing dependency parser by Covington (1990) to Latin. Koster (2005) describes a rule-based top-down chart parser automatically generated and

14 http://www.hf.uio.no/ifikk/english/research/projects/proiel/index.html.

developed from a grammar, and a lexicon built according to the formalism of the two-level AGFL grammar (Affix Grammar over a Finite Lattice; (Koster, 1991)).

McGillivray et al. (2009), Passarotti and Ruffolo (2009), and Passarotti and Dell'Orletta (2010) describe experiments with different statistical parsers for Latin. Passarotti and Dell'Orletta (2010) adapted the DeSR parser (Dependency Shift-Reduce; Attardi 2006) to the structure of Latin sentences. They designed a feature model specific to Medieval Latin aiming at best capturing the syntactic characteristics in Thomas' prose. Using a training set of 61,024 tokens (2,820 sentences), this led to an improvement of the previous accuracy rates, reaching 80.02% for LAS (Labeled Attachment Score, i.e. percentage of tokens with correct head and relation label), 85.23% for UAS (Unlabeled Attachment Score, i.e. percentage of tokens with the correct head), and 87.79% for LA (Label Accuracy, i.e. percentage of tokens with the correct relation label; Buchholz and Marsi 2006).

2.4 Semantic Resources

Research on annotating Latin corpora from a semantic point of view and on creating semantic resources for Latin started only recently, and therefore does not cover a very high number of Latin words. It is however worth reporting on it, since it represents the most advanced level of processing of Latin texts so far, and is a very valuable starting point for studies on Latin semantics.

2.4.1 *Annotating Semantics*

The PROIEL Project already mentioned in section 2.3.3 has annotated its corpus from the point of view of semantics, information structure, and discourse structure. For reasons of economy, the semantic annotation is performed at the lemma level and then adjusted at the token level. It covers animacy, aktionsart, and noun relationality for a limited number of sentences in the corpus. The information structure annotation has focussed on givenness and anaphoricity.

The IT-TB has started to add a semantic/pragmantic annotation layer to the syntactic annotation of a limited number of its sentences (Passarotti, 2010). The theoretical background to this work is Functional Generative Description (Sgall et al., 1986), a Dependency Grammar framework developed in Prague and used for the creation of the Prague Dependency Treebank (Hajič et al., 1999). The tectogrammatical annotation covers semantic roles in argument structure dependencies, as well as sentential information structure, ellipsis, anaphora resolution, and coreferential relations.

2.4.2 *Lexical Databases*

Several Latin dictionaries and lexicons are available online or on CD-ROM: the Lewis and Short dictionary provided by the Perseus Digital Library website, the *Thesaurus Linguae Latinae* from the Bayerische Akademie der Wissenschaften in Munich, the *Thesaurus Formarum* (TF-CILF) from the CTLO, and the *Neulateinische Wortliste* made available by Johann Ramminger,[15] to mention a few.

Here I will focus on the Latin WordNet (LWN) database (Minozzi, 2009), particularly important for its applications to computational semantic tasks like information extraction, data mining, word sense disambiguation, and topic classification. LWN plays also a crucial role in the automatic system for acquisition of verbal selectional preferences illustrated in chapter 4.

2.4.2.1 Latin WordNet

LWN is an ongoing project within the MultiWordNet project,[16] which aims at realizing a large-scale multilingual computational lexicon based on WordNet (WN; Miller et al. 1990).

WN is a semantic network, developed at Princeton University for the English language. WN organizes lexical items into sets of synonyms called *synsets*, which represent lexical concepts. The links among the synsets are defined by means of semantic and lexical relations, such as hyponymy, hyperonymy and meronymy. The synsets are also linked to higher-level synsets (hypernyms) via tree structures until the top nodes. For example, the English noun *bird* has five synsets; the first one ("warm-blooded egg-laying vertebrates characterized by feathers and forelimbs modified as wings") is linked to the top node [ENTITY, SOMETHING] via the intermediate hypernym nodes [vertebrate, craniate], [chordate], [animal, animate_being, beast, brute, creature, fauna], and [life_form, organism, being, living_thing].

The size of LWN is currently around 10,000 lemmas, with 9,000 synsets and 25,000 word senses.

2.5 Summary

This brief overview on existing computational resources and tools for Latin covered annotated corpora, various NLP tools, and lexical databases. This has highlighted a gap in the state of the art which concerns both the size of the

15 http://www.lrz-muenchen.de/ramminger/.

16 http://multiwordnet.fbk.eu/english/home.php.

annotated corpora nowadays available for Latin, and the still limited number of computational tools, especially for semantic processing of Latin texts.

In this context, the lexicon I describe in chapter 3 contributes to expanding the number of linguistic resources containing syntactic information on Latin. Moreover, the system for acquiring selectional preferences (see chapter 4) shows an important application of computational semantic models to the special case of Latin data.

CHAPTER 3

Verbs in Corpora, Lexicon *ex machina*

This chapter presents the first of a series of three case studies concerning various aspects of argument structure of Latin verbs. In accordance with the overall methodological aims of the book, here I will focus on the value of a computational resource for Latin: the first corpus-based valency lexicon for Latin verbs. Rather than being a theoretical study on valency in Latin, this is hence a concrete example of a resource built from annotated corpora. My goal will mainly pertain to the details of the design and creation of the lexicon.

3.1 Why Valency?

Predicates tend to occur with other constituents. However, this co-occurrence is not random. Once we specify a predicate, to some extent we can also predict its co-occurrence with certain other constituents. Such constituents are called *arguments* to distinguish them from *adjuncts*, which do not display this property. In the sentence *She gave him the book yesterday*, the presence of the three arguments for the verb *give* (*she* for the person giving, *him* for the person receiving, and *the book* for the thing given) is predictable based on the verb *give*. On the other hand, the presence of the adjunct *yesterday* cannot be expected based on the verb *give* only, because other complements (adverbials) could occur with this verb: *She gave him the book in the garden*, *She gave him the book with the bill*, and so on.

The number and type of arguments typically occurring with a verb is a lexical feature of the verb itself and is connected with its semantics, although there is a debate in linguistic theories on the nature of this link. Different linguistic approaches have called this feature with different names: argument structure in English linguistics (Levin, 1993; Levin and Rappaport Hovav, 2005; Goldberg, 2006), valency in Dependency Grammar (DG) and Valency Theory (Tesnière, 1959; Mel'čuk, 1988; Pinkster, 1990), subcategorization in Lexical Semantics and Computational Linguistics (McCarthy, 2001; Korhonen, 2002). Since DG is the theoretical framework of the data I have started from, I will use the term 'valency'. However, as I show throughout this chapter, the corpus-based, distributional nature of my approach means that my operational definition of valency differs in some respects from the theoretical definitions generally found in the theoretical literature.

 | DOI: 10.1163/9789004260122_004

Valency is a crucial property of verbs. Knowing verbal valency enables us to predict to some extent the relative position of verbs, their subjects, and their objects (word order) in a sentence, which is very important for categorizing languages in linguistic typology. Just to give another example, valency properties of verbs are also widely used to predict the correct syntactic analysis of a sentence (parsing) and the semantic roles of predicates, two crucial tasks in Computational Linguistics. It is therefore perhaps not surprising that valency is a central topic in the investigation of computational approaches to Latin verbs covered in the three case studies of this book.

This chapter focusses on a lexical resource that gives information about Latin verbal valency and is based on two syntactically annotated corpora. Because the data have been annotated syntactically and morphologically (but not semantically), I will concentrate on the syntactic aspects of verbal valency. So, valency here will refer to the number and type of verbal arguments occurring in the corpora as independent lexical entities, in terms of their syntactic roles (subject, object, etc.) and morphological-lexical features (case/mood, part-of-speech, lemma) explicitly annotated in the corpora used, rather than in terms of their semantic roles (such as agent or patient) or pragmatic features (topic/focus, ellipsis). The corpus-based distributional perspective will offer me the chance to discuss the interesting impact that this methodological decision has on the type of valency information recorded in the lexicon.

3.2 Valency in Lexicons

A typical way to represent verbal valency is through *valency patterns*, which are sequences of verbal arguments. For example, a valency pattern for the English verb *go* is 'NP, PP(*to*)' (phrase structure representation) or 'Subject, (*to*)Object' (dependency representation), as in sentences like *They are going to the beach tomorrow*.

A *valency lexicon* collects valency patterns of verbs in a database/dictionary-like structure, where verbs correspond to lexical entries which can be searched or looked up to investigate their valency behaviour. For instance, we can find which valency patterns are typical of the verb *connect* or which verbs require a source complement with the preposition *from*. But how to find out about verbal valency when we want to build a valency lexicon in the first place?

A linguist asked to compile valency patterns for a verb in an extant language would probably combine her native speaker's intuition with some knowledge from existing resources (such as dictionaries) and linguistic evidence from various sources. She would ask herself questions like "Is the verb *consider* transitive?", "Is its second object (the object complement) optional?", "Which sense of this verb is associated with a transitive valency pattern?". However, in the case of an extinct language like Latin, native speaker intuition is not available, and the main source of information is represented by textual evidence and dictionaries. This introduces the challenge of finding valency properties in textual data.

Some record of verbal valency has always been part of traditional (Latin) lexicography, but we may wonder how this information was gathered and turned into dictionary content. Dictionary entries typically contain references about the arguments required by words in the form of the grammatical category of government. The entry for *advenio* 'arrive' in the Latin monolingual dictionary Forcellini (1940) records the case governed by *advenio* and the prepositions used with it, for example *ab* or *ex* + ablative. For sake of illustration, examples from different Latin authors usually follow such valency statements. The reader can imagine that those, necessarily few, examples have been used as an inductive basis for the lexicographer's work, but does not know if more (and how many) examples have been scanned before selecting those few ones. In other words, the user cannot know to what extent those examples are just illustrations or constituted the empirical evidence for the compiler of the dictionary. The dictionary cannot (and is not supposed to) answer questions like "Is *advenio* used more often with an adverb or with a prepositional phrase to express the locative argument?", "How has the proportion of such usages changed over time?" Instead, it succeeds in answering questions like "Has *advenio* ever occurred with an adverb? If so, who is one of the authors that used this construction?"

Likewise, the *Thesaurus Linguae Latinae* (Bayerische Akademie der Wissenschaften, 2002) gives morpho-syntactic features of verbal arguments (and sometimes adjuncts), either in explicit terms by using the case involved ('dat'), or implicitly by using the indefinite pronoun declined in that case ('alicui'), or sometimes single words, phrases, or larger fragments of texts. In a *continuum* between morpho-syntactic and lexical realization of arguments, the *Thesaurus* offers valency information to the reader in order to display the semantics of verbs and the variety of contexts these verbs occur in. Each sense is exemplified by selected quotations from a very large corpus, containing all Latin texts from the beginning of Latin literature up to the second century AD, and most of the later texts until the fourth century AD. Only the entries of less frequent lemmas record all fragments containing them, while more common entries provide just a selection of passages. As pointed out in the introduction to the *Thesaurus*, the number of quoted passages cannot be considered proportional to the material available in the corpus, due to the emphasis on the diachronic evolution of words and their idiosyncratic properties, rather than on a strictly quantitative account of their syntactic behaviour.

In such traditional lexical resources, we cannot draw a line between the role played by the textual sources and the lexicographers' contribution. The reason lies in the way those resources are conceived. They are printed (or are digital editions of printed originals), which implies that the amount of space available for each entry is limited and some selection is necessary; thus, they cannot contain an explicit quantitative account of a word's behaviour in a reference corpus, but just a selection of passages. Because these resources are made by lexicographers to be consulted by readers interested in the semantic and constructional features of words, it is not considered relevant to provide the complete set of occurrences of a word or to explain in detail how the examples have been selected. Part of the lexicographer's work is precisely to summarize the variety of different patterns found in language into a general and schematic account of valency, while at the same time recording idiosyncratic behaviour.

In a similar fashion, valency lexicons have traditionally been built following a combination of support from text sources and manual selection, and the distinction between these two components has not always been explicit. Happ (1976)'s lexicon—the only existing hand-made valency lexicon for Latin to my knowledge—is based on a corpus of 800 verbal occurrences in Cicero's *Orationes*, which the author manually analysed from the point of view of valency. The lexicon reports a list of Latin verbs, along with their valencies and some quotations from the corpus; the quotations were chosen to exemplify the valency patterns illustrated, rather than to systematically describe the corpus, and the valency analysis of the corpus itself is not available to the reader.

3.2.1 *A Corpus-Based Distributional Attitude*

If we turn to lexical resources built in the field of Computational Linguistics, we find a radically different approach. Computational lexicons like PDT-Vallex (Hajič et al., 2003), FrameNet (Baker et al., 1998), or PropBank (Kingsbury and Palmer, 2002) are based on *annotated* corpora, where each sentence has been syntactically analysed by annotators. This means that the relation between the lexical resource and the corpus is more explicit than that found in traditional resources. Crucially, arguments and adjuncts of verbs are detected during a first phase, where the corpus is annotated. In the second phase, the lexicon is built based on the set of annotated sentences. The reader can thus clearly see where the valency patterns came from (i.e. the corpus) and how the annotators have analysed them. A set of annotated sentences for a verb display the different valency patterns, which are in turn recorded in the lexicon. The user can check the annotation at any point to find out how the lexicographers inferred those patterns.

Going even further in this methodological direction, we find valency lexicons *automatically extracted* from annotated corpora. These lexicons give a systematic account of the valency behaviour of verbs in the corpora, thus minimizing the risk of omissions and inconsistencies typical of manual resources. The valency patterns in these lexicons are categorized lists of all patterns found in the corpora, with no further selection. Instead of resulting from a theoretical definition of valency, such patterns reflect a *distributional* approach to valency.

Distributional approaches to semantics follow the so-called distributional hypothesis (Sahlgren, 2008), according to which words that appear in similar contexts have similar semantic properties; for an overview of this approach, see Lenci (2008). From a computational point of view, this approach implies that it is possible to investigate the lexical-semantic properties of words from a quantitative analysis of their contexts. If we apply this view to verbal arguments, the analysis of their patterns of occurrence in corpora can give us important information about their valency properties. A computational lexicon that was built along these lines is Valex (Korhonen et al., 2006), which provides valency patterns for English verbs, together with their frequencies and actual occurrences in five automatically syntactically annotated (i.e. parsed) corpora.

The only lexicon of this kind built for Latin is the one described in Bamman and Crane (2008). This lexicon was automatically extracted from a 3.5 million-word Latin parsed corpus based on the Perseus Digital Library, and provides the user with an explicit description of the valency behaviour found in the corpus. This is a major difference from traditional resources, where the lexicographer somehow elaborates on the valency information and presents it in a synthetic form to the reader, who cannot access the corpus and reconstruct the process that led to the dictionary content. Another important difference is that a corpus with valency annotation allows the compiler of the lexicon to give frequency data, which quantify the relevance of different valency patterns in the corpus and can be the basis for distributional models of verbs' semantics.

Drawing on the work done in Corpus Linguistics and Computational Linguistics on building corpus-based computational lexicons, the lexicon I propose here is the first available lexicon that applies such an approach to Latin.

TABLE 3.1 *Example of annotation of the Latin sentence* sese iactabit audacia *'audacity will throw itself'*

id='1'	form='sese'	lemma='se'	case='acc'	syn_fun='object'	head='2'
id='2'	form='iactabit'	lemma='iacto'	mood='ind'	syn_fun='predicate'	head='0'
id='3'	form='audacia'	lemma='audacia'	case='nom'	syn_fun='subject'	head='2'

3.2.2 *Consequences for the Definition of Valency*

Because it is an electronic lexical resource from its design, the lexicon does not have space issues and thus is not limited by them. This means that it can afford to give a *systematic* account of the behaviour of verbs in the corpus, and its relation with the textual sources is totally explicit. The sources of evidence for it are not just collections of texts, they are morpho-syntactically annotated corpora (*treebanks*), namely the Latin Dependency Treebank (LDT; Bamman and Crane 2007) and the *Index Thomisticus* Treebank (IT-TB; Passarotti 2007b). What does this mean for the valency information recorded in the lexicon?

An annotated corpus is a corpus where some kind of linguistic information has been made explicit in the annotation phase. A syntactic annotation like the one of the treebanks I use implies that each word in the corpora has been analysed from the point of view of its morphological form and its syntactic role in the sentence. For a constructed example of a basic morpho-syntactic annotation of the Latin sentence *sese iactabit audacia* 'audacity will throw itself', let us look at Table 3.1.

Each of the three word forms of the sentence (*sese*, *iactabit*, and *audacia*) is followed by a list of attributes: 'id' for identifying the word form itself, 'form' for the actual form of the word, 'lemma' for its lemma, 'case' for its case (if it is a nominal form), 'mood' for its mood (if it is a verbal form), 'syn_fun' for its syntactic function in the sentence, and 'head' for the id of its dependency head.

Verbal arguments have thus been labelled by the annotators in the treebanks with specific syntactic tags, together with the dependency relations with their verbal heads. In the previous example, the annotators would have marked the fact that *iacto* 'throw' is found with an accusative argument and an expressed subject; this makes up the valency pattern 'Subject[nom], Object[acc]' for *iacto*.

Therefore, while compiling the lexicon I did not have to detect verbal arguments in the corpus sentences, because the annotators had already done this; this is in accordance with the collaborative research paradigm I described in chapter 1. My task was to make this information explicit and integrate it into the lexicon. From this point of view, we can see the lexicon as an 'interface' to the corpora, because it allows the user to easily search the complex valency information which is implicitly embedded in the corpora.

Consistently with this approach, the lexicon lists which annotated arguments occur with each verb in the corpora. Such lists form the valency patterns that make up the lexicon. Precisely because of the way they were obtained, these patterns differ from the valency patterns found in theoretical statements about Latin verbs. A theoretically important consequence that follows from this has to do with the way Latin lexically expresses verbal arguments, and deserves a small digression.

3.2.3 *Argument Optionality*

Knowing which arguments tend to occur with a verb helps us better understand its semantics, because the arguments of a verb are distinguished from its adjuncts precisely by the fact that they are specific to that verb (and to all verbs which have the same valency behaviour, like *give-donate-offer*, for example), and are not equally likely to occur with other verbs.

However, not all arguments behave in the same way, and this is especially important when trying to generalize from the different occurrences of verbal arguments in real texts to abstract patterns of valency. Some verbal arguments are obligatory because they cannot be missing while at the same keeping the sense of the predicate constant and the sentence grammatical. For example, the verb *consider* means 'have a certain opinion of something/someone' in a sentence like *I consider you dangerous*, but it means 'take into consideration something/someone' if the adjective is not present (*I will consider the matter*). Consequently, the respective patterns for those two senses of *consider* are: 'Subject, Object, Object' (*I consider you dangerous*) and 'Subject, Object' (*I will consider the matter*).

Optional arguments, on the other hand, are required by the predicate, but their absence does not affect the sense of the verb nor the grammaticality of the sentence. For example, sentences (1) and (2) show that the English verb *eat* (differently from its synonym *devour*) has an optional direct object, whose omission causes a shift in telicity but not in sense.

(1) She is eating an apple.
(2) She is eating.

The missing object in (2) is sometimes called "indefinite argument" because the activity of eating is autonomous and does not require the reader to recover its object from the context. On the contrary, the object of *watch* in sentence

(3) is not expressed, but the reader needs to recover it from the context, and is therefore a "definite argument" (Cruse, 2011, 285–286).

(3) Be careful: they're watching.

A similar optional presence of certain arguments can be found in Latin, too. In fact, the omission of direct objects of transitive verbs takes place frequently in Latin (and in ancient Greek), when they refer to definite antecedents (and are thus called 'definite referential null objects'); this happens, for example, in coordinated clauses sharing the same object (Luraghi, 1998).

(4) Caesar exercitum re-duxit et ...
Caesar:NOM.M.SG army:ACC.M.SG. back-lead:IND.PF.3SG and ...
in hibernis conlocavit
in winter camp:ABL.N.PL lodge:IND.PF.3SG
'Caesar led his army back and lodged it in the winter camp'. (Caes., *B.G. III,* 29)

In sentence (4) the direct object of *conlocavit* in the second clause refers to *exercitum*, which only occurs in the first clause.

Sentence (5) shows the omission of the indirect argument *ei* 'to her' of the verb *do* 'give', but that argument can be understood from the context.

(5) Orabo ut mihi pallam reddat
ask:IND.FUT.1SG that me:DAT.SG mantle:ACC.F.SG give back:SBJV.PRS.3SG
quam dudum dedi
which:ACC.F.SG a short time ago give:IND.PF.1SG
'I am going to ask her to give me back the mantle I gave her a short time ago'. (Plaut., *Men.*, 672)

If we turn to subjects, there are important differences between the surface expression of these arguments in English and in Latin. Herbst et al. (2004) call 'structural necessity' the fact that English declarative main clauses normally have an expressed subject; see also (Hewson and Bubenik, 2006, 3–4). In pro-drop languages such as Latin and Italian this is not the case. Consider sentences (6) and (7).

(6) Mangia.
eat:PRS.IND.3SG
'He/she eats.'

(7) Edit.
eat:PRS.IND.3SG
'He/she eats.'

In (6) and (7) the third person singular morphological form of the verb accounts for the presence of the subject. This property of the subjects of Latin verbs is crucial for any account of their valency. The fact that their lexical presence may not appear as independent from the verb's inflectional form (as in *Edit*) can affect subsequent accounts of Latin verbal valency that are purely distributional and solely consider overtly expressed arguments; such accounts will probably not record a subject if it is not explicitly realized as an independent entity (for example with a pronoun).

3.2.4 *An Operational Definition of Valency*

As a consequence of the corpus-based perspective I adopted, the argument patterns found in the lexicon are somewhat different from valency patterns one would expect to find in a traditional, intuition-based lexicon.

As I mentioned in section 3.2.3, since Latin is a pro-drop language, the subjects of verbs are not always lexically realized independently from the verb inflection. For instance, in sentence (8), the subject is understood by the first person of the verb *laudo*.

(8) Laudo te.
praise:PRS.IND.1SG you:ACC.SG
'I praise you.'

This entails that the 'surface' morpho-syntactic annotation of sentence (8) is only possible for the lexical items *laudo* and *te*, so the valency pattern for *laudo* in (8) would be 'Object[acc]'. Likewise, consistently with the annotation of the source corpus data, if there is ellipsis of an argument, the lexicon does not go as far as resolving it and appending the elided argument(s) to the expressed ones. This is because the lexicon does not add any information that is not already present in the annotation.

Going back to sentence (5), a strictly corpus-based approach to valency lexicon building would record the pattern observed in (5) for *do* as 'Object[acc]' (realized by the word *quam*). If we collect all patterns for *do* observed in the corpora, especially as the corpus size increases, we are likely to find some that display a dative object as well ('Object[acc], Object[dat]'), and maybe also some where the subject is lexically expressed by a noun or a pronoun ('Subject[nom], Object[acc]', 'Subject[nom], Object[dat]', and 'Subject[nom],

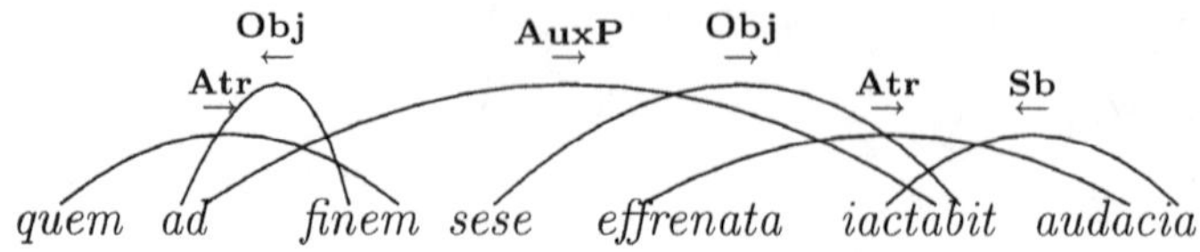

FIGURE 3.1 *A DG representation of sentence* (9)

Object[acc], Object[dat]'). Putting together all these patterns, we would obtain something similar to the theoretically expected valency behaviour of *do* ('Subject[nom], Object[acc], Object[dat]').

These differences between the operational definition of valency I have adopted and theoretical definitions of valency explain the broad sense of 'valency' I will use when referring to the lexicon described in this book.

3.3 The Annotation of the Treebanks

As I said, the lexicon contains valency information as it is annotated in the corpora, so it reflects the theoretical choices that the annotators made concerning the argument status of constituents and the role of arguments. In order to understand the formalism of the lexicon it is thus necessary to know how the annotation works.

Latin is an inflectionally rich language with a relatively free word order. Such variability is possible because Latin morphology is rich, so the syntactic role of a constituent is usually given by its case (nominative for subjects, accusative for direct objects, etc.), rather than by its position in the sentence. Free word order is also related to non-projectivity, which is realized when constituents in a sentence can be broken up by elements belonging to other constituents. Latin texts display quite complex sequences of discontinuous constituents, as we can see in Figure 3.1 for sentence (9).

(9) quem ad finem sese effrenata
which:ACC.M.SG to end:ACC.M.SG oneself:ACC.SG unbridled:NOM.F.SG
iactabit audacia?
throw:IND.FUT.3SG audacity:NOM.F.SG
'To what end will your unbridled audacity throw itself?' (Cic., *Cat.*, speech I, ch. 1)

DG is best suited to represent the syntax of morphologically rich languages with free word order and high non-projectivity such as Latin. For this reason, the LDT and the IT-TB have collaborated since the beginning of their respective projects and decided to adapt the guidelines for the so-called 'analytical layer' of annotation of the Prague Dependency Treebank (Hajič et al. 1999) to Latin syntax.

The Prague Dependency Treebank is annotated at different layers, going from the morphological one to the tectogrammatical one. The analytical layer aims at describing the surface syntax of sentences, while the tectogrammatical layer builds on it, and gives a representation of the meaning of sentences by combining deep syntactic, semantic, and pragmatic analysis (for example by adding basic coreferential links, topic/focus articulation, and semantic labeling of every sentence unit). The tectogrammatical annotation of the IT-TB started only recently and does not provide enough data to be used for building a lexicon like the one I present here; consequently, the lexicon was built from the analytical annotation of the treebanks. However, while extracting the lexicon from the analytical layer (the only one for which a considerable amount of data from both treebanks is available), I developed a methodology that can also be used on the tectogrammatical data, allowing interesting comparisons between the patterns found at those two levels of annotation. Moreover, a relatively shallow annotation is sought after by distributional approaches to semantics, which aim at letting semantic similarity features between words emerge from the analysis of their syntactic contexts.

In what follows I will give a few illustrative examples of the annotation of the treebanks. The annotation assigns a rooted tree to each sentence; the nodes of the tree correspond to word tokens (including punctuation marks) and the edges represent either binary dependency relations between node pairs, or other phenomena such as coordination, apposition, punctuation, etc. Table 3.2 lists all the syntactic tags currently in use in the LDT and the IT-TB.[1]

When it is read from left to right, the tree records the original order of the elements in the sentence. As an example, see Figure 3.2, which presents the dependency tree of sentence (10) from the IT-TB.

(10) Praedicatum enim habet rationem formae.
Predicate:NOM.N.SG indeed have:IND.PRS.3SG account:ACC.F.SG form:GEN.F.SG
'The predicate indeed accounts for the form.' (Th., *Sent. P. L.*, I, Q. 1)

1 In the row for the 'Atv'/'AtvV' tag, 'complement' refers to NPs like *leati* in *Galli laeti in castra pergunt* 'the Gauls happily enter the camp', which agrees with *Galli*.

TABLE 3.2 *Complete Latin tagset adopted by the LDT and the IT-TB*

Pred	predicate
Sb	subject
Obj	object
Atr	attributive
Adv	adverbial
Atv/AtvV	complement
PNom	predicate nominal
OComp	object complement
Coord	coordinator
Apos	apposing element
AuxP	preposition
AuxC	conjunction
AuxR	reflexive passive
AuxV	auxiliary verb
AuxX	commas
AuxG	bracketing punctuation
AuxK	terminal punctuation
AuxY	sentence adverbial
AuxZ	emphasizing particle
AuxS	root of the tree
ExD	ellipsis

In sentence (10), there is a subject ('Sb') relation between the word *praedicatum* and the word *habet*, an object ('Obj') relation between *rationem* and *habet*, and an attribute ('Atr') relation between *formae* and *rationem*. The finite verb ('Pred_Co') depends on the coordinating conjunction *enim*, which in turn depends on the top node, labelled as 'AuxS' and representing the whole sentence. The punctuation mark (tagged as 'AuxK') is also dependent on the top node.

In general, the 'Pred' tag is used for predicate(s) of the main clause(s). It is worth saying that predicates occurring in subordinate clauses are tagged according to the role of the corresponding clause in the sentence: the predicate of a subject clause is tagged as 'Sb' (subject) and the predicate of an adverbial clause is tagged as 'Adv'. Other important syntactic labels are 'Pnom', which annotates predicate nominals (i.e. the determining complements of subjects) and 'OComp', which annotates object complements (i.e. the determining complements of objects). For example, let us consider sentence (11), represented in

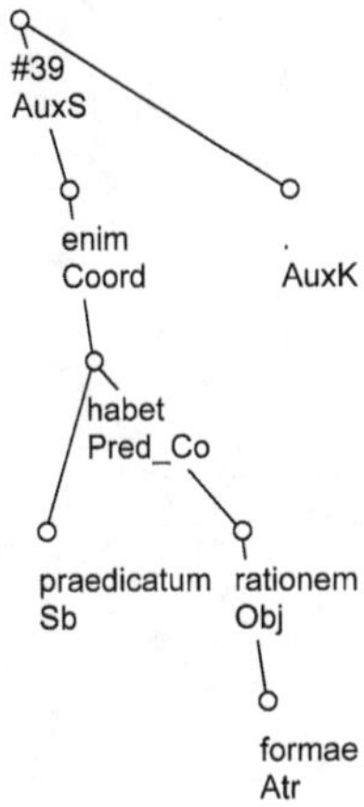

FIG. 3.2 *Dependency tree of sentence (10) from the IT-TB*

Figure 3.3, where the 'Pnom' node *certior* (which I will call *certior*-24 because it is the 24th word in the sentence) refers to *Caesar*-3 and depends on *fiebat*-25.

(11) **Cum esset Caesar in citeriore**
when be:SBJV.IMPF.3SG Caesar:NOM.M.SG in Hither:ABL.F.SG
Gallia in hibernis, ita uti supra
Gaul:ABL.F.SG in winter quarters:ABL.N.PL, so as above
demonstravimus, crebri ad eum
show:IND.PF.1PL, frequent:NOM.M.PL to he:ACC.M.SG
rumores adferebantur litteris -que
rumour:NOM.M.PL bring:IND.IMPF.3PL.PASS letter:ABL.F.PL and
item Labieni certior fiebat
likewise Labienus:GEN.M.SG inform:IND.IMPF.3SG.PASS
omnes Belgas, quam tertiam
all:ACC.M.PL Belgian:ACC.M.PL, who:ACC.F.SG third:ACC.F.SG
esse Galliae partem dixeramus, contra
be:INF.PRS Gaul:GEN.F.SG part:ACC.F.SG say:IND.PPRF.1PL, against
populum Romanum coniurare
people:ACC.M.SG Roman:ACC.M.SG conspire:INF.PRS
obsides -que inter se dare.
hostage:ACC.M.PL and between oneself:ACC.SG give:INF.PRS
'While Caesar was in winter quarters in Hither Gaul, as we have shown above, frequent rumours were brought to him, and he was also informed by letters from Labienus that all the Belgae, whom we have already described as a third of Gaul, were conspiring against the Roman people and giving hostages to each other.' (Caes., *B. G.*, II, 1)

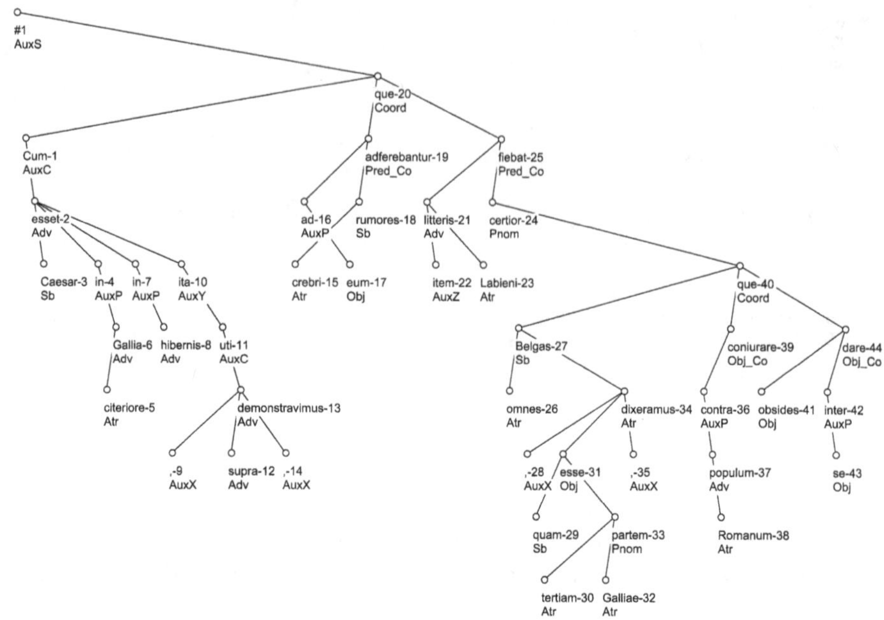

FIG. 3.3 *Dependency tree of sentence (11) from the LDT*

Another peculiarity of syntactic annotations that follow the Prague Dependency Treebank's guidelines is that prepositions and conjunctions are viewed as 'bridge' auxiliary structures and are annotated respectively with 'AuxP' and 'AuxC'. Similarly, in subordinate clauses (except for relative clauses) the conjunction is the bridge between the head verb and the verb of the subordinate clause: see the node *uti*-11 in Figure 3.3, introducing the subordinate clause *uti supra demonstravimus*.

In relative clauses, the predicate is tagged as 'Atr' and the relative pronoun is tagged as 'Sb' or 'Obj', depending on its syntactic function. For example, in Figure 3.3, the predicate *dixeramus*-34 of the relative clause *quam dixeramus* is attached to the noun it refers to (*Belgas*-27) as 'Atr', whereas *quam*-29 is the subject of the relative clause and depends on *esse*-31 AS 'Sb'.

In a coordination the coordinating node (i.e. the conjunction) is the head and its dependents are the coordinated elements appended with the suffix '_Co'. For instance, the coordinating enclitic node *que*-40 links the two verbs *coniurare*-39 ('Obj_Co') and *dare*-44 ('Obj_Co') in Figure 3.3. Similarly, in an apposing construction the apposition is the head and its dependents are tagged with the suffix '_Ap'.

Finally, the LDT and the IT-TB annotate ablative absolutes as subordinate clauses; so, the predicate (i.e. the participle, when it is present) depends on the main verb as an adverbial and the ablative NP (noun or pronoun, etc.) depends

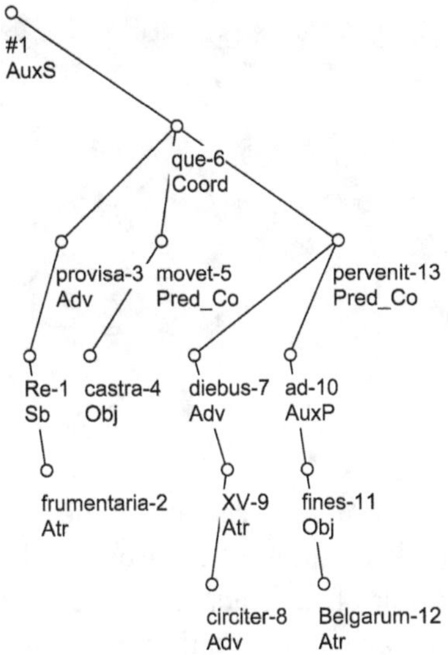

FIG. 3.4 *Dependency tree of sentence (12) from the LDT*

on the participle as a subject; cf. the ablative absolute *re frumentaria provisa* in Figure 3.4 for sentence (12), where the participle *provisa*-3 depends on the main verb *pervenit*-13 via the coordination *que*-6 and the ablative noun *re*-1 depends on *provisa* as a subject.

(12) Re frumentaria provisa castra
Provisions:ABL.F.SG provide:PTCP.PF.ABL.F.SG camp:ACC.N.PL
movet diebus -que circiter XV ad
move:IND.PRS.3SG day:ABL.M.PL and about:ADV fifteen to
fines Belgarum pervenit
border:ACC.M.PL Belgian:GEN.M.PL arrive:IND.PF.3SG
'After providing his provisions, he moved his camp, and in about fifteen days reached the borders of the Belgae' (Caes., *B. G.*, II, 2)

3.3.1 *Extracting Argument Patterns from the Treebanks*

I have created the lexicon as a database. To do that, I first loaded the treebanks into two database tables, because they differ slightly in the annotation format and so they require different search queries. To get an idea of what these tables look like, see Figure 3.5, which is a screen shot of the portion of the database table relative to sentence (9) on page 40 (Figure 3.1). Each row is a word of the sentence and each column is one of its attributes: ID (unique identifier for the word token), form (the form of the word, e.g. *quem* in (9)), lemma (*quis*), part-of-speech ('p' for 'pronoun'), person, number ('s' for 'singular'), tense,

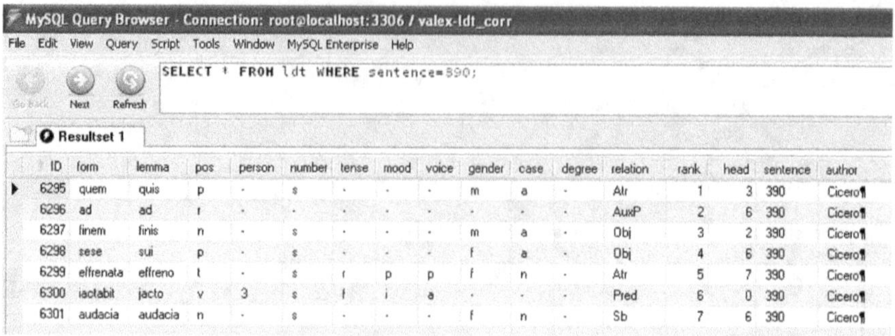

FIG. 3.5 *Database table for sentence (9) (page 40)*

mood, voice, gender ('m' for 'masculine'), case ('a' for 'accusative'), degree, dependency relation ('Atr' for 'attribute'), rank (position of the word in the sentence, e.g. '1' for the first word), head (rank of its head, e.g. '3' because *quem* depends on the third word of sentence (9)), sentence number ('390'), and author (*Cicero*).

Once the databases were ready, I searched them through MySQL queries I wrote specifically for this task. Because of the dependency annotation, the procedure was to first search for verbal tokens (occurrences of verbs in the treebanks), and then their arguments. Because the annotation contains the part-of-speech of each word in the treebanks (see column 'pos' in Figure 3.5), I just extracted all words with part-of-speech 'v' (verb) or 't' (participle). Moreover, the annotation of the treebanks gives the syntactic function of each word (subject, predicate, coordination, etc.) and the node it depends on. For each verb, I then searched for its arguments, i.e. nodes that have relation 'Sb' (subject), 'Obj' (direct and indirect object), 'Pnom' (predicate nominal), or 'OComp' (object complement), and depend on verbal nodes.

The dependency between a verbal head and its argument node can be direct or indirect. In the former case, the argument node is immediately under the head, as *praedicatum* and *habet* in Figure 3.2 on page 43. To extract this type of dependency it is enough to search for nodes whose value for 'head' is the rank of the verb. In the case of indirect dependencies, 'bridge' nodes intervene between the verbal headword and its arguments; these intermediate nodes can be prepositions, conjunctions, coordinating elements, or apposing elements. Figure 3.3 on page 44 shows the argument *eum* depending on the verb *adferebatur*-19 via the preposition *ad*, while Figure 3.3 on page 44 shows two coordinated objects of the predicate *certior fiebat*: *coniurare*-39 and *dare*-44. In the case of indirect dependencies, the database queries were more complex, because they had to account for all possible intermediate nodes (and their combinations).

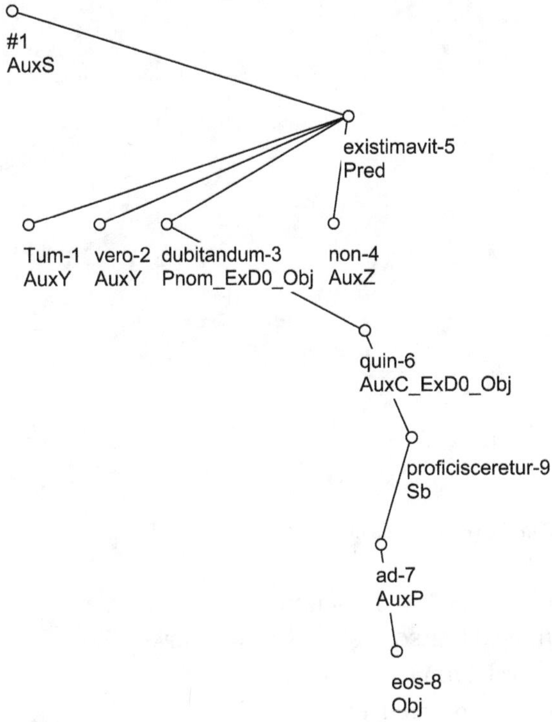

FIG. 3.6 *Dependency tree of sentence (13) from the LDT*

As an example of a conjunction intervening between a predicate and its argument, see (13) represented in Figure 3.6. Here, *proficisceretur* is the predicate of the subject clause *ad eos proficisceretur* and depends on the predicate *dubitandum* (*esse*) via the conjunction *quin*, so the argument pattern for *dubito* in this sentence is '(*quin*)Sb'.

(13) Tum vero dubitandum non existimavit
Then actually doubt:GERUNDIVE.ACC.N.SG NEG think:IND.PF.3SG
quin ad eos proficisceretur
that:CONJ to:PREP they:ACC.M.PL move:SBJV.IMPF.3SG
'Then accordingly he thought that he must no longer hesitate about moving towards them' (Caes., *B. G.*, II, 2)

A more complicated case is when there are multiple coordinated PPs (introduced by 'AuxP'), so that the affix '_Co' is appended to the children of the 'AuxP' node, as the annotation guidelines prescribe. See Figure 3.7 for sentence (14), where the verb *impono* has two coordinated objects (*quidditate* and *forma*) and the pattern for *impono* is 'P_(*a*)Obj_Co[abl],(*a*)Obj_Co[abl],Sb[nom]'.

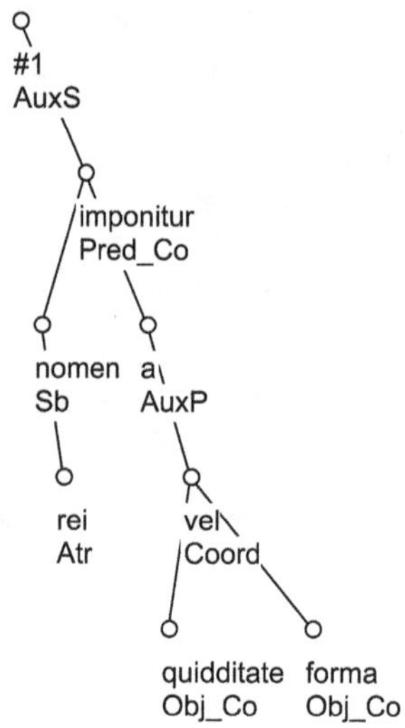

FIG. 3.7 *Dependency tree of sentence (14) from the LDT*

(14) Sed nomen rei imponitur a
but name:NOM.N.SG thing:GEN.F.SG assign:IND.PRS.3SG.PASS by
quidditate vel forma
quidditas:ABL.F.SG or form:ABL.F.SG
'Conversely the name *reality* is assigned by *quidditas* or by the form'. (Th., *Sent. P. L.*, I, D. 25, Q. 1)

3.4 Content and Look of the Lexicon

Once I extracted the verbal arguments, I combined them into patterns. The simplest type of pattern only contains the voice of the verb ('A' for active and 'P' for passive),[2] followed by the list of syntactic labels of the arguments, ordered alphabetically, for example, 'A_Obj, OComp, Sb' for verbs like *considero* 'consider'.

While the valency patterns of English verbs are best represented with syntactic labels, a good valency lexicon for Latin verbs represents patterns with morpho-syntactic features, given the vital role played by morphology in Latin argument realization.

2 Because the distinction between deponent and active verbs in the IT-TB is based on their lemmas only, the data from IT-TB also have a 'D' label for deponent verbs; on the other hand, the LDT distinguishes the semantically passive verbal forms from the semantically active ones for deponent verbs as well, so the LDT data only have 'A' and 'P'.

In addition to being syntactically tagged, the corpora are lemmatized and morphologically annotated, which means that, for each word, we know its lemma and its complete morphological analysis, in terms of part-of-speech, gender, and case (for nominal forms), and mood and voice (for verbal forms). This allowed me to enrich the lexicon with information on case/mood and lemma of the arguments. So, a sentence like

(15) intellectus componit privationem cum
intellect:NOM.M.SG link:IND.PRS.3SG privation:ACC.F.SG with
subiecto
subject:ABL.N.SG
'The intellect links privation to a subject'. (Th., *Sent. P. L.*, II, 37)

leads to the following valency pattern for the verb *compono* 'link':

A_(*cum*)Obj[abl], Obj[acc], Sb[nom].

You might have noticed that the intermediate nodes introducing the arguments (such as the preposition *cum*) are displayed between round brackets. If I wanted to add the lemmas of the arguments, I would get the pattern

A_(*cum*)Obj[abl]{*subjectum*}, Obj[acc]{*privatio*}, Sb[nom]{*intellectus*}.

Knowing the lemmas of the arguments is very important for corpus-based lexical studies like the one presented in chapter 6, and also for studying the verbs' lexical preferences on their arguments (so-called *selectional preferences*), which I will discuss in chapter 4.

In addition to morphological features, there is another peculiarity of the lexicon. Being Latin a so-called free word order language, it is very important to keep track of the relative order of a predicate and its arguments. For this reason, I have used a type of valency structure called *valency frames*. A valency frame lists the verb ('V') and its arguments in the order in which they appear in the sentence, and connects them with the symbol '+'. For example, sentence (15) corresponds to the frame

A_Sb[nom]{*intellectus*} + V + Obj[acc]{*privatio*} + (*cum*)Obj[abl]{*subjectum*}

because the nominative subject precedes the verb, which is followed by an accusative object and an ablative object depending on the preposition *cum*.

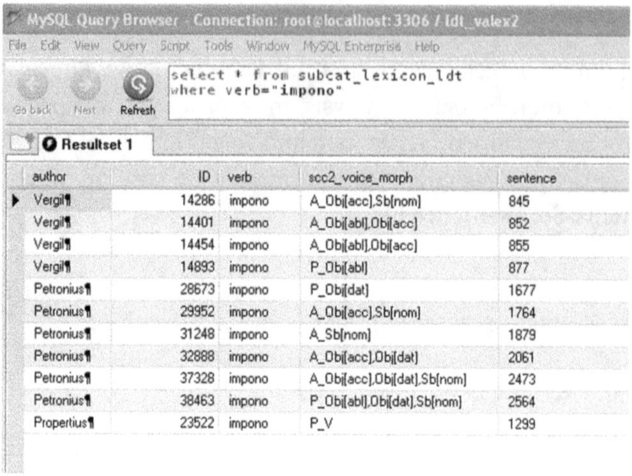

author	ID	verb	scc2_voice_morph	sentence
Vergil¶	14286	impono	A_Obj[acc],Sb[nom]	845
Vergil¶	14401	impono	A_Obj[abl],Obj[acc]	852
Vergil¶	14454	impono	A_Obj[abl],Obj[acc]	855
Vergil¶	14893	impono	P_Obj[abl]	877
Petronius¶	28673	impono	P_Obj[dat]	1677
Petronius¶	29952	impono	A_Obj[acc],Sb[nom]	1764
Petronius¶	31248	impono	A_Sb[nom]	1879
Petronius¶	32888	impono	A_Obj[acc],Obj[dat]	2061
Petronius¶	37328	impono	A_Obj[acc],Obj[dat],Sb[nom]	2473
Petronius¶	38463	impono	P_Obj[abl],Obj[dat],Sb[nom]	2564
Propertius¶	23522	impono	P_V	1299

FIG. 3.8 *Lexical entry for the verb impono from the lexicon for the LDT. The pattern is called 'scc2_voice_morph' because it shows the voice and the morphological features of the arguments.*

Depending of the user's needs, the lexicon can display any combination of the features I just illustrated, which makes it a very flexible resource. The user can thus decide to view the voice of the verb, the lemmas of prepositions and conjunctions intervening between the predicate and its arguments, the syntactic labels of the arguments, and/or their morphological features and lemmas.

In addition, the person of the verb can be added to the valency patterns. This allows the users to identify those cases where the subject is omitted, but the information about it is part of the verbal inflection.

(16) Bibo
drink:IND.PRS.1SG
'I drink'

So, a sentence like (16), has the pattern 'V-1sg'.

3.4.1 *Interface*

I originally represented the lexicon as database tables. The two parts of the lexicon have been deposited in the Oxford Text Archive.[3] As a way of example,

3 They are available at http://www.ota.ox.ac.uk/desc/2546 (LDT lexicon) and http://www.ota.ox.ac.uk/desc/2547 (IT-TB lexicon).

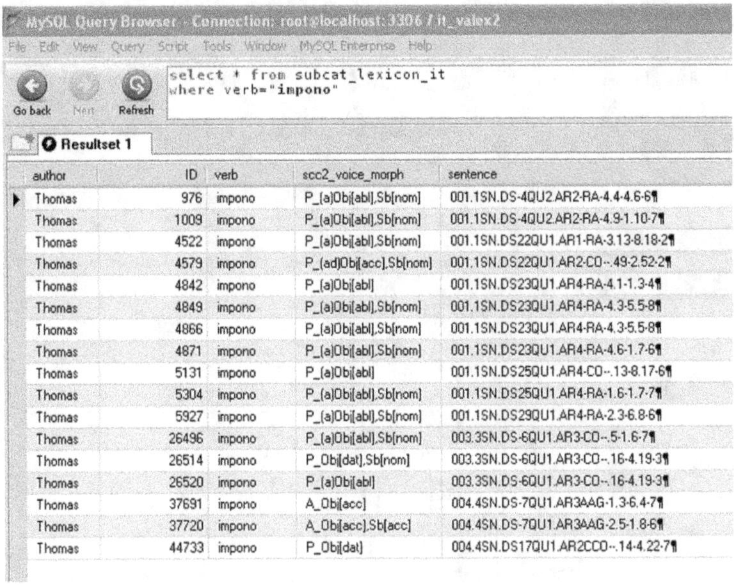

author	ID	verb	scc2_voice_morph	sentence
Thomas	976	impono	P_(a)Obj[abl],Sb[nom]	001.1SN.DS-4QU2.AR2-RA-4.4-4.6-6¶
Thomas	1009	impono	P_(a)Obj[abl],Sb[nom]	001.1SN.DS-4QU2.AR2-RA-4.9-1.10-7¶
Thomas	4522	impono	P_(a)Obj[abl],Sb[nom]	001.1SN.DS22QU1.AR1-RA-3.13-8.18-2¶
Thomas	4579	impono	P_(ad)Obj[acc],Sb[nom]	001.1SN.DS22QU1.AR2-CO--.49-2.52-2¶
Thomas	4842	impono	P_(a)Obj[abl]	001.1SN.DS23QU1.AR4-RA-4.1-1.3-4¶
Thomas	4849	impono	P_(a)Obj[abl],Sb[nom]	001.1SN.DS23QU1.AR4-RA-4.3-5.5-8¶
Thomas	4866	impono	P_(a)Obj[abl],Sb[nom]	001.1SN.DS23QU1.AR4-RA-4.3-5.5-8¶
Thomas	4871	impono	P_(a)Obj[abl],Sb[nom]	001.1SN.DS23QU1.AR4-RA-4.6-1.7-6¶
Thomas	5131	impono	P_(a)Obj[abl]	001.1SN.DS25QU1.AR4-CO--.13-8.17-6¶
Thomas	5304	impono	P_(a)Obj[abl],Sb[nom]	001.1SN.DS25QU1.AR4-RA-1.6-1.7-7¶
Thomas	5927	impono	P_(a)Obj[abl],Sb[nom]	001.1SN.DS29QU1.AR4-RA-2.3-6.8-6¶
Thomas	26496	impono	P_(a)Obj[abl],Sb[nom]	003.3SN.DS-6QU1.AR3-CO--.5-1.6-7¶
Thomas	26514	impono	P_Obj[dat],Sb[nom]	003.3SN.DS-6QU1.AR3-CO--.16-4.19-3¶
Thomas	26520	impono	P_(a)Obj[abl]	003.3SN.DS-6QU1.AR3-CO--.16-4.19-3¶
Thomas	37691	impono	A_Obj[acc]	004.4SN.DS-7QU1.AR3AAG-1.3-6.4-7¶
Thomas	37720	impono	A_Obj[acc],Sb[acc]	004.4SN.DS-7QU1.AR3AAG-2.5-1.8-6¶
Thomas	44733	impono	P_Obj[dat]	004.4SN.DS17QU1.AR2CCO--.14-4.22-7¶

FIG. 3.9 *Lexical entry for the verb impono from the lexicon for the IT-TB*

Figure 3.8 displays the entry for the verb *impono* in the portion of the lexicon extracted from the LDT, whereas Figure 3.9 displays the same information extracted from the IT-TB portion. Note that the tenth row in Figure 3.9 corresponds to sentence (14) (Figure 3.7 on page 48).

In order to make it more user-friendly, I have also designed a graphical interface for the IT-TB-based part of the lexicon, which was then implemented by the CIRCSE research center at the Catholic University of Milan.[4] The interface is described more in detail in (McGillivray and Passarotti, 2012) and enables the user to both browse and search the lexicon.

The screen shot in Figure 3.10 shows the home page of the interface, with the list of verbs in the IT-TB lexicon and their frequency counts. By clicking on each verb the user is redirected to the list of annotated sentences containing that verb. The user can also click on the left-hand side of the page to run searches on the lexicon specifying a verb or certain features of the arguments: number (e.g. which verbs have zero/one/two/three/four arguments?), order (e.g. which verbs display valency patterns where the subject precedes an object?), syntactic function and case/mood (e.g. which verbs have valency patterns with an accusative object introduced by the preposition *ad*?)

4 http://centridiricerca.unicatt.it/circse_78.html, http://itreebank.marginalia.it/itvalex.

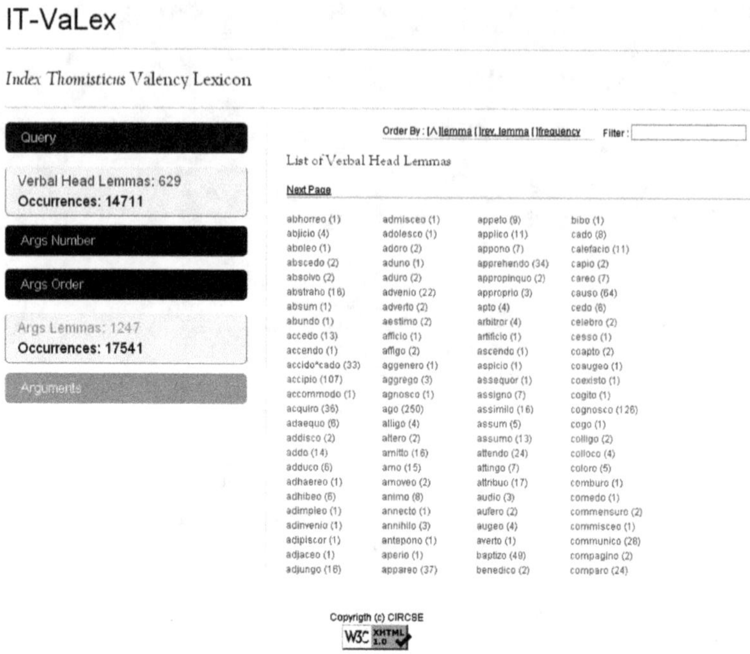

FIG. 3.10 *The home page of the graphical interface for the IT-TB portion of the lexicon*

3.5 Quantitative Data

The lexicon is a valuable source of information on Latin verbs. The fact that it is corpus-based means that it gives a faithful picture of the behaviour of the verbs in the treebanks. In fact, this is the first time that such information is freely available to a wide audience of Latin linguists, and its potential is great.

An example of some basic but important information one can straightforwardly get out of the lexicon is the distribution of verb frequencies in the two treebanks. Table 3.3 shows the number of different verbal tokens (forms and lemmas) and the number of verbal types (forms and lemmas) by author.

Perhaps not surprisingly, Saint Thomas uses much fewer verb types than the authors in the LDT (see the row headed 'TOTAL' in Table 3.3), which means that the lexical richness of verbs is lower in the IT-TB than in the LDT. This result is confirmed when we compare the type/token ratios displayed in the last column of Table 3.3: these ratios are much lower in the IT-TB than in the LDT.[5]

---

5 The measure for the overall lexical richness for all the words in the corpora follows the same trend: $\frac{|V_{Tf}|}{|T|} = \frac{14021}{53143} = 0.26$, $\frac{|V_{Tl}|}{|T|} = \frac{5986}{53143} = 0.11$ (LDT) and $\frac{|V_{Tf}|}{|T|} = \frac{5183}{54878} = 0.09$, $\frac{|V_{Tl}|}{|T|} = \frac{1873}{54878} = 0.03$ (IT-TB).

TABLE 3.3 *Number of verbal tokens ($|T|$) and verbal types (forms $|V_{Tf}|$ and lemmas $|V_{Tl}|$) in the lexicon by author. $\frac{|V_{Tf}|}{|T|}$ and $\frac{|V_{Tl}|}{|T|}$ are the type/token ratios*

Treebank	Author	$\|T\|$	$\|V_{Tf}\|$	$\frac{\|V_{Tf}\|}{\|T\|}$	$\|V_{Tl}\|$	$\frac{\|V_{Tl}\|}{\|T\|}$
LDT	Caesar	295	247	0.84	169	0.57
↓	Cicero	1283	933	0.73	458	0.36
	Jerome	1770	774	0.44	274	0.16
	Ovid	1092	845	0.77	474	0.43
	Petronius	2901	1748	0.60	731	0.25
	Propertius	1039	767	0.74	400	0.38
	Sallust	2294	1509	0.66	631	0.28
	Vergil	511	460	0.90	317	0.62
	TOTAL	11185	7283	0.65	3454	0.31
IT	Thomas	9072	2108	0.23	560	0.06

Also, one may wonder what are the most frequent realized valency patterns in the Classical authors of the LDT and in a medieval author like Thomas (IT-TB). The lexicon gives an answer to this too.

If we focus on patterns displaying the voice of the verbs and morphological features of the arguments, Table 3.4 displays the 15 most frequent patterns in the lexicon.

From Table 3.4 we can see an expectedly large number of "empty" patterns ('A_V' for active verbal forms and 'P_V' for passive ones), that is when the verbs do not occur with any explicitly realized arguments, thus appearing in the zero-valency class of the lexicon. Only a subset of such cases include genuinely zero-valency usages of verbs. This means that an empty pattern may occur in different cases:

- the verb is zerovalent according to valency theories, e.g. *pluit* '(it) rains';
- the verb has valency one (or greater) according to valency theories, but its instance has one or more (definite or indefinite) omitted arguments and its subject is not overtly expressed, as in *bibimus* 'we drink'.

For example, in the lexicon the sentence *Dixerat, et flebant* (Ovid, *Met.*, I, 367) 'He spoke, and they were crying' displays an empty pattern for the verb

TABLE 3.4 *15 most frequent valency patterns with voice and morphological information, and their frequencies in the LDT and IT-TB lexicons*

LDT		IT-TB	
A_V	1669	P_V	1188
A_Obj[acc]	1668	A_V	1047
A_Obj[acc],Sb[nom]	1052	A_Pnom[nom],Sb[nom]	955
A_Sb[nom]	963	A_Sb[nom]	855
P_V	843	P_Sb[nom]	629
A_Obj[inf]	363	A_Obj[acc],Sb[nom]	578
P_Sb[nom]	294	A_Obj[acc]	499
A_Pnom[nom],Sb[nom]	274	A_Pnom[nom]	346
A_Obj[inf],Sb[nom]	260	A_Obj[inf],Sb[nom]	315
P_Sb[abl]	171	A_Obj[inf]	148
A_Pnom[nom]	156	P_Pnom[nom],Sb[nom]	122
A_Obj[acc],Obj[dat]	147	P_Obj[dat],Sb[nom]	101
P_Obj[abl]	126	A_(*quod*)Sb[sbjv]	86
A_Sb[acc]	112	P_Obj[dat]	79
A_Obj[dat],Sb[nom]	105	P_(*a*)Obj[abl]	73

dico in the sense of 'talk', because the subject is dropped and the object is missing. The complete valency structure of *dico* in the usual sense of 'say' would require either just a subject (in its sense of 'talk'), or a subject and an object/complement clause (in the sense 'say').

As to the morphological features (case and mood), in most cases verbal arguments are expressed in the treebanks as we would expect: nominative for subjects and predicate nominals, accusative for direct objects and object complements, dative and ablative for indirect objects. However, Table 3.5 indicates the important role played by alternative constructions, such as ablative absolutes ('Sb[abl]'), accusative + infinitive clauses ('Sb[acc]' and 'Obj[inf]'), and subject clauses ('Sb[ind]' and 'Sb[sbjv]'). In addition, subjects in genitive correspond to gerundives, while nominative objects in most cases belong into reported speech or occur with participial verb forms.

Another feature of the lexicon concerns the display of intermediate nodes occurring between the verb and its arguments. Table 3.6 lists the most frequent ones: coordinations and prepositions, then appositions and conjunctions. Their most frequent lemma is *et* in both corpora; then come other

TABLE 3.5 *Morphological realizations of verbal arguments in the lexicon. Column 'Sb': the rows headed 'acc' and 'abl' refer to subjects in accusative + infinitive constructions and in ablative absolutes, respectively; 'ind' and 'sbjv' refer to subject clauses whose subjects are expressed as verbs in the indicative and subjunctive mood, respectively. For the other cases, see the text.*

LDT							
Sb		**Obj**		**Pnom**		**OComp**	
Case/mood	**Freq**	**Case/mood**	**Freq**	**Case/mood**	**Freq**	**Case/mood**	**Freq**
nom	4528	acc	4657	nom	874	acc	71
acc	606	inf	1014	acc	142	nom	5
abl	230	dat	907	gen	35	–	4
inf	143	abl	833	–	22	gen	2
ind	93	ind	292	abl	19	abl	2
sbjv	49	sbjv	225	dat	16		
–	36	nom	91	inf	10		
gen	24	imp	76	ind	7		
voc	2	gen	57	sbjv	3		
dat	2	–	57	voc	1		
imp	1	voc	3				
		loc	2				
		supine	1				
IT-TB							
nom	4536	acc	1912	nom	1709	acc	35
sbjv	240	abl	553	inf	99	abl	3
acc	160	inf	517	gen	81	ind	1
ind	137	dat	450	acc	60		
inf	128	ind	132	ind	34		
abl	73	sbjv	37	–	4		
–	5	gen	27	sbjv	1		
imp	2	nom	4	abl	1		
adv	1	adv	3	dat	1		
dat	1	–	2				
		imp	1				

TABLE 3.6 *Most frequent syntactic functions and lemmas of the intermediate nodes between the verbs and their arguments in the treebanks*

LDT				IT-TB			
Synt.tag	Freq	Lemma	Freq	Synt.tag	Freq	Lemma	Freq
Coord	1781	*et*	824	Coord	836	*et*	494
AuxP	759	*que*	417	AuxP	790	*quod*	332
Apos	154	*in*	231	AuxC	374	*a*	268
AuxC	67	*atque*	200	AuxC,Coord	79	*ad*	237
AuxP,Coord	62	*ad*	147	Apos	59	*in*	178

coordinating elements (*que* and *atque*)[6] and the preposition *in* in the LDT plus subordinating conjunctions (*quod*) and prepositions (*a, ad, in*) in the IT-TB.

As I said earlier, valency frames in the lexicon record the order of the verb and its arguments; for example 'A_Obj + Obj + Sb_Co + Sb_Co + Sb_Co + V' means that there are two objects followed by three coordinated subjects and an active form of a verb. In order to show how important valency frames are for studying word order properties of Latin syntax, I will describe the results of a small study on word order patterns in the treebanks. A more elaborate investigation of word-order patterns in the two treebanks can be found in Passarotti et al. (2012).

For this study I extracted all frames from the lexicon according to the following criteria: the voice of the verb form was active, and the valency frame contained the labels 'V' for verbs (obligatory), 'Sb' (facultative), and 'Obj' (obligatory). In addition, I excluded the cases where two or more objects occurred to the left and to the right of the verb at the same time. I did not want the data to be biased by the fact that Latin is a pro-drop language; so, I focussed on the alternation between the patterns 'VO' and 'OV', so e.g. 'Obj + Obj + Sb_Co + Sb_Co + Sb_Co + V' counted as 'OV'.

Table 3.7 shows the frequencies of the two patterns in the two portions of the lexicon. Does this mean that there is a significant regularity in the distribution of the two patterns in the treebanks? In order to answer this question I resorted to a chi-square test of independence, which I illustrate in section 7.1. The test

6 According to the annotation guidelines, the comma is considered a coordinating element; its frequency with the 'Coord' tag is the second highest among the lexical items occurring as path nodes in the LDT (482).

TABLE 3.7 *Frequencies of the word order patterns 'VO' and 'OV' in the two portions of the lexicon*

Pattern	LDT portion	IT-TB portion
OV	153	37
VO	116	40

gives a result that is not statistically significant ($p = 0.2141, \chi^2_{(1)} = 1.54$); this might be due to the fact that the LDT contains texts by authors belonging to very different genres and ages. In fact, if I merge the data for Jerome (the latest author in the LDT) with those for Thomas, I get frequencies 152 (LDT without Jerome) and 38 (IT-TB plus Jerome) for 'OV' and 52 (LDT without Jerome) and 107 (IT-TB plus Jerome) for 'VO'. This leads to a significant result ($p < 0.01, \chi^2_{(1)} = 77.79$) and a large effect ($\varphi = 0.474$), which means a strong association between the word order patterns and this new choice of classification by author-based groups.

The result of this case study shows that the data associated with Jerome affect the outcome of the test: the presence of Jerome in the first test pulls the distribution of the LDT data closer to the IT-TB data. This might indicate a diachronic trend from the Classical authors to Jerome+Thomas. However, this first hypothesis should be further tested to see whether factors other than time (like genre) affect the results.

3.6 The Lexicon and Latin Computational Linguistics

The lexicon displays Latin verbal valency on the basis of the actual occurrences of verbs and their arguments in the treebanks LDT and IT-TB. My definition of what constitutes an argument is therefore purely usage-based in the sense that it fully relies on the texts contained in the corpora and on the way the corpora were annotated. The distinction between arguments and adjuncts was already present in the annotated data and so I did not need to acquire it in the extraction step. Consequently, in the extraction system I defined verbal arguments as those nodes depending on a verb (sometimes via certain intermediate nodes) and annotated with some specific syntactic labels ('subject', 'object', etc.).

The operational definition of valency used in the lexicon, which is motivated by the annotational parsimony adopted by the treebanks' designers, has also a methodological advantage. It does not impose too strong theoretical assumptions on the annotated data (for example it does not resolve ellipsis, uninstantiated, or omitted arguments), while at the same time allowing to express distributional properties of Latin lemmas.

According to the distinction between *corpus-based* approaches and *corpus-driven* approaches proposed in Tognini-Bonelli (2001), the lexicon is a corpus-based resource because it automatically detects the structures contained in the corpora on the basis of their annotation, which relies on a specific theoretical framework (Functional Generative Description); the extracted information is thus affected by that annotation schema.

The way I exploited the original corpora to create the lexicon distinguishes it from both traditional and modern lexical resources of the same kind. First, the close connection between the lexicon and the corpora it was obtained from differentiates it from traditional Latin dictionaries and thesauri. These resources typically aim at illustrating the behaviour of words by providing specific examples from texts in a non-systematic fashion. At the same time, these resources usually give a broad overview of Latin, without limiting the analysis to particular works or authors. In contrast, the lexicon aims at comprehensively describing the linguistic evidence represented by the two treebanks used. For this reason, I did not intend the detected valency patterns as representing the general behaviour of Latin verbal arguments: they rather give a picture of the distribution of verbal arguments in the particular corpora at hand. When generalizing these results—as described in chapter 4, for instance—the special composition of the treebanks (time periods, authors, genres) should be considered as an important factor. Further, unlike traditional lexical resources, the lexicon displays frequency data, which is very valuable information for further studies, as I show with an example in chapter 6.

If we compare the lexicon with the other lexicons for Latin (Happ, 1976; Bamman and Crane, 2008), we see that this one presents several advantages. First, its size. Happ (1976)'s lexicon was obtained from a manual inspection of 800 verbal occurrences in Cicero, while Bamman and Crane (2008) extracted a lexicon from an automatically parsed corpus of 3.5 million words. The small size of Happ's corpus is balanced by the high quality of the manually analysed data, but it hardly allows for generalization. On the other hand, the noise present in Bamman and Crane's corpus is compensated for by its large size and the employment of statistical techniques. I propose a lexicon which is obtained from high quality data and is, at the same time, relatively large: it was extracted from two medium-sized treebanks amounting to close to 100,000 word tokens and contains lexical entries for around 20,000 verb tokens. Its size was manageable thanks to the automatic methods I used to extract it. In addition, its high quality makes it possible to perform linguistic studies which target low-frequency phenomena, as well as medium and high-frequency phenomena.

Not only is the lexicon a new resource for Latin that can be automatically updated as the treebanks increase, but it also makes the valency content of the treebanks more accessible to the users and contributes to improving the treebanks themselves. For example, I manually checked the "unexpected" morphological tags in the valency patterns, such as objects in the nominative case or vocative subjects. This allowed me to correct some inconsistencies in the treebank annotation and in the morphological analysis, which were particularly numerous in the LDT. This procedure is an example of a virtuous circle between the creation and annotation of corpora, and the extraction of lexical resources from them. Another interaction between the lexicon and the treebanks concerns ongoing work towards semantic and pragmatic annotation of one of the treebanks (IT-TB; Passarotti (2013)). This additional layer of annotation will make it possible to extract further information on elided arguments and semantic roles, for example, and include them in the lexicon. Among other things, this will allow to make explicit empirical comparisons between the patterns found according to the operational morpho-syntactic definition of valency adopted here and the patterns resulting from the additional semantic annotation level.

In a methodological perspective, the lexicon gives an original contribution to the emerging field of Latin Computational Linguistics: it places itself at the interface between computational lexicography and lexical acquisition on the one hand, and Latin syntax and morphology on the other.

The result is a lexical resource available to all those interested in investigating various aspects of Latin morpho-syntax in a corpus-based fashion: the argument structure of prefixed verbs (analysed in chapter 6), Latin word order (see section 3.5), the semantics of the Dative Subject Construction (Barðdal et al., 2012), just to suggest a few of them.

Dealing with a historical language affects the aims and the audience of the research we carry out. Corpora for modern languages are often exploited in Computational Linguistics as training sets to automatically analyse new unseen texts; on the other hand, corpora for ancient languages combine this aim with the traditional philological interest in the text *per se* and in language change. In this perspective, the lexicon I have extracted can contribute both to Latin corpus linguistic research and to research in NLP for Latin. For what concerns the former, in chapter 6 I will present a linguistic analysis on preverbs based on the lexicons; regarding the latter, in chapter 4 I will proceed towards a further semantic processing of the Latin language, which originates from the morpho-syntactic and lexical information contained in the lexicon.

The literature on Latin Linguistics is still replete with small-scale studies based on manually analysed corpora which are not publicly available (and are often created specifically for those studies), so it is very difficult to check and replicate the results of such analyses. Also, because those studies rely on small amounts of data, they run the risk of presenting results that are not statistically significant. There are very few Latin Linguistics studies based on annotated corpora. In this respect, the lexicon is really in the forefront of a new, corpus-oriented attitude in Latin Linguistics.

All that fits very well in what I see as a desired future attitude in Latin Linguistics, where researchers collaborate in collecting amounts of rich data for large-scale quantitative and replicable linguistic studies. This collaboration means that interrelated but independent projects (such as the annotation of the treebanks and the creation of the lexicon) can build on each other's outcomes. The result is large amounts of data and rich annotation that would not be achievable within the scope of one single project. Each project (whether it is a lexical resource like the lexicon or an analysis tool) could be considered lacking in coverage (for example by showing a syntax-driven approach to valency or by reporting on a selection of authors), but put together they contribute to the bigger picture, which in turn makes it possible for the scientific field to proceed forward.

CHAPTER 4

The Agonies of Choice: Automatic Selectional Preferences

4.1 Automatic Selectional Preferences for Latin Verbs

In chapter 3 I described the first corpus-based valency lexicon for Latin verbs. The lexicon gives a quantitative account of the morpho-syntactic properties of verbal arguments in terms of case (for nominal forms) and mood (for verbal forms) of lemmas of verbal arguments. Additionally, the lexicon records a number of other important properties, like the voice of the verb, the syntactic labels of the arguments (subject, predicate nominal, etc.), their lemmas, prepositions, and conjunctions introducing the arguments, and coordinations and appositions linking the arguments.

Thanks to the lexicon, the user finds out that, for example, the passive forms of the verb *impono* 'impose' occur 12 times in Thomas with an ablative argument introduced by the preposition *a* 'from'. The nouns/pronouns found in this argument position are: *qui* 'who' (7 times), *proprietas* 'property' (1), *forma* 'form' (3), *quidditas* 'quidditas' (1, coordinated with *forma*), *actus* 'act' (1). We can group the valency patterns of *impono* according to any of the afore-mentioned features, for example we can count how many times *impono* is found with a noun in the ablative case coordinated with *forma* and introduced by *a*. But what if we wanted to carry out a wider lexical study on the arguments of *impono*? For example, we may wonder if its direct objects tend to be inanimate or animate entities, and how this distribution changes by author. We may also want to know which proportion of the subjects of *venio* are more likely to be filled by nouns referring to human beings vs. animals. In Computational Linguistics such lexical preferences of verbs on their arguments are conventionally called *selectional preferences* (SPs).

It is possible to obtain SPs through a manual analysis, that is by manually assigning semantic classes to nouns. However, this has several drawbacks. It is a very difficult task, on which little agreement between different annotators is likely to be found. It is also very costly and thus usually limited to relatively small samples. Besides, whenever we need to update the source data, we have to perform the analysis again. Instead, automatic methods allow to process large amounts of data and are, by definition, replicable at (almost) no extra effort. Moreover, having large amounts of analysed data makes it possible to draw

 | DOI: 10.1163/9789004260122_005

more general conclusions, which is the goal of many linguistic studies. In addition, manual procedures are prone to omissions and inconsistencies that are very difficult to detect; instead, automatic methods are in a way more reliable because they are, by definition, consistent. Finally, the high number of variables potentially affecting a semantic phenomenon is not made explicit in a manual analysis, whereas in a computational model we can define and exactly quantify the role played by each variable. For example, if we wanted to build a model for semantically clustering nouns based on their part-of-speech, syntactic role, and lemma, we could assign different weights to each of these variables until the classes we obtain are sufficiently similar to a gold standard. This way, we would be able to quantify the relative importance of each morphological, syntactic and lexical feature.

Over the past two decades research into automatic acquisition of SPs from corpora has led to a number of different computational systems. This chapter shows that it is possible to automatically extract SPs from Latin syntactically annotated corpora by adapting the research in Computational Linguistics to Latin data. The starting point is a count of many times the triples (verb, syntactic relation, and argument's lemma) occur in the corpus (I will refer to the arguments' lemmas as *lexical fillers*). It is possible to get this information from a valency lexicon like the one I described in chapter 3. For example, for the accusative objects of *bibo* 'drink', I found the fillers *aqua* 'water', *toxicum* 'poison', *vinum* 'wine', and *lac* 'milk', each with frequency one in the lexicon. The main idea here is to generalize from the individual lexical fillers to wider classes (for example LIQUID or FLUID). The question I aim at answering is thus: how can I generalize over the corpus occurrences in order to describe the preferences of the verb *bibo* towards its accusative objects? In other words: which nouns or semantic classes other than the lexical fillers listed above are we likely to find as accusative objects of *bibo*?

4.1.1 *The Diachronic Dimension*

As Piotrowski (2012, 100) points out, the typical situation in Computational Linguistics involves large, usually homogeneous, synchronic corpora created for modern languages, and these corpora are usually employed to train statistical computational models. When one single model or tool is used for a whole diachronic historical corpus, the potential linguistic differences across the parts of the corpus may lead to a poor performance.

The diachronic dimension is therefore an additional variable that needs to be taken into account whenever applying computational models developed for (synchronic) corpora of modern languages to a historical corpus. The corpus I used is certainly diachronic, and covers a time span from Cicero to Saint

Thomas. As far as the work presented in this chapter is concerned, the critical question is thus whether diachrony affects selectional preferences of verbs.

One way to tackle this question would be to model SPs based on each of the two main diachronic eras represented in the corpus, and then compare the SPs obtained this way, to see if there is a significant difference between them. However, this solution is not viable due to the characteristics of the corpus. Splitting the corpus into its diachronic parts does not solve the problem, because these parts are too small for training statistical models like the one described here (Piotrowski, 2012, 100). Instead, I will conduct a preliminary study on the original corpus data, to see whether the following assumption can be confirmed.

> There is no statistically significant difference between the diachronic sections of the input to the SP model in terms of verbal lexical preferences.

How to operationalize this assumption? SPs are defined for a given verb-syntactic slot pair, for example, *habeo* 'have' + A_Obj[acc] for the accusative objects of the active forms of *habeo*. SPs are calculated based on the lexical fillers of each verb-slot pair in the corpus (and their frequencies). As I will show in this chapter, I have developed two systems for calculating SPs as probability distributions over a set of semantic classes. In this preliminary study, I will aim at testing whether the assumption above is to be confirmed by considering the diachronic distributions of the lexical realizations of verbal arguments in the corpus in terms of their semantic properties.

The composition of the corpus used for the work described here is that of the LDT and the IT-TB, displayed in Table 1.1 (excluding Plautus). The differences among these authors concern various aspects, including genre and era. Here, I will concentrate on the chronological aspect, but the methodology is valid for differences in the other aspects, too, such as genre. The two main chronological gaps occur between Petronius (ca. 27–66 AD) and Jerome (ca. 347–420) and between Jerome and Thomas Aquinas (ca. 1225–1274 AD). I will thus consider two sets defined in the two following scenarios:

1. (first scenario)
    (a) LDT authors (Cicero, Caesar, Sallust, Vergil, Propertius, Ovid, Petronius, and Jerome)
    (b) IT-TB author (Thomas Aquinas)
2. (second scenario)
    (a) LDT authors excluding Jerome (Cicero, Caesar, Sallust, Vergil, Propertius, Ovid, and Petronius)
    (b) IT-TB author (Thomas Aquinas) and Jerome

First of all, I need to make a distinction between the verb-slot pairs shared by the two parts of the corpus and all the other verb-slot pairs. For the former ones, it makes sense to detect the degree of overlap between their preferences; in the latter case, the fact that a verb-slot pair occurred in one portion of the corpus but not in the other is not enough information to imply that the verb-slot would have different SPs.

I will therefore focus on the verb-slot pairs that occur in both sets in the two scenarios. In the first scenario, the number of shared verb-slot pairs is 505; in the latter it is 653. It is no surprise that in both cases these pairs correspond to high-frequency, common verbs, like *accedo* 'approach' + A_(ad)Obj[acc], *accipio* 'take' + A_Sb, or *advenio* 'arrive' + A_Sb.

If we look at the number of shared fillers for each of these shared pairs, perhaps unsurprisingly, we find out that it is very small: 79 in the first scenario and 103 in the second one. Some examples are:

- *sum* 'be' + A_Sb (shared fillers *potentia* 'power', *oculus* 'eye', *tempus* 'time', *aqua* 'water')
- *sum* 'be' + A_Pnom (shared fillers *servus* 'servant, slave', *bonus* 'good')
- *do* 'give' + A_Sb (shared filler *pater* 'father')
- *impono* 'impose' + A_Obj[acc] (shared filler *manus* 'hand')

The range of topics covered in the works by the different authors of the corpus has an impact on the range of lexical fillers. It would thus be unrealistic to expect a high degree of overlap between the fillers in the two sets, given the size of the corpus. However, since SPs concern the semantic properties of the lexical fillers of the verbs, it is reasonable to consider the overlap between these semantic properties as a measure of the similarity between the SPs across eras.

If I associate each filler to the set of top nodes found in Latin WordNet (LWN, described in section 4.2), I get the following results: 365 out of 505 shared verb-slot pairs have at least one LWN top node in common in the first scenario, and 451 out of 653 in the second one. For example, the fillers for the subjects of the passive forms of the verb *accendo* 'fire, light' are: *ignis* 'fire' (frequency 1) in IT-TB, and *animus* 'soul' (frequency 1) and *libido* 'desire' (frequency 1) in the LDT. The LWN top nodes for *ignis* are:

- ACTIO, ACTUS (ACT, HUMAN ACTION, HUMAN ACTIVITY)
- PSYCHOLOGICAL FEATURE
- OXIDATION, OXIDISATION, OXIDIZATION

The top nodes for *animus* are:

- BEING, LIFE FORM, LIVING THING, ORGANISM
- ENTITY, SOMETHING
- EVILDOING, TRANSGRESSION
- TRAIT
- BODY PART
- PSYCHOLOGICAL FEATURE
- BASIC COGNITIVE PROCESS
- MEMORY, REMEMBERING
- BEING, LIFE FORM, LIVING THING, ORGANISM
- SPIRIT

The ones for *libido* are:

- EVILDOING, TRANSGRESSION
- EMOTIONALISM, EMOTIONALITY
- ATTRIBUTE
- PSYCHOLOGICAL FEATURE
- DECIDING, DECISION MAKING
- AROUSAL

So, the overlap between the top LWN classes in the two eras consists of the class [PSYCHOLOGICAL FEATURE].

In order to check whether the number of verb-slot pairs with overlapping LWN top nodes (which I consider as successes) is significantly higher than chance, it is useful to perform a *binomial test* using the statistics software R (R Development Core Team, 2008) (see pages 112 ff. for an explanation of this test). The results are summarized in Table 4.1 and show that in both scenarios the number of successes is significantly higher than the number of failures (i.e. opposite outcome), and significantly higher than what would be expected by chance. To sum up, a significant majority of verb-slot pairs shared across the two eras (according to both scenarios) also share the broad semantic classes of their fillers, intended as the LWN top nodes. This exploration does not of course imply that verbal selectional preferences are not affected by the diachronic variable in Latin. Such a statement would need to be tested on a larger corpus and with a wider variety of texts, which would fall outside the scope of the present study. The results of this investigation confirm the initial assumption, and legitimize the methodology followed in the next sections, where the fillers from both parts of the corpus are considered together as the corpus basis for the computational model.

TABLE 4.1 *Summary of the results of the test for the assumption on page 63. The first scenario compares the amount of overlap in the set of LWN nodes for the shared verb-slot pairs in LDT and IT-TB; the second scenario compares the LDT authors excluding Jerome and Saint Thomas plus Jerome.*

	No. shared verbs-slots	No. shared fill.	No. shared top nodes	95% conf.int.	P(success)
1st scen.	505	79	365*	[0.68,0.76]	0.72
2nd scen.	653	103	451*	[0.65,0.73]	0.69

4.2 The Knowledge-Based Approach

Knowledge-based approaches to SP acquisition like Resnik (1997), Li and Abe (1998), and McCarthy (2001) use a lexical ontology to find semantic classes of noun fillers. This ontology is usually WordNet (WN, Miller et al. 1990), a lexicon-oriented semantic network, developed at Princeton University for the English language and introduced in section 2.4.2.1. WN is a standard in linguistics; it is freely available and has a wide coverage of the English lexicon. In WN, lexical items are organized into sets of synonyms called *synsets* and representing lexical concepts; links between synsets are defined by means of semantic and lexical relations such as hyponymy, hyperonymy and meronymy. In particular, each synset is linked to higher-level synsets (hypernyms) all the way up to the top nodes via tree structures. For example, the English noun *bird* belongs to five synsets; the first one ("warm-blooded egg-laying vertebrates characterized by feathers and forelimbs modified as wings") is linked to the top node [ENTITY, SOMETHING] via the intermediate hypernym nodes [VERTEBRATE, CRANIATE], [CHORDATE], [ANIMAL, ANIMATE BEING, BEAST, BRUTE, CREATURE, FAUNA], and [LIFE FORM, ORGANISM, BEING, LIVING THING].

The great news is that a Latin version of WN exists and is called Latin WordNet (LWN; Minozzi 2009). LWN is an ongoing project integrated within MultiWordNet,[1] which is aimed at building a large-scale multilingual computational lexicon based on WN. Presently, the size of LWN is around 10,000 lemmas, with 9,000 synsets and 25,000 word senses, approximately a tenth of the English WN. To give an idea of how LWN is structured, let us go back to the example on *bibo*: *aqua* belongs into nine synsets in LWN, *lac* into four synsets, and *toxicum*

1 http://multiwordnet.fbk.eu/english/home.php.

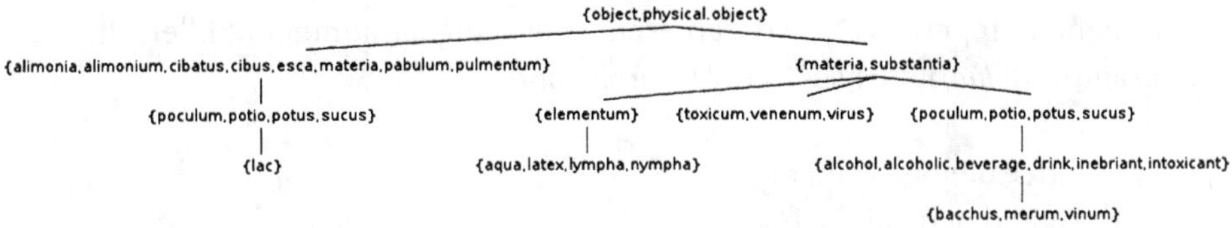

FIG. 4.1 *Example portion of the LWN hierarchy containing one synset for each of the accusative objects of* bibo *'drink' in the corpora:* aqua *'water',* lac *'milk',* toxicum *'poison', and* vinum *'wine'*

and *vinum* into one each. Figure 4.1 represents a portion of LWN where the leaf nodes contain one synset for each of *aqua, lac, toxicum,* and *vinum*, and the synsets are represented by lists of synonyms.

In order to develop the system, I look for nodes in LWN that can faithfully represent the accusative objects of *bibo* and generalize over their corpus fillers. To find those nodes I follow the paths from the fillers' leaf nodes up the hierarchy; I will call each node in those paths a *semantic property*.

In Figure 4.1, [MATERIA, SUBSTANTIA] is a parent node of *toxicum, vinum,* and *aqua*, so [MATERIA, SUBSTANTIA] is a semantic property common to *toxicum, vinum,* and *aqua*; moreover, it is a semantic property for other entities that can be drunk, even if they are not attested in the corpora (so-called *unseen events*), like *bacchus, merum, Falernum* 'wine', or *nectar* 'fruit juice'. [MATERIA, SUBSTANTIA] is thus a good candidate for the SPs of *bibo*. Going up to the top level we find [OBJECT, PHYSICAL OBJECT], which is the parent node of all the fillers in the corpora and is a more general class than [MATERIA, SUBSTANTIA]. However, [OBJECT, PHYSICAL OBJECT] also includes things that cannot be drunk: it is probably too general for our purposes, since it would not be able to differentiate between the arguments of *bibo* and the arguments of other verbs. A good generalization should at the same time be comprehensive and reflect the features of the fillers it generalizes from; my model precisely tackles the issue of how to achieve this optimal level of generalization.

4.2.1 *Challenges of the Latin Data*

The corpus fillers are the basis for the generalization. Intuitively, if I had a larger set of fillers to generalize from, the approximation of the SPs for *bibo* would probably improve. Also, the corpus is not semantically annotated at the sense level, which means that, for example, I can only see *lac* in the corpus, but I do not know which of its four senses is used in each occurrence. The best I can do when I assign the fillers to the LWN nodes is to distribute the occurrences of *lac* (and any other noun) evenly among its different senses. However, if there are enough observations, the model assigns a higher probability to the semantic properties that are represented by a higher number of fillers. In the example of *lac*, its senses in LWN correspond to:

1. a source of nourishment
2. the liquid parts of the body
3. dairy product
4. any liquid suitable for drinking

At the beginning of this process I cannot know which sense is the most likely one for the accusative objects of *bibo*; however, if I find other fillers of *bibo* that share certain semantic properties with some of the above-mentioned senses (for example other dairy products), I would feel more confident in assigning them to the SPs for *bibo*. This confidence increases with statistical measures that depend on the corpus frequencies of the fillers, and effectively disambiguate them.

As a matter of fact, previous systems for SP acquisition exploit large corpora as training sets: this increases the probability of capturing a high number of argument fillers from the input. In addition, the size of the corpora allows for the use of statistical techniques that are able to highlight significant differences in frequency between likely and unlikely verbal arguments. My relatively small dataset (around 100,000 tokens) results in a large number of low-frequency verb-noun associations, which may not reflect the actual distributions of Latin verbs. This is particularly problematic in the generalization step, since the set of seen events I try to generalize from may be too small to reflect the actual SP behaviour of Latin verbs. If I then try to generalize from these corpus occurrences to broader classes of nouns, the results may be compromised by the small size. For example, if I find zero or just one instance of an animate subject for *adfirmo* 'state, claim', it may mean that there are too few occurrences of the verb overall, rather than that animate entities are not likely subjects for this verb. In order to (partially) remedy this difficulty I will group the observations into larger entities, *constructions*, so as to increase the number of instances that count as a generalization base for each verb. My definition of 'construction' follows from Alishahi (2008), who builds on the concept of form-meaning pair as defined in Construction Grammar (Goldberg, 1995) and extends it probabilistically, as I shall show now.

4.2.2 *Frames and Constructions*

Let us consider a synonym of *bibo*, *haurio* 'drink', which occurs with the following accusative objects in the lexicon: *flumen* 'river' and *potio* 'drink'. If I join the set of fillers for *bibo* (*aqua* 'water', *toxicum* 'poison', *vinum* 'wine', *lac* 'milk') with this set, I get a wider range covering things that are drunk. *Potio* shares the LWN node [*poculum, potio, potus, sucus*] ('any liquid suitable for drinking') with *lac* and *vinum*, which gives additional reasons to infer a stronger preference of *bibo* for the fourth sense of *lac* ('any liquid suitable for drinking'). In a system that merges the fillers of *bibo* with those of *haurio*, the semantic properties relating to the other less relevant senses of *lac* will receive lower probabilities.

The key step in this process is to group together some of the verbal corpus occurrences of *bibo* with occurrences of other verbs like *haurio*. To decide if a verb instance is suitable to be clustered with a certain occurrence of *bibo*, the system measures its semantic similarity with *bibo*, the closeness between their syntactic patterns containing 'Obj[acc]', and the semantic similarity between their fillers. In other words, rather than stating a general similarity between *bibo* and *haurio*, the system detects those single verb usages where the two predicates behave similarly with respect to syntactic and lexical-semantic criteria. Once those occurrences of *bibo* and *haurio* have been grouped together, they all contribute to the set from which the system generalizes to create the SPs for *bibo*.

My system is inspired by the cognitive model for SP acquisition described in Alishahi (2008). In Alishahi's model each verb usage is defined as a *frame*, that is a collection of syntactic and semantic features, such as the number of verbal arguments, the valency pattern, and the semantic properties of each argument. A *construction* is then defined as a collection of frames probabilistically sharing some syntactic and semantic features, for example the transitive construction. Let us discuss a concrete example.

(1) grando magna sicut talentum
hail:NOM.F.SG big:NOM.F.SG as talentum:NOM.N.SG
descendit de caelo in homines
come down:IND.PF.3SG from sky:ABL.N.SG towards man:ACC.M.PL
'Hailstones, as big as a talent, came down from the sky on men.' (Jerome, *Apocalypse*, 16.)

Sentence (1) represents an active occurrence of the verb *descendo* 'go down' and the valency lexicon records it with the following valency pattern ('A' stands for 'Active', 'Sb' for 'subject', 'Obj' for 'object', 'nom' for 'nominative', 'acc' for 'accusative', and 'abl' for 'ablative'):

(2) *descendo* + A_(*de*)Obj[abl]{*caelum*}, (*in*)Obj[acc]{*homo*}, Sb[nom]{*grando*}

TABLE 4.2 *Frame for sentence* (2)

sentence	
grando magna [...] *descendit de caelo in homines*	
frame	
verb	do
feature$_1$	A_(de)Obj[abl],(in)Obj[acc],Sb
feature$_2$	(de)Obj[abl]: *caelum*↔{sky, celestial sphere, sphere, empyrean, firmament, heavens, vault of heaven, welkin, surface, boundary, bound, bounds, extremity, region, part, location, object, physical object, entity, something} (in)Obj[acc]: *homo*↔{man, adultmale, male, person, individual, someone, somebody, mortal, human, soul, life form, organism, being, living thing, entity, something} Sb[nom]: *grando*↔{hail, precipitation, downfall, weather, weather condition, atmospheric condition, atmospheric phenomenon, physical phenomenon, natural phenomenon, nature, phenomenon}
feature$_3$	*descendo*↔ {descend, fall, go down, come down}

I will call each such verbal occurrence a *frame*. Each frame is identified by the values of three features, accounting for its valency and its lexical-semantic properties.

Morpho-syntactic feature. The argument slots for the active form of *descendo* in sentence (1) are an ablative object with the preposition *de* (A_(*de*)Obj[abl]), an accusative object with *in* (A_(*in*)Obj[acc]), and a nominative subject (A_Sb). The first feature of the frame concerns its morpho-syntactic labels and I will call it *feature*$_1$. The value of this feature in sentence (2) is thus 'A_(*de*)Obj[abl], (*in*)Obj[acc], Sb'. In my system, unlike Alishahi's one, the number of arguments in a frame is not part of the frame's syntactic features, given the high optionality of verbal arguments in Latin and the fact that Latin is a Pro-Drop language. Additionally, I record the case marking of objects (which differentiate patterns of valency in Latin), but I identify subjects, nominal predicates and object complements by their syntactic labels only.

Semantic features of the arguments. In addition to the morpho-syntactic features, I include the lexical fillers of the verbal arguments into each frame (together with their corresponding WN nodes) as a semantic component, which I will call *feature*$_2$. For each argument position, the values of *feature*$_2$ are the set of WN synonyms and hypernyms of the filler(s) for that slot. For example, the semantic properties for the slot A_Sb in (2) are all the hypernyms of the synset for *grando* 'hail': [GRANDO, PRECIPITATION, DOWNFALL, WEATHER, WEATHER CONDITION, ATMOSPHERIC CONDITION, ATMOSPHERIC PHENOMENON, PHYSICAL PHENOMENON, NATURAL PHENOMENON, NATURE, PHENOMENON].

Since LWN only records nouns, verbs, adjectives, and adverbs, I tag all verbs and participles occurring as argument fillers with the labels 'V' and 'Pt' respectively, and all proper nouns either as 'NP' (anthroponyms and ethnonyms), 'NL' (toponyms), 'NO' (names of literary works), or 'NT' (names of time entities). In addition, I exclude all occurrences of pronouns as lexical fillers from the system. The reason for this is that pronouns cannot be associated to noun classes, unless by performing anaphora resolution, which is beyond the scope of the present research.[2]

In order to define a correct mapping between the lexical fillers extracted from the treebanks and the LWN lemmas, and between the lemmas in the LDT and those in the IT-TB, I normalize spelling mismatches, such as spelling variations with or without assimilation of the consonant (*impedio*/*impello*, *adfligo*/*affligo*) or different spellings of the semivowel *i* as *j* (*adiungo*/*adjungo*).

Semantic features of the verb. I define the semantic feature of a frame (*feature*$_3$) as the list of the verb's LWN synsets. In sentence (2) they coincide with the list of all items appearing in the synsets of *descendo*: *cado, defluo, degredior, delabor, demeo* 'descend, fall, go down, come down'. The synsets for *cado* 'fall' and *descendo* 'descend' are represented in Table 4.3. The overlap between the synsets for *descendo* and those for *cado* contains one synset: {*cado, defluo, degredior, delabor, demeo*}. The number of synsets for *F* is 1, so the synset score in this case is $\frac{1}{1} = 1$.

Table 4.2 shows an example of the frame corresponding to sentence (2); for the sake of clarity, I only reported the hypernyms of the English synset

2 Following the proposal on page 50, one could also use the information on the person of the verb to identify animate subjects. The first and the second verbal forms indicate speech act participants, and therefore suggest that they are animate. However, the classification outlined here is more granular that the animate vs. inanimate categorization and requires a more in-depth case-by-case analysis that what information on verb morphology can offer, and has therefore excluded such cases.

TABLE 4.3 *Synsets of* cado *'fall' and* descendo *'descend'. For each sense of these two verbs (e.g. cado/1), the first row contains the LWN synset, while the second row contains their corresponding English synsets in Multi WordNet.*

cado/1	{*cado, defluo, degredior, delabor, demeo*}
	{descend, fall, go down, come down}
cado/2	{*abscedo, degredior, migro, proficiscor*}
	{depart, part, start, start out, set forth, set off, set out, take off}
cado/3	{*averto, declino, deflecto, degredior, derivo, detorqueo, deverto*}
	{deviate, divert}
cado/4	{*degredior*}
	{stoop, descend}
cado/5	{*degredior*}
	{condescend, deign, descend}
cado/6	{*degredior, delabor*}
	{derive, come, descend}
descendo/1	{*cado, defluo, degredior, delabor, demeo*}
	{descend, fall, go down, come down}

corresponding to the synset number 11 of *caelum* in LWN, referring to the sense "outer space as viewed from the earth"; for *homo*, I reported the hypernyms of its sixth synset "an adult male person (as opposed to a woman)"; for *descendo*, I reported the English synset corresponding to the Latin synset {*cado, defluo, degredior, delabor, demeo*} "move downward but not necessarily all the way".

Enriching Latin WordNet. While defining the values for the second and third features, which involve mapping the corpus fillers onto LWN, it becomes clear that the coverage of LWN is low with respect to the data: 1027 corpus fillers out of 2934 and 90 verbs out of 559 are not present in it. A way to increase the number of LWN lemmas matching the fillers is to create a procedure for semi-automatically adding new Latin lemmas to the LWN hierarchy. For each lemma, I collect its Italian and/or English translations by using Latin-to-Italian and Latin-to-English dictionaries. For example, the lemma *ianua* 'door' does not appear in LWN; its Italian and English translations in the dictionaries Lewis and Short (1879) and Castiglioni and Mariotti (1993) are: *porta, uscio, entrata, door*, and *entrance*. Then, I extract the synsets of these translations from the Italian version of MultiWordNet (MWN) and from the English WN.

In accordance with the semantics of each Latin noun, I manually select those synsets of its translation(s) that are relevant to its senses. For *ianua*,

TABLE 4.4 *Synsets of* porta, entrata, door, *and* entrance *in MWN*

Italian synset	Latin synset
porta/1	{foris, porta}
porta/2	none
porta/6	none
entrata/2	{accessus, aditus, foris, ingressus, initus, introitus, limen, porta, vestibulum}
door/1	{foris, porta}
door/3	none
entrance/1	{accessus, aditus, foris, ingressus, initus, introitus, limen, porta, vestibulum}
entrance/3	{aditus, foris, ingressus, initus, introitus, limen, porta, vestibulum}

Table 4.4 contains the LWN synsets corresponding to the selected senses of its translations. Therefore, I select 'porta/1', 'porta/2', 'porta/6', 'entrata/2', 'door/1', 'door/3', 'entrance/1', and 'entrance/3'.

Finally, thanks to the alignment between MWN, LWN and WN, I can retrieve the Latin synsets corresponding to the selected Italian and English synsets from the previous step, when they are present, and assign them to the Latin word. In the previous example, this means assigning the lemma *ianua* to the following synsets: {*accessus, aditus, foris, ingressus, initus, introitus, limen, porta, vestibulum*}, {*foris, porta*}, and {*aditus, foris, ingressus, initus, introitus, limen, porta, vestibulum*}. This procedure makes it possible to add 401 new noun lemmas and 90 verb lemmas to 2056 already existing Latin synsets.

4.2.3 *Clustering Frames*

I have defined a frame as a pattern identified by the values of three following features:

- *feature*$_1$ (morpho-syntactic): verb lemma + voice + syntactic and morphological tags of its arguments: e.g. '*descendo* + A_(*de*)Obj[abl]'
- *feature*$_2$ (semantic): WN synonyms and hypernyms (semantic properties) of the lexical fillers of the verb's arguments: e.g. ATMOSPHERIC PHENOMENON, ENTITY
- *feature*$_3$ (semantic): WN synonyms of the verb: e.g. *cado, descendo*

TABLE 4.5 *Schema of the clustering algorithm*

step 0	$\{F_1\}$	$\{F_2\}$	...	$\{F_x\}$	...	$\{F_N\}$
step 1	$\emptyset$	$\{F_2\}$	...	$\{F_1,F_x\}$	...	$\{F_N\}$
...			...			

Each verbal occurrence in the corpora corresponds to a frame. In order to create a reasonably large set of frames from which to generalize, I then cluster them into constructions (see sections 5.2.2 and 5.2.3 for an illustration of clustering). My system acquires these clusters by means of the incremental process from Alishahi (2008), which I describe more in detail in section 5.4.2. and which is summarized in Table 4.5.

Here I will focus on the conceptual core of the algorithm.

A construction collects frames that are similar from the point of view of their syntactic and semantic features, and I define this similarity by specific *similarity scores*. For example, let us consider the following frames *F*:

descendo + A_(*de*)Obj[abl]{*caelum*}, (*in*)Obj[acc]{*homo*}, Sb{*grando*}

and *h*:

descendo + A_(*de*)Obj[abl]{*caelum*}, (*in*)Obj[acc]{*terra*}.

F is clustered together with *h* on the basis of the similarity between the valency patterns of the two frames, the number of shared semantic properties of the two pairs of fillers for the slot '(*de*)Obj[abl]' (*caelum*) and the slot '(*in*)Obj[acc]' (*homo* and *terra*), and the similarity/identity between the verbs of the frames.

For measuring the similarity between the valency patterns I use *syntactic scores*. The syntactic score between two frames is the number of syntactic slots they shared, divided by the number of slots in the first frame; the syntactic score accounts for the degree to which the frames' valency patterns differ. The syntactic score between *F* and *h* is given by the number of slots shared by *F* and *h* (which is 2), divided by the total number of slots in *F* (which is 3), hence it is $\frac{2}{3}$.

Semantic scores account for the degree of overlap between the semantic properties of the argument fillers in frames, divided by the number of semantic properties of the fillers in the first frame. In the above-mentioned frames *F* and *h*, *terra* 'earth' and *homo* 'man' are the lexical fillers of the slot '(in)Obj[acc]' for *h* and *F*, respectively. The semantic score relative to the slot '(in)Obj[acc]' is $\frac{5}{58} = 0.09$, because the intersection between the semantic properties of the two words contains 5 items (*caelum, classis, mundus, natio* and *res*) out of 58 (which are all the semantic properties for *terra*); see section 5.1.2 for the full sets of semantic properties for *terra* and *homo*.

Finally, for the semantic properties of the verbs, I calculate the *synset scores* between the verbs in the two frames. The synset score is the degree of overlap between the synonyms of the verb in the two frames divided by the number of synsets for the verb in the first frame. For example, let us compare *F*

descendo + A_(*de*)Obj[abl]{*caelum*},(*in*)Obj[acc]{*homo*},Sb{*grando*}

and *h*

cado+ A_Sb{*angelus*}.

The overlap between the synsets for *descendo* and those for *cado* contains one synset: {*cado, defluo, degredior, delabor, demeo*}; the number of synsets for *F* is 1, so the synset score is $\frac{1}{1} = 1$. The reason why verb features are only extracted from its synset and not its hypernyms is that the definition of hyperonymy for verbs is less straightforward than for nouns; see for example Richens (2008), who shows the flaws of WordNet's verb hierarchy.

Another way to calculate the similarity between two fillers or two verbs would be to use a WN-based measure, such as the score defined in Wu and Palmer (1994); this score is based on the depth of two nodes in WN, and thus it heavily relies on the theoretical assumptions underlying the WN hierarchy. On the other hand, the overlap between synsets is not dependent on the depth of the hierarchy and measures the similarity of two words based solely on the amount of shared lexical content of their synsets. For this reason, it relies on fewer assumptions and is a simpler model, which is the main reason for choosing it for this specific purpose.

4.2.3.1 Results

When the algorithm is run on the dataset containing the lexicon described in chapter 3, it produces 11478 distinct frames with a total frequency of 15509. The number of distinct syntactic patterns (such as 'A_(*ex*)Obj[abl], Obj[acc]') is 697 and the distinct pairs verb-syntactic pattern are 5309. The output of the algorithm consists of 7105 constructions. For example, the 13 frames where the verb *abeo* 'go from, leave' occurs (frequency =13) are split into 6 different constructions, listed in Table 4.6.

TABLE 4.6 *Constructions for the frames containing the verb* abeo *'go from, leave'*

Construction	Frames
1	*abeo*+A_(*ad*)Obj[acc]{*angelus*} *eo*+A_(*ad*)Obj[acc]{*conspectus*} *exeo*+A_(*ad*)Obj[acc]{*frigida*}
2	*abeo*+A_(*ad*)Obj[acc]{*multus*} *eo*+A_(*ad*)Obj[acc]{*conspectus*} *exeo*+A_(*ad*)Obj[acc]{*frigida*}
3	*abeo*+A_(*in*)Obj[acc]{*villus*},A_Sb[nom]{*vestis*} *abscondo*+A_(*in*)Obj[abl]{*petra*},A_Obj[acc]{*PR*},A_Sb[nom]{*dives*} *abstraho*+A_(*a*)Obj[abl]{*pulvis*},A_Obj[acc]{*PR*},A_Sb[nom]{*amor*} *abstraho*+A_(*a*)Obj[abl]{*materia*},A_Sb[acc]{*forma*}
5	*abeo*+A_Obj[abl]{*domina*}
6	*abeo*+A_Obj[acc]{*domus*} *dimitto*+A_Obj[acc]{*domus*},A_Obj[acc]{*PR*}
7	*abeo*+A_Obj[acc]{*terra*}
8	*abeo*+A_Sb[-]{*carica*} *cado*+A_Sb[nom]{*NL*}
9	*abeo*+A_Sb[acc]{*PR*} *pereo*+A_Sb[acc]{*PR*}
10	*abeo*+A_Sb[nom]{*caelum*},A_Sb[nom]{*terra*}
11	*abeo*+A_Sb[nom]{*NP*}
12	*abeo*+A_Sb[nom]{*primus*} *abeo*+A_Sb[nom]{*secundus*}

Construction	Frames
13	*abeo*+A_Sb[nom]{*vinus*} *decedo*+A_Sb[nom]{*delicatus*},A_Sb[nom]{*margaritum*} *deficio*+A_(*a*)Obj[abl]{*repraesentatio*},A_Sb[abl]{*PR*} *morior*+A_Sb[nom]{*PR*} *recedo*+A_(*a*)Obj[abl]{*PR*},A_Sb[nom]{*PR*}

Note the semantic similarity between the three verbs involved in construction 1 (*abeo* 'go from, leave', *eo* 'go', and *exeo* 'go out of') and between the subject fillers in construction 6 (*domus*).

Among the constructions acquired, 3011 contain one frame, 3836 contain 2 frames, 242 contain 3 frames, 13 contain 4 frames, 2 contain 5 frames, and one contains 6 frames. The small number of frames per construction and the consequent high number of constructions can be explained by the coverage of LWN with respect to the fillers in the dataset. In fact, the system is not able to assign 782 fillers out of 2408 to any LWN synset; for these lemmas the semantic scores with all the other nouns is 0, which results in assigning the frame to a singleton construction consisting of the frame itself.

Furthermore, a large number of frames (6588 out of 19581, or 33%) contain verbs, participles, pronouns and proper nouns as their fillers; consequently, they are clustered with frames containing the same fillers, since this is the only case where the semantic score is not 0.

In addition, in the system frequent senses do not contribute more than unfrequent ones. Instead, senses with longer paths to the root nodes contribute more than the others, because the number of their hypernyms is higher; this biases the actual frequency distributions of senses in the corpora. As an example, take the two nouns *felicitas* and *laetitia*. According to Lewis and Short (1879), the first meaning of *felicitas* is 'fruitfulness, fertility', the second being 'happiness, felicity', considered as the predominant sense; the third one is the deity Felicitas. For *laetitia*, Lewis and Short (1879) list 'unrestrained joyfulness, gladness, pleasure, delight' and then the transferred sense of 'pleasing appearance, beauty'. Although the semantics of these two nouns may appear quite similar, their semantic score is lower than 0.5, because the intersection between the semantic properties of *felicitas* and those of *laetitia* contains only 12 items, while the union contains 51.

All these difficulties make the constructions defined in the dataset less general than those found by Alishahi (2008). This may also be caused by the fact that she uses more homogeneous corpora: the children language corpus *Childes* and the general language corpus British National Corpus. However, the constructions turn out to be good enough to give rise to quite interesting SPs.

4.2.4 *Probabilistic Selectional Preferences*

I defined SPs as probability distributions over the set of semantic properties, which are elements of WN nodes (cf. section 4.2.3), for example ENTITY or OBJECT. So, for example, if the probability of OBJECT as an accusative object of *abeo* is higher than LOCATION, it means that OBJECT is more likely than LOCATION in that position for *abeo*. I calculate this probability based on the constructions containing the verb *abeo* itself. Moreover, to expand the generalization set even further, I consider the constructions containing verbs which appear in the same synset(s) as *abeo*, like *abscedo*, and assign different weights to those verbs according to their semantic similarity with *abeo*. This contribution from verbs sharing a synset with the verb is an innovation from the system by Alishahi (2008) and is tailored to the dataset, where the low frequencies in many cases would not allow the generalization step.

As I explain more in detail in section 5.4.3, the probability of a semantic property for a certain verb and a given argument position is obtained by summing the probabilities of that semantic property for all constructions containing the verb or its WN-synonyms. I calculate each of these probabilities by accounting for the degree to which the verbs in the constructions are similar to the target verb, and the degree to which the fillers of the frames in the constructions are similar to the semantic property.

4.3 The Knowledge-Free Approach

Unlike knowledge-based approaches which refer to external knowledge bases like WN, knowledge-free approaches in computational semantics aim at collecting information on a word's semantics by looking at its corpus context, following the famous statement by Firth (1957, 11): "You shall know a word by the company it keeps!". This view has led to distributional approaches to semantics in Computational Linguistics. In the case of SP acquisition, distributional methods produce semantic classes directly from the corpus evidence on the words' co-occurrence contexts, as exemplified in what follows.

4.3.1 *Distributional Similarity*

As a toy example, suppose we are interested in the subjects of *fly*, for which I have collected the following fillers and corpus frequencies: *bee* (3), *bug* (2), *bird*

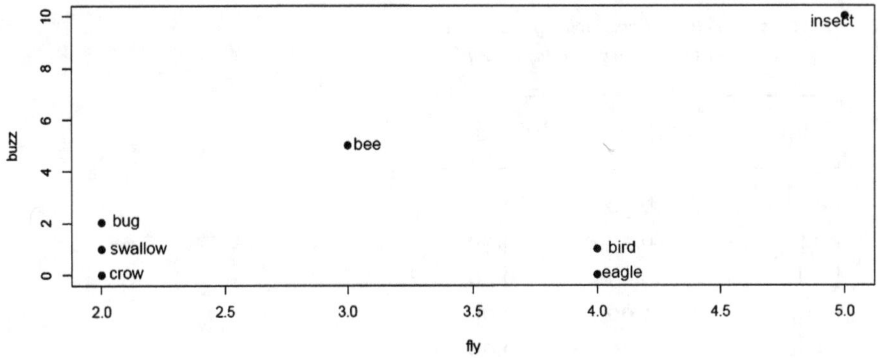

FIG. 4.2 *Two-dimensional plot representing the subjects of* fly *and* buzz (*absolute frequencies*) *in a toy example*

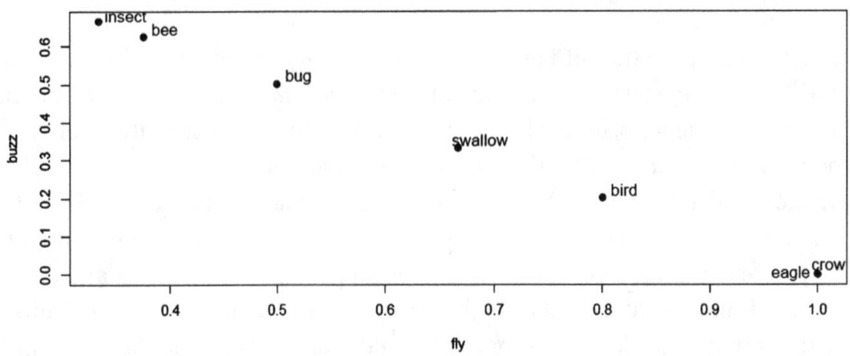

FIG. 4.3 *Two-dimensional plot for the subjects of* fly *and* buzz (*relative frequencies*) *in a toy example*

(4), *crow* (2), *eagle* (4), *insect* (5), *swallow* (2). I may want to split this set of nouns into coherent subgroups; for this, I could decide to place similar nouns into the same group. For example, I may expect *crow* and *eagle* to be more similar than, say, *crow* and *bee*. To confirm this intuition I could extract the contexts of these nouns as the verb lemmas with which they occur and see if *crow* and *eagle* share more contexts than *crow* and *bee*: in this case I would say that they are *distributionally similar* and distributional similarity would be a model for semantic similarity.

Imagine that *buzz* occurs with the following frequencies: *bee* (5), *bug* (2), *bird* (1), *crow* (0), *eagle* (0), *insect* (10), *swallow* (1). I can now identify those seven nouns in geometrical terms by their co-occurrence with the two verbs *fly* and *buzz*: this means representing them as points in a space defined by two dimensions, one associated with *fly* and one with *buzz*, as shown in Figure 4.2.

TABLE 4.7 *Relative frequencies of the subjects of* fly *and* buzz *in a toy example*

Noun	With *fly*	With *buzz*
bee	0.38	0.63
bug	0.50	0.50
bird	0.80	0.20
crow	1.00	0.00
eagle	1.00	0.00
insect	0.33	0.66
swallow	0.66	0.33

From an inspection of Figure 4.2 we notice that the points *crow, swallow,* and *bug* lie very close together, just like *bird* and *eagle*: this is because of their absolute frequencies, from which I may conclude that the distributions of these points are similar. If I plot their relative frequencies instead (Table 4.7), i.e. I divide each verb-filler frequency count by the frequency of the filler (e.g. the relative frequency of *bee* with *fly* is $\frac{3}{3+5} = \frac{3}{8} = 0.375$), I get a different picture. In Figure 4.3 *insect* and *bee* are now close together, just like *crow* and *eagle.* In fact, I may be interested in highlighting that *insect* appears twice as often with *buzz* as with *fly* (that is, one third and two thirds of its total frequency, respectively): this allows us to notice the similarity between *eagle* and *crow*, in spite of their different raw frequencies.

4.3.2 *Distributional Selectional Preferences*

In the SP system I described in section 4.2, I choose the synset score and semantic score as measures of the similarity between verbs and nouns, respectively. These scores rely on the structure and content of LWN, so that a high score means that the two words are highly related with respect to the WN relations. According to the syntax-semantics interface hypothesis, two verbs sharing syntactic features such as valency patterns also share meaning components (Levin, 1993; McCarthy, 2001; Schulte im Walde, 2003). By combining this hypothesis with a distributional approach to semantics, I want to provide the algorithm for SP acquisition with an alternative measure of semantic similarity, and calculate this measure between words based on the frequencies of their distributions in corpora (as the cosine distance between the corresponding vectors, see section 5.2.2).

In order to get higher frequency counts and a better performance, I use larger corpora than the treebanks. These corpora are portions of the *Perseus Digital Library* (10 million tokens; Bamman and Crane 2008)[3] and the *Index Thomisticus* (11 million tokens; Busa 1980).[4] Two subsets of over 3 million tokens each have been extracted from these corpora and automatically syntactically parsed (Bamman and Crane, 2008; McGillivray et al., 2009; Passarotti and Ruffolo, 2009).

So, I now try using these two parsed corpora as input to the database queries for the extraction of the valency lexicon described in chapter 3, and use the new lexicon obtained this way as a corpus basis for measuring semantic similarity between words. The idea is to consider two verbs semantically similar according to the valency slots they share. Similarly to the second toy example on *fly* and *buzz*, I measure the similarity between two verbs by using their relative frequencies with each valency slot. In other words, it is not important how many times a verb (say *voco* 'call') occurs with a slot (say 'A_Sb'), but which *proportion* of the total occurrences of *voco* are found with A_Sb. To measure how similar two noun fillers are, I use their relative frequency with the verb-slot pairs, for example *abeo* 'go from, leave' with A_Obj[acc], and calculate their distance based on the angle between their corresponding vectors.

In section 5.3 I give the details of how I calculate these similarity measures. Here, I would like to stress the conceptual difference between this approach to semantic similarity and the WN-based one illustrated in sections 4.2.3 and 4.2.4. Rather than referring to an ontology where, for example, *dico* 'say' and *narro* 'tell' share six synsets and are therefore semantically close to each other, this approach puts more emphasis on the distributional behaviour of the two verbs in a corpus. The distributional version of the algorithm hence replaces the similarity scores described in sections 4.2.3 and 4.2.4 with this corpus-based distributional similarity measure, and considers two words as similar if they share enough lexical-syntactic contexts.

4.4 Evaluating Preferences

The two versions of the algorithm produce SPs in the form of probabilities of LWN nodes, for example the probability of SUBSTANCE as an object of *bibo*. But how to asses how good these probabilities are?

---

3 http://www.Perseus.tufts.edu/hopper/.

4 http://www.corpusthomisticum.org/.

TABLE 4.8 *15 nouns with the highest probabilities as accusative objects of* appono *'serve, delegate' in the WN model*

Noun	SP probability
actio 'act'	0.04443662
actus 'act'	0.04443662
forma 'form'	0.04443662
entity	0.04443662
instrumentality	0.04443662
instrumentation	0.04443662
object	0.04443662
physical object	0.04443662
psychological feature	0.04443662
something	0.04443662
eventum 'event'	0.04127941
eventus 'event'	0.04127941
organization	0.04127941
res 'thing'	0.04127941

4.4.1 *The System Calibration*

The first question I want to answer is whether the system is good at distinguishing between high and low probabilities, i.e. between likely and unlikely entities for a verb in a particular argument position: I call this property of the model *calibration.* Since I work with corpus data, I restrict the evaluation to entities that are realized as nouns in the corpora. So, in general, I expect a small set of nouns (preferred nouns) to get a high SP probability, and a large set of nouns (the rest) to get a low probability. Of course, the proportion of preferred nouns will be higher for verbs such as *take* or *like,* which accept a much wider range of entities as their direct object, than that for verbs such as *eat* or *repair*, which divide the "preference space" more clearly.

As a way of example, Table 4.8 displays the 15 nouns with the highest probabilities as direct objects of *appono* 'serve, delegate', according to the WN model of the system. Because the model assigns a probability to each noun in the corpus, I can group together those nouns sharing the same probabilities and plot them onto a cartesian plane. Figure 4.4 shows the SP distribution for the objects of *appono* 'serve, delegate'. The *y* axis displays the SP probability values, while the *x* axis displays the number of semantic properties assigned to a certain SP

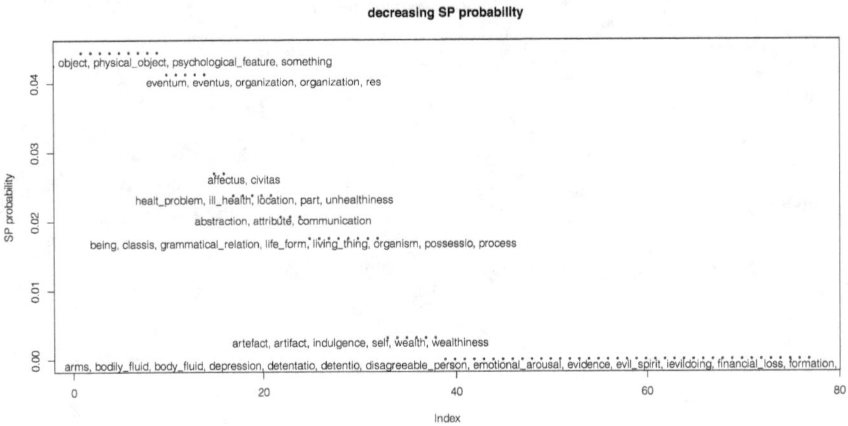

FIG. 4.4 *Decreasing SP probabilities of the LWN leaf nodes for the accusative objects of appono 'serve, delegate'*

probability. In general, the plots have shapes similar to Figure 4.4, which shows that the SP distribution given by the model is skewed for all verbs, with few high-frequency nouns and a larger number of low-frequency nouns. This result is confirmed by measures of statistical dispersion described in section 5.5.1, and is encouraging, because it means that the model does succeed in "preferring" a small set of nouns to all the other nouns.

4.4.2 *The System Discrimination*

The second question I ask is how good the model is at correctly estimating the SP probability of each single noun: I call this property *discrimination*. Previous work on SPs usually evaluates the models' discrimination by using human plausibility judgements on pairs of verbs and their preferred nouns. Since I deal with a language with no native speakers, I approximate plausibility judgements with corpus occurrences. By simulating a random extraction of argument fillers for a list of verbs from a wide variety of Latin texts, I consider these instances as implicit plausibility judgements.

I randomly select a list of 40 verbs (listed in Table 5.13 on page 111) from the valency lexicon, equally distributed in two classes of frequency: high frequency (>51, e.g. *dico* 'say'), and medium frequency (between 11 and 50, e.g. *ascendo* 'ascend'). For each of these verbs I select one argument slot. Then I manually collect a lexical filler for each such pair from the following freely available collections of Latin texts: *Perseus Digital Library*,[5] *Corpus*

5 http://www.Perseus.tufts.edu/hopper/.

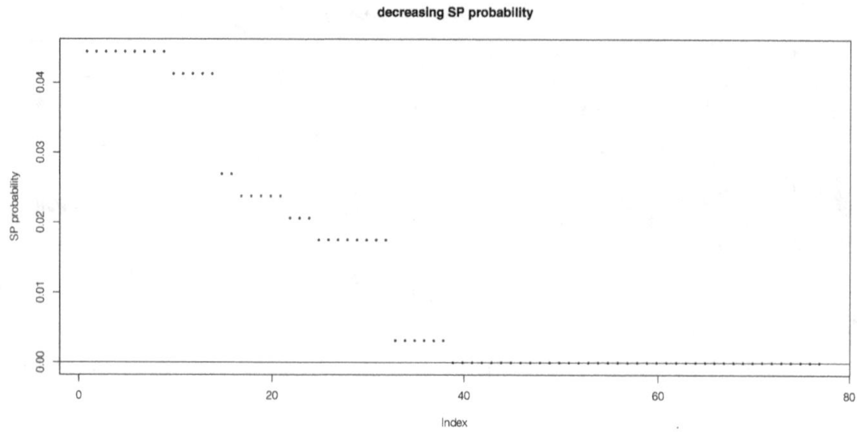

FIG. 4.5 *Median (dark grey line), mean (black), and value of the third quantile (light grey) for the accusative objects of* appono *'serve, delegate'*

Thomisticum,[6] and *The Latin Library*.[7] I exclude those fillers that already occur in the valency lexicon. The list of fillers for each verb-slot pair constitutes the *gold standard*.

For each of the 40 verb-slot pairs, I focus on the probabilities the two versions of the model (knowledge-based and knowledge-free) assigned to the random filler. To determine how good the model's prediction is, I compare these probabilities with three measures of central tendency (defined in section 5.5.1): mean, median, and the value of the third quartile. The mean is the average value among all SP probabilities, the median is calculated by sorting the SP probabilities and picking the middle one; finally, the third quartile is the threshold under which three quarters of the nouns have their probabilities. Figure 4.5 visualizes these measures for the accusative objects of *appono* 'place in front, serve, delegate'.

The idea is that, because I consider the random filler a plausible filler, its probability has to be high, so if the probability assigned by the model to the random filler is higher than these measures (i.e. the outcome is a success), it means that the model's prediction is good. Section 5.5.2 gives the numerical details of this comparison. As shown in the first three rows of Table 4.9, in the WN case, two (mean and median) out of three measures show a significantly higher proportion of successes, while the distributional version has one positive result (median).

6 http://www.corpusthomisticum.org/.

7 http://www.thelatinlibrary.com/.

TABLE 4.9 *Summary of the evaluation results for the knowledge-based and the knowledge-free versions of the algorithm. Each row lists the number of successful cases for each set of evaluation measures, as illustrated in the text. The asterisks mark statistically significant results.*

Set	Knowledge-based successes	Knowledge-free successes
P(rand. fill.)>mean	28*	18
P(rand. fill.)>median	36*	35*
P(rand. fill.)>3rd quartile	24	17
P(rand. fill.)>mean P(39 rand. fill.)	24*	25*
mean P(min-fr. fill.)<mean P(max-fr. fill.)	27*	18
corr. of rankings (gold stand. vs. system)	12	16
mean P(rand. fill.)>mean P(not-a-fill.)	36*	32*

Next, I compare the probabilities assigned by the system to the random filler of each verb with the mean of the probabilities assigned to the 39 random fillers extracted for the other verbs. My assumption is that in most cases the former probability should be higher than the latter (leading to a success), even though in some cases the random filler extracted for a verb-slot pair could be compatible with different verb-slot pairs. In a significantly high proportion of cases (24 out of 40 for the WN version and 25 out of 40 for the distributional version) I obtain a success (see fourth row of Table 4.9).

The approach to evaluation I just described does not take into account the corpus frequency of the random fillers. In other words, their plausibility as argument fillers for specific verbs is based on their single occurrences with those verbs, as observed in the random extraction process. As an alternative approach to evaluation, I decide to collect the frequencies of the fillers of each of the 40 verb-slot pairs in the *Perseus Digital Library* and the *Index Thomisticus* parsed corpora. Now the question is: to what extent is this frequency distribution reflected in the SP probability distribution assigned by the system? In order to test this, I first check if higher frequencies correspond to higher SP probabilities: when the mean of the probabilities assigned to the minimum-frequency fillers is lower than the probability assigned to the maximum-frequency fillers,

I consider the outcome a success. For the WN version of the algorithm, I obtain 27 successes, while for the distributional version I obtain 18 successes. In the former case, a significance test shows that the successes are significantly more likely than the failures, whereas in the latter cases the successes are significantly less likely (see section 5.5.3 for details, and fifth row of Table 4.9).

Now I want to quantify the association between the two distributions: the corpus frequency distribution and the SP probability distribution. To do that, I perform a correlation test which considers the rankings assigned by the two distributions to the fillers extracted from the parsed corpora. The results (reported in section 5.5.3 on page 115 ff.) show that in a significantly higher proportion of cases (28 out of 40 for the knowledge-based version and 24 out of 40 for the knowledge-free version) there is no correlation in the rankings of the two distributions (sixth row of Table 4.9). This might be due to the size of the input data, which depends on the number of fillers extracted from the parsed corpora for each verb. This result shows that, although the system is able to accurately detect the minimum and maximum-frequency fillers in most cases by simply judging from their SP probabilities, its accuracy is significantly lower when trying to assign the same ranking as the frequency distribution.

Finally, I want to compare the ability of the system to distinguish between plausible and implausible argument fillers. For each verb-slot pair I calculate the mean probability of all random fillers extracted from the parsed corpora for that pair, and compare it with the mean probability of the random fillers extracted for the other verb-slot pairs. In this comparison, the successes (i.e. the probabilities of the actual fillers are higher than the probabilities of the "non-fillers") are 36 (knowledge-based) and 32 (knowledge-free version); these are significantly high proportions, providing a positive result. See section 5.5.3 on page 118 ff. for details.

Overall, the WN version succeeded in 5 evaluation tests out of 7, while the distributional one failed in 4. Therefore, the WN algorithm performs better, which might be due to the fact that the parsed data are noisy, and this affects the filler extraction step, on which the similarity measure relies. The noise can be partially removed by more sophisticated parsers, which take into account features specific to Latin, such as the parser described in Passarotti and Dell'Orletta (2010). In addition, distributional measures other than cosine could be tested, to see if the cosine distance is actually the best option.

The results are overall encouraging, and show that the system has a good calibration and a good discrimination. However, its performance can still be improved. What is currently the best version, the WN-based one, assigns a SP probability to an LWN node based on its LWN similarity with the fillers of verbs that are similar to the target verb; consequently, the results depend both on the occurrences in the input corpus and on the structure of LWN.

Varying the input corpus affects the set of seen instances, but not their contribution to the probability assigned to similar nouns. Instead, a combination of the LWN measure and a distributional measure could account for the distinctive features of the input corpus in the similarity measure, too. This may allow for more direct comparisons between results from corpora with different features for genre, era, authors, etc. I will give an example of such a comparison in a diachronic perspective in the next chapter.

4.5 Lessons Learnt

The topic presented in this chapter has given me the chance to conduct an investigation on the obstacles that become apparent when developing a computational model for selectional preferences on Latin data. First of all, the generalization step from the corpus observations to the general linguistic behaviour of verbs is affected by the size of the corpus on which the generalization is based. The current state of Latin annotated corpora forces any attempt in this direction to use relatively small corpora. Therefore, systems need to be in place in order to overcome the data sparseness problem. This work has offered a solution to this, which relies on the semantic similarity information embedded in LWN synsets.

Second, morphological features of Latin nominal forms need to be taken into appropriate account, since they play such an important role in verbal argument realization. This is another crucial aspect that needs to be considered when adapting computational models from English.

Finally, the lack of native speakers for the evaluation phase has meant that corpus occurrences had to be consulted in order to approximate human judgements.

CHAPTER 5

A Closer Look at Automatic Selectional Preferences for Latin

This chapter gives various definitions, mathematical details, and data that complement the argumentation given in chapter 4. I have tried to present the technical content in an way that is accessible to non-experts. My aim is to explain the technical details of the SP model, as well as more general background notions on vector spaces and clustering.

5.1 Data from Latin WordNet

5.1.1 *Synsets*

This section shows the WN synsets relative to some of the nouns used as examples in chapter 4: *homo* 'man', *mundus* 'world', and *terra* 'earth'. I indicate the lemma, followed by an index for each synset, the domain assigned to the synset in MultiWordNet (MWN), and the gloss. Then, I represent the LWN synset between curly brackets, and the corresponding synset in the English Princeton WordNet (PWN). These data are extracted from the MWN interface.[1]

5.1.1.1 *Homo*

homo/1: (Person) [a human being; "there was too much for one person to do"] {anima, animus, caput, corpus, homo, pectus, spiritus} ={person, individual, someone, somebody, mortal, human, soul}

homo/2: (Biology, Person) [any living or extinct member of the family Hominidae] {homo, vir} ={homo, man, human being, human}

homo/3: (Factotum) [a person's body (usually including their clothing); "a weapon was hidden on his person"] {caput, corpus, homo} ={person}

homo/4: (Grammar) [a grammatical category of pronouns and verb forms; "stop talking about yourself in the third person"] {caput, corpus, homo} ={person}

homo/5: (Factotum) [all of the inhabitants of the earth; "all the world loves a lover"] ={caelum, homo, mundus, vir} ={world, human race, humanity, humankind, human beings, humans, mankind, man}

1 http://multiwordnet.fbk.eu/online/multiwordnet.php.

 | DOI: 10.1163/9789004260122_006

homo/6: (Person) [an adult male person (as opposed to a woman); "there were two women and six men on the bus"] {homo, vir} ={man, adult male}
homo/7: (Person) [(informal) a male person who plays a significant role (husband or lover or boyfriend) in the life of a particular woman; "she takes good care of her man"] {homo, vir} ={man}
homo/8: (Person) [an adult male person who has a manly character (virile and courageous competent); "the army will make a man of you"] {homo, vir} ={man}
homo/9: (Person) [a male subordinate; "the chief stationed two men outside the building"; "he awaited word from his man in Havana"] {homo, vir} ={man}
homo/10: (Military) [someone who serves in the armed forces; "two men stood sentry duty"] {homo, vir} ={serviceman, military man, man, military personnel}

5.1.1.2 *Mundus*

mundus/1: (Factotum) [something used to beautify] {mundus, ornamentum} ={decoration, ornament, ornamentation}
mundus/2: (Psychology) [the concerns of the world as distinguished from heaven and the afterlife; "they consider the church to be independent of the world"] {caelum, mundus} ={worldly concern, earthly concern, world, earth}
mundus/3: (Factotum) [all of the inhabitants of the earth; "all the world loves a lover"] {caelum, homo, mundus, vir} ={world, human race, humanity, humankind, human beings, humans, mankind, man}
mundus/4: (Astronomy) [the apparent surface of the imaginary sphere on which celestial bodies appear to be projected] {aethra, caelum, mundus} ={celestial sphere, sphere, empyrean, firmament, heavens, vault of heaven, welkin}
mundus/5: (Astronomy, Physics) [everything that exists anywhere; "they study the evolution of the universe"; "the biggest tree in existence"] {caelum, cosmos, mundus, universitas} ={universe, existence, nature, creation, world, cosmos, macrocosm}
mundus/6: (Astronomy) [the 3rd planet from the sun; the planet on which we live; "the Earth moves around the sun"; "he sailed around the world"] {caelum, globus, humus, mundus, sphaera, tellus, terra} ={Earth, world, globe}

5.1.1.3 *Terra*

terra/1: (Electricity) [a connection between an electrical device and the earth (which is a zero voltage)] {humus, tellus, terra} ={ground, earth}
terra/2: (Anatomy) [a part of an animal that has a special function or is supplied by a given artery or nerve; "in the abdominal region"] {arvum, cardo, orbis, pars, plaga, populus, regio, terra, tractus} ={area, region}
terra/3: (Politics) [the people of a nation or country or a community of persons bound by a common heritage; "a nation of Catholics"; "the whole country worshipped

him'"] {gens, humus, natio, populus, solum, tellus, terra} ={nation, nationality, land, country, a people}

terra/4: (Politics) [a politically organized body of people under a single government; "the state has elected a new president"] {adfectus, civitas, gens, humus, populus, solum, tellus, terra} ={state, nation, country, land, commonwealth, res publica, body politic}

terra/5: (Geography) [a particular geographical region of indefinite boundary (usually serving some special purpose or distinguished by its people or culture or geography); "it was a mountainous area"; "Bible country"] {area, arvum, cardo, humus, mensura, regio, spatium, tellus, terra} ={area, country}

terra/6: (Administration, Geography) [the territory occupied by a nation; "he returned to the land of his birth"; "he visited several European countries"] {adfectus, arvum, civitas, gens, gleba, humus, natio, populus, solum, tellus, terra} ={ country, state, land, nation}

terra/7: (Religion) [the abode of mortals (as contrasted with heaven or hell); "it was hell on earth"] {humus, tellus, terra} ={Earth}

terra/8: (Factotum) [a large indefinite location on the surface of the Earth; "penguins inhabit the polar regions'"] {arvum, orbis, pars, plaga, populus, regio, terra, tractus} ={region}

terra/9: (Geography) [the solid part of the earth's surface; "the plane turned away from the sea and moved back over land'"; "the earth shook for several minutes"; "he dropped the logs on the ground"] {arvum, gleba, humus, tellus, terra} ={land, dry land, earth, ground, solid ground, terra firma}

terra/10: (Geography) [what plants grow in (especially with reference to its quality or use); "the land had never been plowed"; "good agricultural soil"] {ager, arvum, gleba, humus, solum, tellus, terra} ={land, ground, soil}

terra/11: (Astronomy) [the 3rd planet from the sun; the planet on which I live; "the Earth moves around the sun"; "he sailed around the world"] {caelum, globus, humus, mundus, sphaera, tellus, terra} ={Earth, world, globe}

terra/12: (Economy) [extensive landed property (especially in the country) retained by the owner for his own use; "the family owned a large estate on Long Island"] {ager, fundus, gleba, humus, praedium, solum, tellus, terra, villa} ={estate, land, landed estate, acres, demesne}

terra/13: (Geology) [the loose soft material that makes up a large part of the surface of the land surface; "They dug into the earth outside the church"] {humus, solum, tellus, terra} ={earth, ground}

terra/14: (Philosophy) [(archaic) once thought to be one of four elements composing the universe] {humus, tellus, terra} ={earth}

5.1.2 *Semantic Properties*

In this section I list the semantic properties for *homo* 'man', *mundus* 'world', and *terra* 'earth'. Semantic properties are defined in section 4.2.

5.1.2.1 *Homo*

{adsecla, adsectator, anatomy, anima, animus, being, bod, build, caelum, caput, causa, chassis, classis, cognatio, corpus, entity, familia, figure, flesh, focus, form, frame, genus, grammatical category, grex, hominid, homo, human body, life form, living thing, male, male person, material body, mundus, natio, ordo, organism, pectus, physical body, physique, res, shape, skilled worker, soma, something, spiritus, subordinate, subsidiary, syntactic category, trained worker, underling, vir}

5.1.2.2 *Mundus*

{adfectus, aethra, artefact, artifact, astrum, caelum, circumscriptio, civitas, classis, cognitive state, commodum, concern, confine, cosmos, curiosity, entity, extremitas, fenus, finis, globus, homo, humus, location, meta, modus, mundus, natural object, object, ornamentum, part, physical object, planeta, region, something, sphaera, state of mind, stella, surface, tellus, termen, terminus, terra, terrestrial planet, universitas, usura, vir, wonder}

5.1.2.3 *Terra*

{administrative district, administrative division, affectus, ager, area, arvum, body part, caelum, cardo, census, civitas, classis, complexio, detentatio, detentio, elementum, fundus, gens, glaeba, globus, humus, instrumentality, instrumentation, location, materia, mensura, mundus, natio, natural object, object, orbis, organization, pars, physical object, plaga, planeta, political unit, populus, possessio, praedium, real estate, real property, realty, regio, res, solum, spatium, sphaera, stella, substantia, tellus, terra, terrestrial planet, territorial division, toparchia, tractus, villa}

5.2 Vectors and Linguistic Variables

Vectors in multidimensional spaces are a necessary notion for understanding the SP system I described in chapter 4. In data analysis we usually deal with tables whose rows correspond to *observations* and column to *variables*. For example, we can collect the occurrences of verbs in a corpus (observations) and, for each of them, record the author whose work the verb occurs in, as well as the verb's lemma.

TABLE 5.1 *Constructed example of dataset recording the author and the verb lemma for each verbal occurrence observed*

Verb token	Verb lemma	Author
v_1	*dico*	Plautus
v_2	*do*	Cicero
v_3	*dico*	Caesar
v_4	*do*	Caesar

TABLE 5.2 *Frequency table of the dataset represented in Table 5.1*

Author/verb	*Dico*	*Do*
Caesar	1	1
Cicero	0	1
Plautus	1	0

Table 5.1 shows some constructed data for this example. The cells of the table correspond to the values of each of the variables 'author' and 'verb' relative to each observation; for example, the cell in the first row and third column records the author of the verbal token v_1, i.e. Plautus. Tables like 5.1 can be turned into *frequency tables*, also called *contingency tables*. In the case of two variables (in the previous example 'author' and 'verb'), we can assign rows to the values for the first variable ('author') and columns to the values of the second variable ('verb'). We can then categorize the observations by these two variables and count the frequency of each variable pair, as in Table 5.2.

5.2.1 *Vectors*

The rows (and the columns) in frequency tables like Table 5.2 have a geometrical interpretation as *vectors*. A vector v in a n-dimensional space is identified by an ordered set of n numbers called *coordinates*: $v = (v_1, \ldots, v_n)$. For example, a two-dimensional space can be thought of as the well-known Cartesian plane, defined by two perpendicular lines called x axis and y axis, and meeting in the *origin* 0. In such a space a vector is associated with a pair of coordinates, called *abscissa* and *ordinate*. In the previous example, the points correspond to the

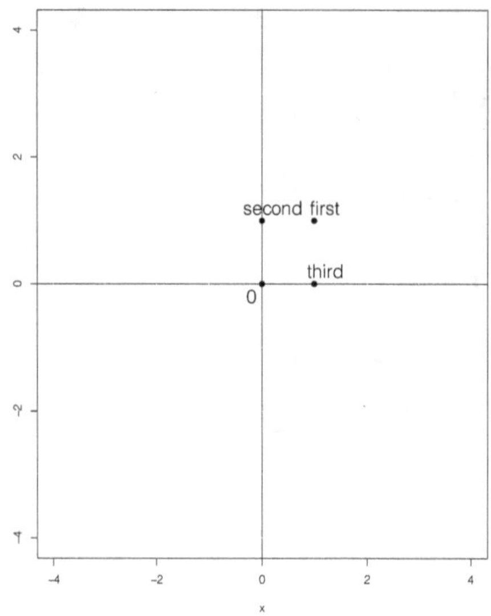

FIG. 5.1 *2-dimensional Cartesian space displaying the points corresponding to the rows of Table 5.2*

first, second and third row of Table 5.2 and have two coordinates, associated with the two verbs *dico* and *do*. These points are plotted on a Cartesian plane in Figure 5.1: 'first' corresponds to the first row of Table 5.2, and so on.

We can generalize this case to a higher-dimensional space with n dimensions, defined by n orthogonal axes. This allows us to work on cases when more than two values for the second variable are observed. For example, we could think of a study where more than two verbs are considered. This is very useful as a starting point for several data analysis techniques, such as clustering.

5.2.2 *A Very Brief Introduction to Clustering*

The term 'clustering' in data analysis denotes a group of statistical techniques that share the aim of grouping an input set of observations into subsets called *clusters*. In clustering, we represent observations as row vectors in a table like Table 5.2, and consider their similarities with respect to some variables (the table columns). Here I will illustrate clustering through a toy example. For a more comprehensive discussion on the uses of clustering in linguistics, I refer to Baayen (2008, 138–148) and Bilisoly (2008, 219–235).

Vector distance. In clustering, observations are grouped together into the same cluster according to a measure of how similar they are. The common way to define similarity between observations is through some kind of *distance* measure. The most intuitive example of distance is the *Euclidean distance*, which measures how far apart two points are as the length of the line connecting them. Its version in two dimensions is

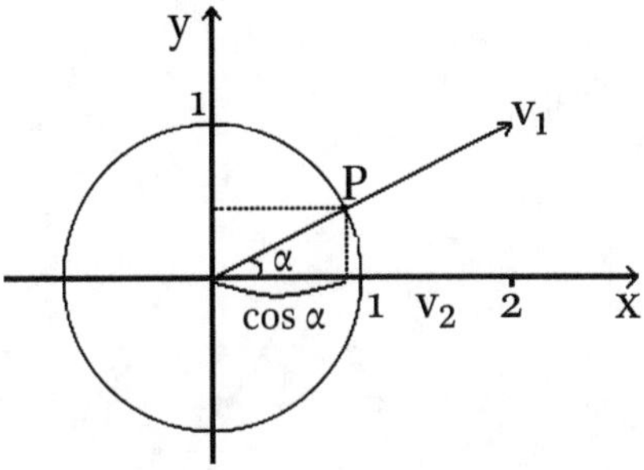

FIG. 5.2 *Unit circle, the two vectors (4,0) and (2,1), the angle α between them, and its cosine*

$$(5.1) \quad d(v_1, v_2) = \sqrt{(x_1 - x_2)^2 + (y_1 - y_2)^2}$$

where $v_1 = (x_1, y_1)$ and $v_2 = (x_2, y_2)$ are two points in a two-dimensional space.

A distance widely used in computational semantics is the *cosine distance*. To illustrate the cosine, I will refer to the unit circle, i.e. the circle with a radius of one (Figure 5.2). In Figure 5.2 we see the vectors $v_1 = (2, 1)$ and $v_2 = (2, 0)$, the angle α, and the point P, which is the intersection between the unit circle and the line through the origin making the angle α with the positive half of the x-axis. The cosine of α is the abscissa of P. The formula for the cosine between two vectors $v_1 = (x_1, x_2)$ and $v_2 = (y_1, y_2)$ is:

$$(5.2) \quad \frac{x_1 x_2 + y_1 y_2}{\sqrt{(x_1^2 + y_1^2) * (x_2^2 + y_2^2)}}$$

The cosine is 0 for $\alpha = 90°$; the cosine distance between two vectors v_1 and v_2 is $d(v_1, v_2) = 1 - cos(v_1, v_2)$, where $cos(v_1, v_2)$ is the *cosine* between v_1 and v_2. The cosine distance is 0 when $v_1 = v_2$ and is 1 when v_1 and v_2 are orthogonal. One nice property of the cosine distance is that it is affected only by the angle between the vectors and not by their length, i.e. it is norm-invariant.

Table 5.3 shows frequencies from a toy example on the subjects of *fly* and *buzz*, and Figure 4.2 on page 79 plots them as points in space; Table 5.4 reports the Euclidean and cosine distances between the pairs *crow-eagle, bird-eagle* and *bug-swallow*.

As can be observed from Table 5.4, according to the Euclidean distance, *bird* and *eagle* are closer together than *crow* and *eagle*, whereas the opposite holds for the cosine distance. This has to do with the fact that the cosine distance is norm-invariant: in fact, the cosine distance between two nouns identified by their absolute frequencies equals the cosine distance between their relative frequencies. For an illustration of this claim on the previous example, see Table 4.7 on page 80 and Figure 4.3 on page 79, which show the same nouns plotted

TABLE 5.3 *Constructed frequencies of the subjects of* fly *and* buzz

Noun	With *fly*	With *buzz*
bee	3	5
bug	2	2
bird	4	1
crow	2	0
eagle	4	0
insect	5	10
swallow	2	1

TABLE 5.4 *Euclidean and cosine distance measures between three pairs of nouns from Table 5.3*

Noun pair	Euclidean distance	Cosine distance
crow-eagle	2	0
bird-eagle	1	0.03
bug-swallow	1	0.05

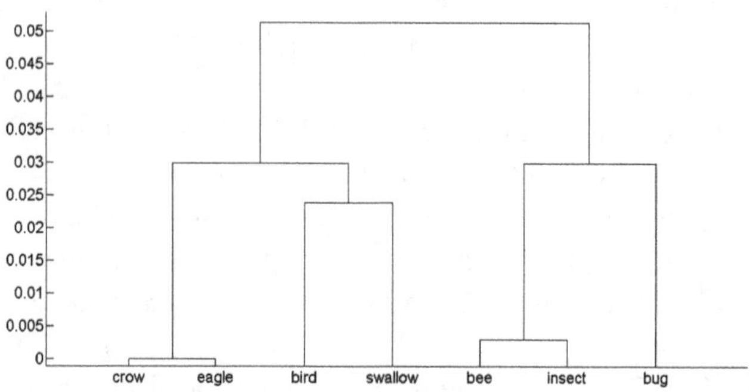

FIG. 5.3 *Dendrogram from a clustering for the subjects of* fly *and* buzz *in a toy example*

as different points depending on whether they are identified in the space by their absolute or relative frequencies.

A clustering algorithm produces a tree (dendrogram) showing the output clusters. For example, the tree in Figure 5.3 displays the output of a clustering on the constructed data from the previous example (Table 5.3), where the chosen distance is the cosine distance.

5.2.3 *Hard Agglomerative Hierarchical Clustering*

Clustering methods can be classified in several ways. For example, there is hard clustering and soft (or fuzzy) clustering, depending on whether overlaps between clusters are allowed or not. In addition, partitional clustering differs from hierarchical clustering in the algorithm used: the former determines the number of clusters at the beginning, while the latter proceeds by merging groups together (agglomerative or bottom-up clustering) or splitting them (divisive or top-down clustering). For the sake of simplicity, I will focus on hard agglomerative hierarchical clustering and illustrate it on the example given in Table 5.3, and will omit the description of more complex types of clustering.

In agglomerative hierarchical clustering, the first step assigns one cluster to each input observation (object). Then, at each step the closest clusters are merged together until one cluster is obtained at the end. This type of clustering produces a tree representation of the clusters detected in the input, usually called *dendrogram*; the special layout of the tree reflects the multilevel hierarchy highlighted by the cluster analysis.

Two clusters are merged by calculating the distance between them and this is achieved in several different ways: for example, the distance can be obtained as the minimum distance between the elements of each cluster (single linkage algorithms), their maximum distance (complete linkage), their average distance (average linkage), and so on.

By way of example, let us consider again the data from Table 5.3. I will proceed in the following way:

1. calculate the distances between all pairs of objects (nouns)
2. group the objects into a cluster tree
3. determine where to divide the tree into clusters

First, I calculate the distances between all pairs of nouns, in this case I decide to employ the cosine distance; Table 5.4 displays the cosine distances between the points in Table 5.3. The next step of the clustering defines one cluster for each object: $cluster_1 = \{bee\}, ..., cluster_7 = \{swallow\}$. Subsequently, I need to group the observations: to do this, a linkage function must be chosen. In this case I will choose the simplest one, the single linkage function, which calculates the shortest distance between the clusters. According to Table 5.5 the closest pair is *crow-eagle*, which constitutes the first cluster. Then the clustering algorithm proceeds by calculating the distances between all the clusters existing at this point: $cluster_1 = \{bee\}$, $cluster_2 = \{bug\}$, $cluster_3 = \{bird\}$, $cluster_4 = \{\}$, $cluster_5 = \{\}$, $cluster_6 = \{insect\}$, $cluster_7 = \{swallow\}$, $cluster_8 = \{crow, eagle\}$. Note that, by convention, $cluster_8$ indicates the new

TABLE 5.5 *Cosine distance measures between all pairs of nouns from Table 5.3*

Noun pair	Cosine distance
bee-bug	0.030
bee-bird	0.290
bee-crow	0.490
bee-eagle	0.490
bee-insect	0.003
bee-swallow	0.160
bug-bird	0.140
bug-crow	0.290
bug-eagle	0.290
bug-insect	0.050
bug-swallow	0.050
bird-crow	0.030
bird-eagle	0.030
bird-insect	0.350
bird-swallow	0.020
crow-eagle	0.000
crow-insect	0.550
crow-swallow	0.110
eagle-insect	0.550
eagle-swallow	0.110
insect-swallow	0.200

cluster created by the grouping of *crow* and *eagle*, while the single clusters previously containing these nouns are now empty. It turns out that the next closest pair are: *bee-insect* (step 3), then *bird-swallow* (step 4), {*crow, eagle*}-{*bird, swallow*} (step 5), *bug*-{*bee, insect*} (step 6), and finally {*crow, eagle, bird,swallow*}-{*bug, bee, insect*} (step 7).

Table 5.6 summarizes all clustering steps. The cluster analysis and the dendrogram were produced using the functions `pdist`, `linkage` and `dendrogram` in MATLAB® (MathWorks Inc., 2004). The x-axis in Figure 5.3 displays the clustered objects, while the y-axis shows the distances between the clusters. For example, the distance between *bird* and *swallow* is between 0.020 and 0.025.

Finally, I divide the tree into clusters by specifying the number of desired clusters, a distance threshold, or other criteria. For example, if I wanted to cut

TABLE 5.6 *Clusters obtained in each step from a single linkage clustering with cosine distance on the data from Table 5.3*

Step number	Cluster merged
2	{crow}∪{eagle}
3	{bee}∪{insect}
4	{bird}∪{swallow}
5	{crow,eagle}∪{bird,swallow}
6	{bug}∪{bee,insect}
7	{crow,eagle,bird,swallow}∪{bug,bee,insect}

TABLE 5.7 *Vectors of the verbs* voco *'call' and* nomino *'name' in a multidimensional space defined by the valency patterns with which these two verbs occur in two 3 million-token parsed corpora. See Table 5.9 for the description of the valency patterns* S_1*, etc.*

	S_1	S_2	S_3	S_4	S_5	S_6	S_7	S_8	S_9	S_{10}	S_{11}	S_{12}	S_{13}	S_{14}	S_{15}
voco	1	1	5	1	0	0	5	0	1	2	0	1	1	10	3
nomino	0	0	3	1	3	1	4	1	0	0	1	0	0	1	1

the tree in Figure 5.3 by setting a distance threshold of 0.031, I would get the following two clusters: {*crow,eagle, bird, swallow*} and {*bee, insect, bug*}.

5.3 A Distributional Measure of Semantic Similarity

In the distributional version of the algorithm (illustrated in section 4.3), I represent each verb as a vector in a multi-dimensional space whose dimensions are all the possible valency patterns recorded in the lexicon. The coordinate of a verb vector in the *i*th dimension is the frequency with which the verb displays the *i*th valency pattern. Table 5.7 shows two example vectors for the verbs *voco* 'call' and *nomino* 'name'. Similarly, I represent the argument fillers occurring in the lexicon as vectors in the space defined by their occurrence with all the verb-slot pairs; Table 5.8 displays the two vectors for *terra* 'earth' and *homo* 'man'.

TABLE 5.8 *Vectors of the nouns* terra *'earth' and* caelum *'sky' in a multidimensional space defined by the first (verb, slot) pairs with which these nouns occur in two 3 million-token parsed corpora. See Table 5.10 for the description of the patterns S_1, etc.*

	S_1	S_2	S_3	S_4	S_5	S_6	S_7	S_8	S_9	S_{10}	S_{11}	S_{12}
terra	1	0	1	1	1	1	1	0	0	1	1	0
caelum	0	1	0	0	0	0	0	1	2	0	0	1

TABLE 5.9 *Description of the valency patterns S_1, S_2, etc. shown in Table 5.7*

S_1	A_(ad)Obj[acc],Obj[acc]
S_2	A_(in)Obj[acc],Obj[acc],Sb
S_3	A_Obj[acc]
S_4	A_Obj[acc],Obj[dat],Sb
S_5	A_Obj[acc],OComp[acc]
S_6	A_Obj[acc],OComp[acc],Sb
S_7	A_Obj[acc],Sb
S_8	P_(a)Obj[abl]
S_9	P_(a)Obj[abl],Sb
S_{10}	P_(ad)Obj[acc],Sb[acc]
S_{11}	P_(per)Obj[acc],Sb[nom]
S_{12}	P_Obj[dat]
S_{13}	P_Pnom
S_{14}	P_Pnom,Sb
S_{15}	P_Sb

TABLE 5.10 *Description of the valency patterns S_1, S_2, etc. shown in Table 5.8*

S_1	abeo+A_Obj[acc]
S_2	abeo+A_Sb[nom]
S_3	adiuvo+A_Sb
S_4	admiror P_Sb
S_5	aduro+A_Obj[acc]
S_6	aperio+A_Sb
S_7	ascendo+A_(de)Obj[abl]

S_8	ascendo+A_(in)Obj[acc]
S_9	cado+A_(de)Obj[abl]
S_{10}	cado+(in)Obj[acc]
S_{11}	cado+A_(super2)Obj[acc]
S_{12}	claudo+A_Obj[acc]

I defined the *cosine* between two vectors in section 5.2.2. The cosine is independent of the norm (length) of the vectors and ranges between 0 (when the two vectors are orthogonal) and 1 (when the vectors are aligned). The cosine distance between two vectors is defined as 1 minus the cosine between the vectors.

As I show in section 4.3, in the algorithm I use the cosine distance between pairs of verbs and pairs of nouns in equation 5.10 as an alternative version of the synset score and the semantic score defined in section 4.2.3. For the verbs in Table 5.7 (*voco* and *nomino*) the cosine is 0.59, and hence their cosine distance is 1−0.59=0.41; for the two nouns in Table 5.8 (*terra* and *caelum*), the cosine distance is 1, i.e. they are maximally distant because there is no overlap in their verb-slot pairs.

5.4 Formulae for the Probabilistic Model

In this section I will give the formulae for the SP acquisition system, introduced in sections 4.2.3 and 4.2.4. In order to understand the principles behind the algorithm, it is important to first know the concept of conditional probability.

5.4.1 *Conditional Probability*

The conditional probability of a hypothesis H given some evidence D is the probability of H after D has been observed.

The conditional probability $P(H|D)$ is defined as:

$$P(H|D) = \frac{P(H \cap D)}{P(D)}$$

where the *joint* probability of H and D, i.e. $P(H \cap D)$, is the probability of H and D occurring together. According to Bayes' theorem:

$$P(H|D) = \frac{P(D|H)P(H)}{P(D)} \qquad (5.3)$$

In (5.3) $P(H)$ is multiplied by the factor $\frac{P(D|H)}{P(D)}$ to obtain $P(H|D)$: this factor is greater than one if it is likely that the data D would be observed when H is true, but unlikely that D would have been the outcome of the observation; otherwise, $P(H)$ is multiplied by a number smaller than one, resulting in $P(H|D) < P(H)$.

5.4.2 *Clustering Frames*

The steps of the SP algorithm described in chapter 4 can be formalized as follows.

1. The input to the clustering algorithm in the system is the set of all frames observed in the valency lexicon, each of which forms a construction containing the frame itself.
2. Then, I consider a random first frame F_1 and calculate the similarity scores between F_1 and all other frames (i.e. constructions), including the baseline construction $k_0 = \{F_1\}$. These scores contribute to the probability $P(k|F_1)$, which is the conditional probability of a construction k given F_1.
3. If I find a specific construction $K = \{F_x\}$ for which the probability $P(k|F_1)$ is maximized and greater than the baseline probability $P(k_0|F_1)$, then I assign F_1 to K, which then consists of two frames: F_x and F_1. K contains the frame that is the most similar to F_1 according to *feature*$_1$, *feature*$_2$, and *feature*$_3$, as measured by the similarity scores. If such a construction cannot be found, this means that no frame is sufficiently similar to F_1, which is then assigned the singleton construction $\{F_1\}$.
4. In a similar way, the second frame F_2 is compared with all the other constructions and assigned the most similar construction according to the similarity scores.
5. The algorithm keeps on considering a frame at a time until each frame is assigned to a construction.

During the clustering, a frame F is assigned to a construction K if K maximizes the probability $P(k|F)$ over all constructions k. After Bayes' theorem (see 5.3), this is equivalent to maximizing the product $P(k)P(F|k)$. The prior probability $P(k)$ measures how much k is "attested" in the corpora and is calculated as the number of frames contained in k divided by the total number of frames. I calculate $P(F|k)$ by looking at the degree of syntactic and semantic similarity between F and the frames already included in k. In other words, $P(F|k)$ calculates the overlap between the values of the features (*feature*$_1$, *feature*$_2$ and *feature*$_3$) in F and the values of the same features in the other frames belonging to k.

If I assume that the frame features are independent, $P(F|k)$ is the product of the conditional probability that each feature displays the same value it has in F and in k. Let F be a frame, defined according to the criteria given in 4.2.2. A construction K is assigned to F by the clustering algorithm if K maximizes the probability $P(k|F)$ over all constructions k, including the baseline $k_0 = \{F\}$: $K = arg\,max_k\, P(k|F)$. After Bayes' theorem, since $P(F)$ is constant for all k: $K = arg\,max_k\, P(k)P(F|k)$.

– $P(k)$ is calculated as the number n_k of frames contained in k divided by N+1, where N is the total number of frames: $P(k) = \frac{n_k}{N+1}$. Hence, the prior probability of a new construction is $P(k_0) = \frac{1}{N+1}$.

– If I assume that the frame features are independent, $P(F|k)$ is the product of $P_i(feature_i(F)|k)$ for i=1,2,3:

$$P(F|k) = \prod_{i=1,2,3} P_i(feature_i(F)|k), \tag{5.4}$$

where $P_i(feature_i(F)|k)$ is the probability that the ith feature displays the same value in F and in k, i.e. $feature_i(F)$.

– *Feature*$_1$. I estimate $P(feature_1(F)|k)$ by using the following smoothed Maximum Likelihood Estimation formula:

$$P(feature_1(F)|k) = \frac{(\sum_{h \in k} synt\_score(h,F)) + \lambda}{n_k + \lambda\alpha_1}$$

where the *syntactic score* is the number of syntactic slots shared by h and F over the number of slots in F, and n_k is the number of frames in k:

$$synt\_score(h,F) = \frac{|SCS(h) \cap SCS(F)|}{|SCS(F)|}$$

The smoothing factor α_1 is set to an estimate of the number of possible values that $feature_1$ can have. Thus, $\alpha_1 = 1537$, the number of all slots realized in the dataset; I set $\lambda = 10^{-7}$. See Alishahi (2008, 49) for a discussion on ways to set λ.

– *Feature*$_2$. Let $nslots(F)$ be the number of argument slots in F; for each such slot a, $P(feature_2(F)|k)$ is

$$P(feature_2(F)|k) = \frac{\sum_a[\sum_{h \in k} sem\_score_a(h,F)] + \lambda}{n_k * nslots(F) + \lambda\alpha_2} \tag{5.5}$$

where the *semantic score* accounts for the degree of overlap between the semantic properties $S(h)$ of h and the semantic properties $S(F)$ of F (for argument a):

$$sem\_score_a(h, F) = \frac{|S(h) \cap S(F)|}{|S(F)|}$$

α_2 is the number of semantic properties of all fillers in the treebanks (697)

– $Feature_3$: the probability of displaying the same value for $feature_3$ in F and in k is

(5.6) $$P(feature_3(F)|k) = \frac{\sum_{h \in k} syn\_score(h,F) + \lambda}{n_k + \lambda\alpha_3}$$

where the *synset score* calculates the degree of overlap between the synsets for the verb in h and the synsets for the verb in F over the number of synsets for the verb in F:

$$syn\_score(h, F) = \frac{|Synsets(verb(h)) \cap Synsets(verb(F))|}{|Synsets(verb(F))|}$$

5.4.3 *Selectional Preferences as Probability Distributions*

In section 4.2.4 I defined SPs in terms of the probability that certain WN nodes (like ENTITY or OBJECT) are selected by a verb for a given syntactic position (like accusative objects of *abeo* 'leave'). In this section, I will give more details of how I calculate this probability.

If s is a semantic property and a an argument position for a verb v, in the SP algorithm I developed, I calculate the probability $P_a(s|v)$ as the sum of $P_a(s, k|v)$ over all constructions k containing v or a WN-synonym of v. By Bayes' rule (see 5.3), this leads me to calculate $P_a(s|k, v)$, which is obtained by accounting for the degree to which the verbs in the constructions k are similar to v, and the degree to which the fillers of the frames in k are similar to s. The probability of a semantic property s in an argument position a for a verb v is calculated as follows:

$$P_a(s|v) = \sum_k P_a(s, k|v) \propto \sum_k \frac{P(k,v)P_a(s|k,v)}{P(v)}.$$

– $P(k, v)$ is estimated as

$$P(k, v) = \frac{n_k * freq(k,v)}{\sum_{k'} n_k freq(k',v)}$$

where n_k is the number of frames contained in k whose verbs share a synset with v.

– I define the similarity score as the frequency of h, multiplied by the synset score between v and the verbs in each frame h belonging to k, multiplied by the frequency of h and the semantic score between s and h:

(5.7) $$SP\_sim\_score_a(h, v, s) = freq(h) * syn\_score(v, verbs(h)) * \\ * sem\_score(s, h)$$

with

(5.8) $$syn\_score(v, verbs(h)) = \frac{|Synsets(v) \cap Synsets(verbs(h))|}{|Synsets(v) \cup Synsets(verbs(h))|}$$

and

(5.9) $$sem\_score(s, h) = \frac{\sum_f sem\_score(s, S(f))}{N_{fillers(h,a)}} = \frac{\sum_f \frac{|s \cap S(f)|}{|s \cup S(f)|}}{N_{fillers(h,a)}}$$

$S(f)$ in (5.9) is the set of semantic properties of each filler f of $verbs(h)$ for a and $N_{fillers(h,a)}$ is the number of fillers f for a in h. This way the value in (5.7) ranges between 0 (when $syn\_score(v, verbs(h)) = 0$ and/or $sem\_score(s, h) = 0$) and $freq(h)$ (when $syn\_score(v, verbs(h) = 1$ and $sem\_score(s, h) = 1$).

– If I sum these similarity scores over all frames in k, I divide this sum by the total frequency of the frames in k that contain v or its synonyms, and finally normalize, I get a measure of how likely it is to find the semantic property s in the argument position a for v in the construction k: $P_a(s|k, v)$.

Therefore, I estimate $P_a(s|k, v)$ by normalizing over all k

(5.10) $$\frac{\sum_h SP\_sim\_score_a(h,v,s) + \lambda\alpha_s}{(\sum_h freq(h,v)) + \lambda\alpha}$$

In 5.10 h is summed over all frames in k whose verbs share the same synset with v. λ, α and α_s are smoothing factors: α_s is set as the relative frequency of s among all fillers and α is the sum of all α_s. I set $\lambda = 10^{-7}$, as in the clustering step. See Alishahi (2008, 128) for a discussion on how to set λ.

Formulae for the evaluation phase. As I explained in section 4.4, in the evaluation phase I am interested in calculating the probability of a specific noun n occurring in an argument position a for a verb v. Therefore, I change formula (5.7) into the following one:

(5.11) $$SP\_sim\_score_a(h, v, s) = freq(h) * syn\_score(v, verbs(h)) * \frac{\sum_f sem\_score(S(n),S(f))}{N_{fillers(h,a)}}$$

where the semantic score is calculated between the set of semantic properties of n and those of each filler f for a in h. The other quantities remain the same as in section 5.4.3.

Cosine distance. In the distributional version of the algorithm I calculate the similarity scores on the basis of the cosine distance. For each noun lemma n in the input parsed corpora, $P_a(n|k, v)$ is

(5.12) $$freq(h) * cosine\_distance(v, verbs(h)) * \frac{\sum_f cosine\_distance(n,f)}{N_{fillers(h,a)}}$$

where the first cosine distance is calculated between the vector representations of v and the verb(s) in h; the second cosine distance is calculated between the noun n and each filler f for a in h. Correspondingly, $P_a(n|k, v)$ is calculated as

(5.13) $$\frac{\sum_h SP\_sim\_score_a(h,v,n)+\lambda\alpha_n}{\sum_h freq(h,v)+\lambda\beta}$$

The smoothing factor α_n is set as the relative frequency of n among all fillers in the parsed corpora and β is the sum of all α_n.

5.5 Formulae for the Evaluation of the System

In this section I give the technical details on the evaluation of the SP acquisition system described in section 4.4.

5.5.1 *Statistical Dispersion*

In order to assess how skewed the SP probability distribution given by the WN-based model is, I calculate the values of two measures of statistical dispersion on the evaluation set:

- *Interquartile Range* (IQR)
- *Median Absolute Deviation* (MAD)

The IQR is defined as the difference between the third quartile and the first quartile. By definition, the IQR is less sensitive to outliers than the usual range, which measures the difference between the maximum and the minimum values of a set.

TABLE 5.11 *Interquartile Range (IQR) and Median Absolute Deviation (MAD) of the SP probability distributions given by the WN-based system for each verb in the evaluation set. 'Accido2' and 'dico2' refer to the 'fall' and 'say' senses of the two verbs, respectively.*

	IQR	MAD
accido2	2.50e-04	1.89e-09
agito	3.11e-04	1.81e-04
ascendo	3.15e-04	1.56e-04
canto	1.18e-04	1.94e-06
cognosco	2.64e-04	1.59e-04
comparo	3.29e-04	1.86e-04
constituo	3.12e-04	1.75e-04
convenio	2.91e-04	2.07e-04
cupio	2.88e-04	1.87e-04
determino	1.99e-09	1.16e-09
dico2	2.63e-04	1.92e-04
dimitto	1.24e-04	1.01e-09
do	2.66e-04	1.96e-04
facio	2.23e-04	1.65e-04
fero	2.87e-04	1.72e-04
induco	3.05e-04	1.82e-04
intellego	2.82e-09	1.86e-09
intro	2.62e-04	9.82e-10
invenio	2.93e-04	2.04e-04
maneo	2.68e-04	1.95e-04
moveo	3.08e-04	1.89e-04
multiplico	2.56e-04	1.90e-04
nego	2.96e-04	1.75e-04
paro	2.89e-04	1.36e-04
pateo	2.42e-04	1.82e-04
pono	2.59e-04	1.78e-04
praecedo	2.62e-04	1.94e-04
praedico	2.35e-04	7.38e-10
profero	1.24e-04	7.17e-10
recipio	2.34e-04	1.71e-04
refero	4.29e-09	2.82e-09
resulto	3.18e-04	1.86e-04

TABLE 5.11 *IQR and MAD, Continued.*

	IQR	MAD
scio	2.05e-04	1.52e-10
sequor	2.76e-04	1.62e-04
subeo	2.64e-04	2.36e-09
sum	2.22e-04	1.44e-04
tento	3.07e-04	2.02e-04
timeo	1.76e-04	2.25e-09
venio	2.62e-04	1.24e-04
volo	2.89e-04	1.65e-04

The MAD is calculated by taking the median of the absolute deviations from the distributions' medians:[2]

$$MAD(v) = median(|P_a(n_i|v) - median(P_a(*|v))|)$$

For instance, the median of the set $(1, 2, 4, 5, 5, 9)$ is 4.5 and the absolute deviations from the median are $(3.5, 2.5, 0.5, 0.5, 0.5, 4.5)$; the median of the latter set is 2.22, which is the MAD of the original set.

Table 5.11 shows the IQR and MAD values for all 40 verbs in the evaluation set.

Both measures are calculated on the distributions of 40 random verbs extracted from the corpora.

5.5.2 *Central Tendency*

In order to evaluate the system, I analyse the probability distributions obtained for 40 random verbs, for which an example is given in Figure 4.4 on page 83. I consider the 40 functions that assign the SP probability to each noun belonging to the set of the 4724 LWN leaf nodes.

There are several ways to synthetically describe the typical value of a distribution. First, I calculate the *mean* of the values of the probability distribution:

$$\frac{\sum_{n \in N} P_a(n|v)}{4724}$$

For example, the mean for *dico* 'say' with the slot 'A_Obj[acc]' is 0.00021.

2 For a definition of median see the next paragraph.

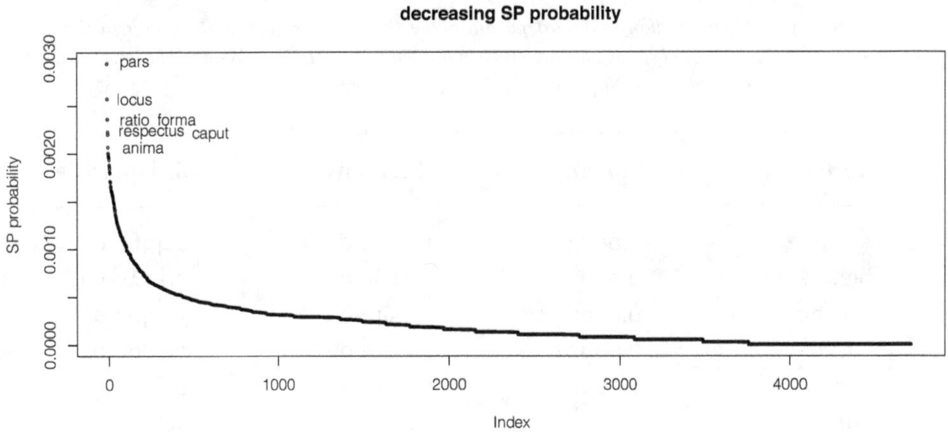

FIG. 5.4 *SP probability distribution for the objects of* dico *'say'*

Second, I calculate the *median*: I sort the values $P_a(n|v)$ in descending order and pick the noun in the middle of this sequence, or the mean of the two middle points in case of an even number of observations. The set N is thus split in two subsets: half the nouns have a probability lower than the median and half have a higher probability. For example, the median for *dico* is 0.00013.

Third, I calculate the values at the third quartile. I divide the set of 4724 nouns into four equal-sized parts (*quartiles*); this way, 25 % of the nouns have a probability higher than the value at the third quartile. For example, the value of the third quartile for *dico* is 0.0003. Figure 5.4 shows the mean, median, and third quartile values for the distribution of the direct objects of *dico*, while Table 5.12 shows the mean, median, and value of third quartile for each of the 40 verbs I used for evaluation.

For each verb v and syntactic slot position a, I calculate the value $P_a(f|v)$ predicted by the model for the random filler f and compare it with the measures of central tendency I just illustrated. Table 5.13 records each of the 40 verbs in the evaluation set, together with its frequency, its respective random filler, its SP probability, and whether or not this probability is higher than each of the three measures of central tendency.

The last row of Table 5.13 shows the total number of pairs for which the SP probability of the random filler was higher than the measure of random tendency: 28 (mean), 36 (median) and 24 (third quartile). Now, I want to answer the following question: are these proportions significantly higher than I would expect by chance?

TABLE 5.12 *Mean, median, and third quartile of the SP probability distributions given by the WN-based system, for each verb in the evaluation set. 'Accido2' and 'dico2' refer to the 'fall' and 'say' senses of the two verbs, respectively.*

Verb	Mean	Median	Third quartile
accido2	0.00021	1.273e-09	2.496e-04
agito	0.00021	1.218e-04	3.114e-04
ascendo	0.00021	1.054e-04	3.150e-04
canto	0.00021	1.310e-06	1.180e-04
cognosco	0.00021	1.074e-04	2.635e-04
comparo	0.00021	1.257e-04	3.286e-04
constituo	0.00021	1.181e-04	3.120e-04
convenio	0.00021	1.398e-04	3.157e-04
cupio	0.00021	1.264e-04	2.88e-04
determino	0.00021	8.575e-10	2.118e-09
dico2	0.00021	1.292e-04	2.897e-04
dimitto	0.00021	6.903e-10	1.244e-04
do	0.00021	1.325e-04	2.930e-04
facio	0.00021	1.489e-04	2.790e-04
fero	0.00021	1.162e-04	3.156e-04
induco	0.00021	1.229e-04	3.049e-04
intellego	0.00021	1.401e-09	3.049e-09
intro	0.00021	6.726e-10	2.624e-04
invenio	0.00021	1.376e-04	3.280e-04
maneo	0.00021	1.316e-04	2.951e-04
moveo	0.00021	1.272e-04	3.085e-04
multiplico	0.00021	1.282e-04	2.565e-04
nego	0.00021	1.178e-04	2.958e-04
paro	0.00021	9.173e-05	2.918e-04
pateo	0.00021	1.230e-04	2.816e-04
pono	0.00021	1.200e-04	2.827e-04
praecedo	0.00021	1.309e-04	2.621e-04
praedico	0.00021	5.183e-10	2.348e-04
profero	0.00021	4.892e-10	1.238e-04
recipio	0.00021	1.152e-04	2.623e-04
refero	0.00021	2.126e-09	4.632e-09
resulto	0.00021	1.256e-04	3.180e-04
scio	0.00021	1.042e-10	2.049e-04
sequor	0.00021	1.090e-04	2.762e-04

Verb	Mean	Median	Third quartile
subeo	0.00021	1.594e-09	2.642e-04
sum	0.00021	1.523e-04	2.773e-04
tento	0.00021	1.360e-04	3.073e-04
timeo	0.00021	1.519e-09	1.760e-04
venio	0.00021	8.343e-05	2.623e-04
volo	0.00021	1.114e-04	2.887e-04

TABLE 5.13 *Frequency and random filler for each verb in the evaluation set, followed by a binary value indicating whether the SP probability of the random filler is higher than the mean, median, and third quartile, respectively. 'Accido2' and 'dico2' refer to the 'fall' and 'say' senses of the two verbs, respectively.*

v	fr.	slot (a)	rand. filler f	$P_a(f\|v)$ >mean?	$P_a(f\|v)$ >median?	$P_a(f\|v)$ > 3rd q.?
accido2	58	Obj[dat]	homo	0	1	0
agito	18	A_Obj[acc]	nubes	1	1	1
ascendo	17	A_(de)Obj[abl]	aqua	1	1	1
canto	14	A_Sb	virgo	1	1	1
cognosco	90	A_Sb	pater	1	1	1
comparo	13	P_(ad)Obj[acc]	meritum	1	1	1
constituo	32	A_Obj[acc]	numerus	1	1	1
convenio	65	A_Obj[dat]	sapientia	0	1	0
cupio	15	A_Obj[acc]	cibus	0	1	0
determino	74	A_Sb	potentia	1	1	1
dico2	466	A_Obj[acc]	sententia	1	1	1
dimitto	13	Sb	baptisma	0	1	0
do	207	A_Obj[dat]	pater	1	1	1
facio	466	A_Obj[acc]	abstinentia	1	1	1
fero	56	A_Obj[acc]	lex	1	1	1
induco	82	A_(in)Obj[acc]	cornu	1	1	0
intellego	19	A_Sb	homo	1	1	1
intro	25	A_(in)Obj[acc]	atrium	1	1	1
invenio	67	A_Obj[acc]	diversitas	1	1	1
maneo	56	A_Sb	virgo	1	1	1
moveo	67	A_(ad)Obj[acc]	baculum	1	1	0

TABLE 5.13 *Frequency and random filler for each verb in the evaluation set, Continued.*

v	fr.	slot (a)	rand. filler f	$P_a(f\vert v)$ >mean?	$P_a(f\vert v)$ >median?	$P_a(f\vert v)$ > 3rd q.?
multiplico	15	A_Obj[acc]	munus	1	1	1
nego	18	A_Obj[acc]	cursus	1	1	1
paro	27	Obj[acc]	rabies	0	1	0
pateo	497	A_Sb	arca	1	1	0
pono	185	A_Obj[acc]	causa	1	1	1
praecedo	30	A_Obj[acc]	tempus	1	1	1
praedico	59	A_Sb	fides	1	1	1
profero	30	A_Sb	tabula	0	0	0
recipio	140	Obj[acc]	similitudo	0	0	0
refero	39	A_(ad)Obj[acc]	rex	0	1	0
resulto	16	A_Sb	cauda	0	0	0
scio	72	A_Sb	anima	1	1	1
sequor	77	A_Obj[acc]	squalor	0	0	0
subeo	14	A_Obj[acc]	vinculum	0	1	0
sum	4010	A_Sb	provincia	1	1	1
tento	18	A_Obj[acc]	fides	1	1	1
timeo	36	A_Sb	praeda	1	1	1
venio	143	A_(ad)Obj[acc]	auris	0	1	0
volo	82	A_Sb	libertas	1	1	0
			TOTAL	28	36	24

Binomial test. To answer this question I perform a *binomial test* using the statistics software R (R Development Core Team, 2008), which tests the null hypothesis that the successes (probability higher than the measure of central tendency) and the failures (probability lower than the measure of central tendency) are equally likely.

The results, reported in Table 5.14 are: 28 successes for the mean, 36 for the median, and 24 for the third quartile. This means that the probability of the random filler is higher than the mean in 28 cases out of 40, and it is higher than the median in 36 cases. Finally, in 24 cases the random filler is placed in the high-probability quarter of the plot, which is where the arguments preferred by the verb tend to gather. A binomial test finds that the success

TABLE 5.14 *Summary of the first set of results obtained by the WN version of the SP system, evaluated on a set of 40 random fillers (one for each verb-slot pair) extracted from large corpora. The first column contains the condition for a success, realized when the SP probability assigned by the system to the random filler is higher than the measure of central tendency (mean, median, and third quartile). The second column shows the number of verb-slot pairs for which the probability assigned by the WN version of the SP system is higher than the corresponding measure of central tendency (i.e. success). The third column contains the 95% confidence interval calculated by a binomial test on these results, and the last column the probability of success calculated by the test. The stars flag significant results.*

Condition	No. successes	95% conf.int.	Est.p.succ.
prob >mean	28*	[0.53,0.83]	0.7
prob>median	36*	[0.76,0.97]	0.9
prob> 3rd q.	24	[0.43,0.75]	0.6

rate is statistically significant at the 5% level for the first two measures and not statistically significant at the 5% level for the third measure. For the 28 successes (mean), the test gives the 95% confidence interval [0. 53, 0. 83] and estimates the probability of success as 0.7. For the 36 successes (median), the 95% confidence interval is [0. 76, 0. 97] and the estimated probability of success is 0.9. For the 24 successes (third quartile), the 95% confidence interval is [0. 43, 0. 75] and the estimated probability of success is 0.6. In all cases the estimated probability of success falls around the mid point of the interval, which is a good result; moreover, the intervals are narrow and their first endpoint is higher than 0.5 in the first two cases, which means that I can be 95% sure that the success happens in more than 50% of the cases. In other words, the success is more likely than the failure, which means a good result for the evaluation.

Random filler vs. remaining 39 random fillers. Table 5.15 shows the results I obtain if I compare the probability assigned by the system to each verb's random filler with the mean of the probabilities assigned to the 39 random fillers extracted for the other verbs.

In 24 cases out of 40 the former probability is higher than the latter probability. A binomial test on these data shows that the proportion of successes is significantly higher than the proportion of failures (confidence interval [0. 43, 0. 75], estimated probability of success 0.6).

TABLE 5.15 *Summary of the second set of results obtained by the WN version of the SP system, evaluated on a set of 40 random noun fillers (one for each verb-slot pair) extracted from large corpora. This time the random filler corresponding to each verb-slot pair is compared with the other 39 fillers, under the assumption that a success is realized if the probability assigned by the system to that noun is higher than the mean of the probabilities assigned to the other 39 nouns. The first column shows the condition for a success. The second column contains the number of verb-slot pairs for which a success is realized. The third column contains the 95 % confidence interval calculated by a binomial test on these results, and the last column the probability of success calculated by the test. The stars flag significant results.*

Condition	No. successes	95 % conf.int.	Est.p.succ.
p(fill.)>mean p(39 fill.)	24*	[0.43,0.75]	0.6

5.5.3 *Corpus Frequencies*

Finally, I extract the fillers of the 40 verb-slot pairs from the two automatically parsed corpora. Each of these pairs of verbs and slots has a noun with the highest frequency, and one or more nouns with the lowest frequency. So, I calculate the SP probabilities of these maximum-frequency fillers and the mean of the SP probabilities of the minimum-frequency fillers, as shown in Table 5.17. I consider successes the cases where the former is higher than the latter, because this means that the SP probability distribution assigned by the system behaves similarly to the corpus frequency distribution, as far as the opposition between preferred nouns (i.e. high probability and high frequency) and dispreferred nouns (low probability and low frequency) are concerned. For example, the fillers for the slot 'A_(in)Obj[acc]' of *intro* 'enter' are:

- *mundus* 'world' (frequency 22)
- *homo* 'man' (3)
- *gloria* 'glory' (3)
- *paradisus* 'heaven' (3)
- *orbis* 'world' (2)
- *definitio* 'boundary' (1)
- *cognitio* 'knowledge' (1)
- *terra* 'earth' (1)
- *constitutio* 'regulation' (1)
- *possessio* 'possession' (1)

The maximum-frequency filler is *mundus*, which is assigned a SP probability of 0.0013. The minimum-frequency fillers are *definitio*, *cognitio*, *terra*, *constitutio*,

TABLE 5.16 *Summary of the third set of results obtained by the WN version of the SP system, evaluated on a set of 40 random noun fillers (one for each verb-slot pair) extracted from large corpora. In this case, I consider a success the event in which the SP probabilities of the maximum-frequency nouns are higher than the mean of the probabilities of the minimum-frequency nouns. The first column shows the condition for a success. The second column contains the number of verb-slot pairs for which a success is realized. The third column contains the 95 % confidence interval calculated by a binomial test on these results, and the last column the probability of success calculated by the test. The star flags a significant result.*

Condition	No. successes	95 % conf.int.	Est.p.succ.
p(max-freq. fill.)>mean p(min-freq fill.)	27*	[0.51,0.81]	0.7

and *possessio*; the mean of their SP probabilities is 0.0011: *Intro* is thus an instance of success, because it is the preferred filler for *intro* (and the slot 'A_(*in*)Obj[acc]') and its probability (0.0013) is higher than the mean of the probabilities of the dispreferred nouns (0.0011).

Of the 40 pairs, 27 are successes. Among the failures I consider *ascendo* for which only one filler is extracted. A binomial test on these data gives the 95 % confidence interval [0. 51, 0. 81] and an estimated probability of success of 0.7 (see Table 5.16).

Correlation test. In order to judge how good the SP probability distribution given by the model is, I compare it with the frequency distributions found in the automatically parsed corpora. For this, I need a test that compares the similarity between two rankings. I therefore perform a Spearman rank correlation test computed in R (R Development Core Team, 2008). This test converts the frequencies to ranks and is an ordinal version of the Pearson correlation test; for an explanation of this test, see Hinton (2004, 279–281). The Spearman test calculates a coefficient (called the Spearman coefficient) r and then decides on its significance based on tables of critical values. The formula for r is

$$r = 1 - \frac{6\sum_{i=1}^{N} D_i^2}{N^3 - N}$$

where $(D_1, \ldots, D_N)$ is the vector containing the differences between the two ranks and N is the number of observations.

TABLE 5.17 *Comparison between the corpus frequencies and the SP probabilities assigned by the WN system. Both values refer to the maximum-frequency and minimum-frequency fillers extracted from the parsed corpora. Column A contains the maximum frequency of the fillers; column B contains the probability of the maximum-frequency filler; column C contains the mean frequencies of the minimum-frequency fillers, column D contains the mean of the probabilities of the minimum-frequency fillers; the column E contains the binary answers to the question "is the probability of the maximum-frequency filler higher than the mean of the probabilities of the minimum-frequency fillers?"; column F contains the mean of the probabilities assigned to the fillers; column G contains the mean of the probabilities assigned to the "non fillers"; column H contains the binary answers to the question "is the mean of the probabilities of the fillers higher than the mean of the probabilities of the 'non fillers'?"*

Verb	Slot	A	B	C	D	E	F	G	H
accido2	A_Obj[dat]	7	0.00048	1	0.00047	1	0.00044	0.00029	1
agito	A_Obj[acc]	7	0.00072	1	0.00036	1	0.00038	0.00029	1
ascendo	A_(de)Obj[abl]	1	0.00026	1	0.00026	0	0.00026	0.00029	0
canto	A_Sb	5	0.00013	2	0.00140	0	0.00054	0.00024	1
cognosco	A_Sb	84	0.00100	1	0.00046	1	0.00057	0.00026	1
comparo	P_(ad)Obj[acc]	13	0.00066	1	0.00061	1	0.00064	0.00028	1
constituo	A_Obj[acc]	34	0.00340	1	0.00041	1	0.00049	0.00028	1
convenio	A_Obj[dat]	64	0.00064	1	0.00046	1	0.00050	0.00027	1
cupio	A_Obj[acc]	4	0.00070	1	0.00051	1	0.00049	0.00026	1
determino	A_Sb	96	2.8361e-09	1	0.00029	0	0.00030	0.00034	0
dico2	A_Obj[acc]	81	0.00196	1	0.00031	1	0.00038	0.00027	1
dimitto	A_Sb	4	0.00126	1	0.00078	1	0.00080	0.00024	1
do	A_Obj[dat]	30	0.00139	1	0.00040	1	0.00041	0.00028	1
facio	A_Obj[acc]	55	5.6077e-05	1	0.00030	0	0.00035	0.00027	1
fero	A_Obj[acc]	47	0.00079	1	0.00034	1	0.00038	0.00028	1
induco	A_(in)Obj[acc]	3	0.00090	1	0.00066	1	0.00064	0.00029	1
intellego	A_Sb	150	0.00194	1	0.00032	1	0.00025	0.00035	0
intro	A_(in)Obj[acc]	22	0.00127	1	0.00107	1	0.00099	0.00029	1
invenio	A_Obj[acc]	13	0.00054	1	0.00035	1	0.00039	0.00027	1
maneo	A_Sb	25	0.00040	1	0.00040	0	0.00051	0.00028	1
moveo	A_(ad)Obj[acc]	6	0.00105	1	0.00035	1	0.00050	0.00027	1
multiplico	A_Obj[acc]	7	1.556e-12	1	0.00043	0	0.00035	0.00029	1
nego	A_Obj[acc]	7	0.00043	1	0.00035	1	0.00042	0.00030	1
paro	A_Obj[acc]	23	0.00030	1	0.00037	0	0.00038	0.00030	1
pateo	A_Sb	272	7.8697e-05	1	0.00058	0	0.00058	0.00029	1
pono	A_Obj[acc]	48	0.00101	1	0.00035	1	0.00042	0.00026	1

Verb	Slot	A	B	C	D	E	F	G	H
praecedo	A_Obj[acc]	23	0.00059	1	0.00039	1	0.00046	0.00028	1
praedico	A_Sb	8	0.00040	1	0.00037	1	0.00047	0.00026	1
profero	A_Sb	20	2.0889e-10	1	0.00078	0	0.00072	0.00024	1
recipio	A_Obj[acc]	29	0.00153	1	0.00043	1	0.00050	0.00028	1
refero	A_(ad)Obj[acc]	7	1.1266e-08	1	0.00045	0	0.00047	0.00034	1
resulto	A_Sb	7	8.547e-05	1	0.00037	0	0.00056	0.00028	1
scio	A_Sb	16	0.00089	1	0.00044	1	0.00047	0.00021	1
sequor	A_Obj[acc]	5	0.00111	1	0.00044	1	0.00048	0.00028	1
subeo	A_Obj[acc]	7	0.00074	1	0.00035	1	0.00039	0.00029	1
sum	A_Sb	638	0.00122	1	0.00024	1	0.00027	0.00032	0
tento	A_Obj[acc]	7	0.00174	1	0.00049	1	0.00054	0.00028	1
timeo	A_Sb	10	0.00017	1	0.00043	0	0.00056	0.00026	1
venio	A_(ad)Obj[acc]	13	0.00027	1	0.00041	0	0.00046	0.00029	1
volo	A_Sb	78	0.00077	1	0.00047	1	0.00051	0.00026	1

TABLE 5.18 *Corpus frequency and SP probabilities of the arguments of* intro *'enter' for the slot 'A_(in)Obj[acc]'*

Index	Filler	Frequency	SP prob.	Freq. rank	Prob. rank
1	*mundus*	22	1.27e-03	10	7
2	*homo*	3	3.35e-04	9	5
3	*gloria*	3	1.39e-03	8	8
4	*paradisus*	3	1.69e-10	7	1
5	*orbis*	2	1.57e-03	6	9
6	*definitio*	1	3.93e-10	5	2
7	*cognitio*	1	2.60e-04	4	4
8	*terra*	1	4.76e-03	3	10
9	*constitutio*	1	3.44e-04	2	6
10	*possessio*	1	4.98e-10	1	3

As a way of example, Table 5.18 shows the two distributions for the arguments of *intro* 'enter' for the slot 'A_(in)Obj[acc]', i.e. the accusative arguments introduced by the preposition *in* 'into, to'. The SP probabilities displayed correspond to the fillers for *intro* in the parsed corpora. The two last columns contain the ranks of the two distributions (frequency distribution and SP probability distribution). Note that two synonyms like *mundus* 'world' and *terra* 'earth' do not appear in the same position in the two rankings: *mundus* is first by frequency in the parsed corpora and *terra* is first in the SP probability distribution. This may be due to the their semantic score: $\frac{15}{90} = 0.17$ (see sections 5.1.2.3 and 5.1.2.2). This score is low because the WN-based measure of similarity adopted does not distinguish between common and less common senses of words.

In the case of *intro*: $N = 10$, $D = (10-7, 9-5, 8-8, 7-1, 6-9, 5-2, 4-4, 3-10, 2-6, 1-3) = (3, 4, 0, 6, -3, 3, 0, -7, -4, -2)$, $D^2 = (3^2, 4^2, 0^2, 6^2, (-3)^2, 3^2, 0^2, (-7)^2, (-4)^2, (-2)^2) = (9, 16, 0, 36, 9, 9, 0, 49, 16, 4)$, and $\sum D^2 = 148$. Therefore, $r = 1 - \frac{6*148}{10^3-10} = 0.10$. If I look up the critical value for $N = 10$ and 0.01 level of significance in the table of critical values presented in Hinton (2004, 373), I find a critical value of 0.746, which is higher than the r I calculated. This means that there is no significant correlation in the two rankings given by the two distributions.

Table 5.19 shows the correlation coefficients, the p-values, and the statistics of the Spearman tests run on the 40 verb-slot pairs. For 12 pairs (in small caps in Table 5.19) I get p-values lower or equal to 0.05 and r coefficients between 0.13 (*fero*) and 0.43 (*moveo*). For the remaining 28 pairs I get a p-value higher than 0.05, which implies that in 28 out of 40 cases the test gives a non-significant correlation at the 0.05 level. If I had chosen a level of 0.01, the number of significant cases would have been 4 out of 40. A binomial test on 12 successes gives a 95% confidence interval of $[0.166, 0.465]$ and an estimated probability of success of 0.3. Since the interval is narrow and its lower margin is lower than 0.5, I am 95% confident that the 12 successes occurred by chance. The results of a binomial test on 4 successes give the following 95% confidence interval and estimated probability of success: $[0.028, 0.237]$ and 0.1.

Fillers vs. "non-fillers". As a last measure of the goodness for the system, for each verb v and slot a, I compare the mean of the probabilities assigned by the system to the fillers for v and a extracted from the parsed corpora with the mean of the probabilities assigned to the fillers for the other verbs and slots: $P_a(f|v)$ where f is a filler for (v, a) in the parsed corpora vs. $P_a(n|v)$, where n is a filler for pairs other than (v, a).

As shown in Table 5.21, the comparison gives 36 successes, where the mean of $P_a(f|v)$ is higher than the mean of $P_a(n|v)$. A binomial test on 36 successes out of 40 provides a 95% confidence interval of $[0.76, 0.97]$ and an estimated probability of success of 0.9, which says that the proportion of successes is significantly higher than the proportion of failures.

TABLE 5.19 *Correlation coefficients* r, *p-values, and statistics of the Spearman correlation test on the corpus frequency distribution and the SP probability distribution given by the WN version of my model.*

Verb	*r*	p-value	Statistic
accido2	-0.078	0.615	15295.941
agito	0.117	0.443	13400.823
canto	-0.5	0.667	6.000
COGNOSCO	0.230	0.017	157228.776
comparo	0.239	0.062	30231.272
CONSTITUO	0.247	0.004	308573.364
convenio	0.095	0.284	323784.481
cupio	-0.106	0.429	35951.592
determino	-0.067	0.644	22218.496
dico2	0.235	2.115e-07	13840039.950
dimitto	0.112	0.679	603.790
DO	0.165	0.019	1181899.648
facio	0.201	1.560e-07	39867702.500
FERO	0.134	0.011	6731259.403
induco	-0.087	0.693	2199.923
intellego	-0.002	0.989	54837.015
intro	0.111	0.759	146.610
INVENIO	0.181	0.012	965591.911
MANEO	0.307	0.0007	194536.3307
MOVEO	0.430	0.041	1153.452
multiplico	-0.456	0.217	174.772
nego	0.155	0.105	187329.390
paro	0.0128	0.906	115985.660
pateo	0.059	0.677	23351.174
pono	0.203	7.415e-05	7120781.734
PRAECEDO	0.260	0.004	235252.190
PRAEDICO	0.414	0.044	1347.408
profero	-0.185	0.609	195.536
RECIPIO	0.197	0.004	1310847.672
REFERO	0.262	0.015	78173.180
resulto	0.055	0.866	270.388
scio	0.071	0.584	36894.184
sequor	0.287	0.062	9447.610
subeo	0.073	0.475	140924.768

TABLE 5.19 *Correlation coefficients* r, *p-values, and statistics, Continued.*

Verb	*r*	p-value	Statistic
sum	0.135	4.033e-05	110032847.665
tento	0.205	0.102	36393.017
timeo	0.191	0.513	368.151
venio	0.160	0.050	482171.470
VOLO	0.222	0.039	85351.370

TABLE 5.20 *Summary of the fourth set of results obtained by the WN version of the SP system, evaluated on a set of 40 random noun fillers (one for each verb-slot pair) extracted from large corpora. In this case, I consider a success the event in which there is a significant correlation (at the 0.05 level) between the SP probability distribution and the corpus frequency distribution. The second column contains the number of verb-slot pairs for which a success is realized. The third column contains the 95% confidence interval calculated by a binomial test on these results, and the last column the probability of success calculated by the test. The absence of stars indicates that there is the number of success is not significantly higher than the number of failures.*

Condition	No. successes	95% conf.int.	Est.p.succ.
signif.corr. between 2 rankings	12	[0.17,0.47]	0.3

TABLE 5.21 *Summary of the fifth set of results obtained by the WN version of the SP system, evaluated on a set of 40 random noun fillers (one for each verb-slot pair) extracted from large corpora. In this case, I consider a success the event in which the mean of the probabilities assigned by the system to the filler corresponding to a given verb-slot pair is higher than the mean of the probabilities assigned to the fillers corresponding to the other verbs and slots. The second column contains the number of verb-slot pairs for which a success is realized. The third column contains the 95% confidence interval calculated by a binomial test on these results, and the last column the probability of success calculated by the test. The star flags a significant result.*

Condition	No. successes	95% conf.int.	Est.p.succ.
p(fill. for *v-a*)>p(fill. other verbs-slots)	36*	[0.76,0.97]	0.9

TABLE 5.22 *Summary of the first set of results obtained by the distributional version of the SP system, evaluated on a set of 40 random noun fillers (one for each verb-slot pair) extracted from large corpora. The first column contains the condition for a success, realized when the SP probability assigned by the system to the random filler is higher than the measure of central tendency (mean, median, and third quartile). The second column shows the number of verb-slot pairs for which the probability assigned by the WN version of the SP system is higher than the corresponding measure of central tendency (i.e. success). The third column contains the 95% confidence interval calculated by a binomial test on these results, and the last column the probability of success calculated by the test. The star flags significant results.*

Condition	No. successes	95% conf.int.	Est.p.succ.
prob >mean	18	[0.30,0.63]	0.5
prob>median	35*	[0.76,0.97]	0.9
prob> 3rd q.	17	[0.28,0.60]	0.4

5.5.4 *Evaluating the Distributional Model*

In this section I will analyse the evaluation of the distributional version of the SP algorithm.

Central tendency. First, I compare the probability assigned by this algorithm to the random fillers with the mean, median, and value at the third quartile of the distribution for each verb-slot pair.

As Table 5.22 shows, in 18 cases the probability is higher than the mean, showing that the proportion of successes is not higher than the proportion of failures, as confirmed by a binomial test: 95% confidence interval =[0. 30, 0. 63], estimated probability of success =0.46. In 35 cases the probability is higher than the median, which says that the proportion of successes is significantly higher than the proportion of failures: 95% confidence interval =[0. 76, 0. 97], estimated probability of success =0.9. Finally, in 17 cases the probability is higher than the value of the third quartile, which means a significantly lower probability of success: 95% confidence interval =[0. 28, 0. 60], estimated probability of success =0.44.

Random filler vs. remaining 39 random fillers. Table 5.23 shows the results I obtain if I compare the probability assigned by the system to each verb's random filler with the mean of the probabilities assigned to the 39 random fillers extracted for the other verbs.

TABLE 5.23 *Summary of the second set of results obtained by the distributional version of the SP system, evaluated on a set of 40 random noun fillers (one for each verb-slot pair) extracted from large corpora. This time the random filler corresponding to each verb-slot pair is compared with the other 39 fillers, under the assumption that a success is realized if the probability assigned by the system to that noun is higher than the mean of the probabilities assigned to the other 39 nouns. The first column shows the condition for a success. The second column contains the number of verb-slot pairs for which a success is realized. The third column contains the 95% confidence interval calculated by a binomial test on these results, and the last column the probability of success calculated by the test. The star flags significant results.*

Condition	No. successes	95% conf.int.	Est.p.succ.
p(fill.)>mean (39 fill.)	25*	[0.46,0.77]	0.6

Fillers from parsed corpora. I extract the fillers of the 40 verb-slot pairs from two automatically parsed corpora, and then calculate the SP probabilities of the maximum-frequency fillers and the mean of the SP probabilities of the minimum-frequency fillers. The cases when the first is higher than the second are considered as successes. Table 5.24 shows that there are 18 successes. Among the failures I consider *ascendo* for which only one filler is extracted. A binomial test on these data gives the 95% confidence interval [0. 301, 0. 628] and an estimated probability of success of 0.462. Then, for each pair (v, a) I compare the mean of the probabilities of the fillers with the mean of the probabilities of the fillers for the other pairs and consider as successes those cases where the former is higher than the latter. I obtain 32 successes and a binomial test on these data gives a 95% confidence interval of [0. 665, 0. 925] and an estimated probability of success of 0.82 (Table 5.23).

Fillers vs. "non-fillers". For each verb v and slot a, I compare the mean of the probabilities assigned by the system to the fillers for v and a extracted from the parsed corpora with the mean of the probabilities assigned to the fillers for the other verbs and slots: $P_a(f|v)$ where f is a filler for (v, a) in the parsed corpora vs. $P_a(n|v)$, where n is a filler for pairs other than (v, a). As shown in Table 5.25, the comparison gives 32 successes.

Correlation test. I use a Spearman correlation test to compare the frequency distributions found in the automatically parsed corpora with the SP probability distribution given by the model.

TABLE 5.24 *Summary of the third set of results obtained by the distributional version of the SP system, evaluated on a set of 40 random noun fillers (one for each verb-slot pair) extracted from large corpora. In this case, I consider a success the event in which the SP probabilities of the maximum-frequency nouns are higher than the mean of the probabilities of the minimum-frequency nouns. The first column shows the condition for a success. The second column contains the number of verb-slot pairs for which a success is realized. The third column contains the 95 % confidence interval calculated by a binomial test on these results, and the last column the probability of success calculated by the test.*

Condition	No. successes	95 % conf.int.	Est.p.succ.
p(max-freq. fill)>mean p(min-freq fill.)	18	[0.30,0.63]	0.5

TABLE 5.25 *Summary of the fifth set of results obtained by the distributional version of the SP system, evaluated on a set of 40 random noun fillers (one for each verb-slot pair) extracted from large corpora. In this case, I consider a success the event in which the mean of the probabilities assigned by the system to the filler corresponding to a given verb-slot pair is higher than the mean of the probabilities assigned to the fillers corresponding to the other verbs and slots. The second column contains the number of verb-slot pairs for which a success is realized. The third column contains the 95 % confidence interval calculated by a binomial test on these results, and the last column the probability of success calculated by the test. The star flags a significant result.*

Condition	No. successes	95 % conf.int.	Est.p.succ.
p(fil. for *v-a*)>p(fill. other verbs-slots)	32*	[0.64,0.90]	0.8

TABLE 5.26 *Correlation coefficients* r, p*-values and statistics of the Spearman correlation test on the corpus frequency distribution and the SP probability distribution given by the distributional version of the model*

Verb	*r*	*p*-value	Statistic
accido2	0.21	0.09	4.14e+04
agito	0.14	0.23	7.38e+04
canto	1.00	0.00	0.00
cognosco	0.23	<1.00E-03	1.33e+06
comparo	0.49	<1.00E-03	5.57e+04

TABLE 5.26 *Correlation coefficients* r, p-*values and statistics, Continued.*

Verb	*r*	*p*-value	Statistic
constituo	0.21	0.00	1.01e+06
convenio	0.40	1.85E-09	8.98e+05
cupio	0.07	0.49	1.09e+05
determino	0.23	0.04	7.93e+04
dico2	0.12	<1.00E-03	1.30e+08
dimitto	0.07	0.68	5.54e+03
do	0.15	0.00	1.27e+07
facio	0.18	1.43E-10	2.56e+08
fero	0.10	0.02	2.59e+07
induco	0.08	0.68	3.36e+03
intellego	0.32	<1.00E-03	3.55e+05
intro	0.36	0.28	142
invenio	0.11	0.06	3.69e+06
maneo	0.37	5.29E-08	8.92e+05
moveo	0.10	0.59	4.03e+03
multiplico	-0.15	0.66	253
nego	0.13	0.10	5.72e+05
paro	0.09	0.28	3.63e+05
pateo	0.09	0.39	1.39e+05
pono	0.26	3.66E-10	2.44e+07
praecedo	0.07	0.37	7.22e+05
praedico	0.19	0.20	1.7e+04
profero	0.56	0.02	299.00
recipio	0.05	0.38	4.95e+06
refero	0.05	0.61	2.35e+05
resulto	0.23	0.34	1.03e+03
scio	0.13	0.20	1.64e+05
sequor	-0.06	0.66	4.00e+04
subeo	0.11	0.22	3.12e+05
sum	0.05	0.01	2.74e+09
tento	-0.08	0.43	1.41e+05
timeo	0.29	0.11	3.52e+03
venio	0.24	<1.00E-03	2.02e+06
volo	0.08	0.29	8.35e+05

TABLE 5.27 *Summary of the fourth set of results obtained by the distributional version of the SP system, evaluated on a set of 40 random noun fillers (one for each verb-slot pair) extracted from large corpora. In this case, I consider a success the event in which there is a significant correlation (at the 0.05 level) between the SP probability distribution and the corpus frequency distribution. The second column contains the number of verb-slot pairs for which a success is realized. The third column contains the 95% confidence interval calculated by a binomial test on these results, and the last column the probability of success calculated by the test. The absence of stars indicates that there is the number of success is not significantly higher than the number of failures.*

Condition	No. successes	95% conf.int.	Est.p.succ.
signif.corr. between 2 rankings	16	[0.25,0.57]	0.4

Table 5.26 shows the correlation coefficients, the *p*-values and the statistics of Spearman tests run on the 40 verb-slot pairs and Table 5.27 summarizes the results. For 16 pairs (in small caps in Table 5.19) I get *p*-values lower or equal to 0.05 and *r* coefficients between 0.04 (*sum*) and 1 (*canto*) (the number of significant cases at the 0.01 level is 12). For the remaining 24 pairs I get *p*-values higher than 0.05, which implies a non-significant correlation at the 0.05 level. A binomial test on 16 successes gives a 95% confidence interval of [0. 249, 0. 567], and an estimated probability of success of 0.4, which means that I can be 95% confident that the 12 successes occurred by chance.

CHAPTER 6

A Corpus-Based Foray into Latin Preverbs

6.1 New Paradigm

After presenting a computational lexicon for Latin verbal valency in chapter 3 and a system for learning SPs from Latin treebanks in chapters 4 and 5, this chapter gives an example of a quantitative investigation that uses the lexicon data. Given the extremely limited number of quantitative corpus studies concerning linguistic phenomena in Latin, the principal aim of this chapter is to show the potential of such an approach. Therefore, rather than as an exhaustive interpretation of the diachronic development of Latin prefixed verbs, the present study should be considered for its methodological contribution, which shows what can be achieved by using new source data (treebanks and the valency lexicon) and new techniques (multivariate statistics). This methodological focus also explains the emphasis which I intentionally placed on the research design rather than on the steps of a traditional analysis. This case study is meant to show an instance of the collaborative paradigm illustrated in section 1.4.

We can imagine the research process as a *circle* containing the following phases:

0. Create corpora, annotate them
1. observe the phenomenon, assign the label (e.g. 'preverb')
2. do preliminary theoretical work, identifying the phenomenon in different languages and constructing theories on it
3. gather data manually (examples)
4. interpret the example data in light of the theories
5. formulate theoretical hypotheses
6. process corpus data
7. carry out quantitative studies on corpus data
8. prepare first interpretation of the results
9. prepare further interpretation of the results and theoretical considerations such as: "is the label 'preverb' adequate?". Back to step 1.

I consider step number 0 to be independent from the particular phenomenon under investigation, and therefore this step does not enter the iterative process.

 | DOI: 10.1163/9789004260122_007

Given the methodological aims of the book, this study does not cover the whole process; instead, it focusses on phases 1–2 and 5 to 8. It does not include a complete comparison between the results offered by the analyses and the statements contained in previous studies, although it does mention some examples. Moreover, it illustrates the quantitative methodology necessary for further studies on this phenomenon and offers a basis for reconsidering the theories in the light of the analysed corpus data.

I define preverbs as prefixes of verbal stems. For example, *ab-* 'from' is prefixed to the verb *eo* 'go' in the prefixed verb (PV) *abeo* 'go from, depart'. How do these verbs express spatial complements? Does *abeo* express the place from which the subject departs with a simple ablative, or with a PP introduced by *ab* or another preposition? To what extent does the preverb affect the argument realization of the PV? In this chapter I will show how a quantitative analysis of corpus data can contribute to the field of Latin Computational Linguistics by addressing these questions as examples. The investigation presented here will testify the challenge of applying quantitative Corpus Linguistics to Latin data. In addition, this work will employ appropriate statistical techniques that measure the degree of uncertainty in the data, in order to overcome the issues related to small diachronic corpora.

One way to explore this topic is by making some theoretically grounded claims and then illustrate text examples, which is the usual practice in so-called qualitative studies. Another way is to refer to a corpus to carry out a systematic, quantitative account of the arguments of PVs, which means that the corpus is the starting point of an analysis that aims at quantitatively describing the data, and then generalizing the results to the whole population. This is achieved by using statistical techniques that help detect significant patterns in the data. In keeping with the general aim of this book, I will choose the latter approach and use the corpus-based lexicon I described in chapter 3 as the basis for the investigation. The quantitative approach allows me to highlight the advantages of using statistical techniques to explore a complex phenomenon, and quantify the role played in it by several factors.

That the phenomenon of preverbation is complex is made clear by the definition of preverbs given in Booij and van Kemenade (2003): "morphemes that appear in front of a verb, and which form a close semantic unit with that verb". This definition makes an explicit link between the morphological status of preverbs and their semantic properties with respect to the verb they are prefixed to. Although preverbation traditionally pertains to word formation and is therefore a morphological phenomenon, PVs offer the opportunity to explore interesting aspects of the syntax-semantics and syntax-lexicon interfaces. I will show how relevant interactions between the morpho-syntactic realizations of the arguments of PVs and their lexical-semantic properties can diachronically manifest themselves and be effectively detected in corpus data.

Several linguistic subfields have treated preverbs by referring to different theoretical frameworks. Indo-European linguistics has investigated the link between preverbs and adpositions (Benveniste, 1949; Lehmann, 1983; Cuzzolin, 1995; Echarte Cossío, 1998; López Moreda, 1998; Mellado Rodríguez, 2001; Cuzzolin et al., 2006; Hewson and Bubenik, 2006; Luraghi, 2010). Romance linguistics has focussed on the role played by preverbs in the development of Italian phrasal verbs (Masini, 2005; Iacobini, 2005; Simone, 2008). In Latin Linguistics several diachronic and synchronic studies have focussed on the system of Latin prepositions and cases, their semantics, and in particular on the argument structure of PVs (Benveniste, 1949; Lehmann, 1983; Echarte Cossío, 1998; Carvalho, 1998; Moussy, 2005). Some scholars have studied preverbs as *aktionsart* markers (*facio*, 'make', 'do' vs. *perficio*, 'achieve' Romagno 2004; García-Hernández 2005), while attempts have been made in typology to describe common properties of preverbs in different languages (Booij and van Kemenade, 2003; Rousseau, 1995; Heine et al., 1991). Finally, spatial preverbs have been discussed within Talmy (2000)'s typology of motion events and particularly with respect to the distinction between satellite preverbs and relational preverbs (Craig and Hale, 1988; Imbert, 2008). This literature is very interesting; however, a complete overview of the studies on this topic falls outside the scope of this work, which aims at showing a *methodologically new* approach, resorting to annotated corpora and advanced statistical techniques.

The realization of arguments of PVs and in particular the choice between a bare-case realization and a prepositional one is connected with the relation between preverbs and prepositions, and how distinctly these elements are perceived. Also, a relevant question is if the semantics of PVs is considered to be compositional and how this affects their argument structure. This will lead me to explore what scholars have claimed about the evolution of Latin preverbs and prepositions, and the processes behind the semantic evolution of Latin PVs.

6.2 Origin and Development of Latin Preverbs

6.2.1 *Preverbs and Adpositions*

A hypothesis in Indo-European linguistics that goes back to Saussure and was drawn on by Meillet and Vendryes (1963, 199–200, 573–578) associates preverbs to adpositions through their common origin from a class of undifferentiated proto-Indoeuropean adverbial particles. According to this hypothesis, such original adverbial elements were characterized by a rather free status within the sentence both as to their linear order and as to their syntactic functions. In Vedic such particles are often separated from verbs, while this is not the case in Classical Sanskrit (MacDonell, 1953, 285). Homeric Greek too displays various examples of the flexible status of such elements (cf. e.g. Hewson and Bubenik (2006, 57–59; 345)).

A first phase of development of preverbs and adpositions from independent constituents is attested in Latin as well, but evidence is limited to a few archaic texts. An example is the following passage by the grammarian Festus, quoted in Cuzzolin (1995, 130):

(1) Sub vos placo, in precibus fere cum dicitur, significat id, quod supplico, ut in legibus: transque dato et endoque plorato.

'When we say, mostly in prayers, *sub vos placo*, it means the same as *supplico*, like *transque dato* and *endoque plorato* in the laws.'

While talking about the language of early prayers, Festus sets a semantic equivalence between the Classical form *supplico* 'implore, beseech' and its *a posteriori* decomposition into the elements *sub* 'under' (adverb) and *placo* 'reconcile' (verb). In Plautus and Terence *intro-* occurs both as a preverb and as a free adverbial element (Brachet, 2005).

In spite of such few examples, in Latin we typically find a clearly delimited situation with prepositions on the one hand, and preverbs as bound prefixes on the other. This situation has been explained diachronically through a combination of processes referring to word order change and the erosion of the case system, although the individual stages of this evolution are not uncontroversial (Cuzzolin, 1995; Fruyt, 1998; Oniga, 2005; Hewson and Bubenik, 2006; Luraghi, 2010). These scholars have suggested that, as the order of words became more fixed, in some cases the original adverbial elements were morphologically fused with the following verbal forms (univerbation), thus developing into preverbs, and in other cases they syntactically governed the case of the preceding nouns, thus generating postpositions. This development of Latin preverbs and adpositions is also consistent with a grammaticalization account (Cuzzolin, 1995; Fruyt, 1998; Hewson and Bubenik, 2006; Luraghi, 2010). In fact, from an undifferentiated class of Indo-European adverbial elements, preverbs and adpositions evolved distinctly towards "more grammatical" items. It is also important to point out that such differentiation preverbs and adpositions underwent is related to the crucial possibility of attaching these elements to VPs or NPs, respectively.

The further evolution of Latin preverbs seems to conform to a case of univerbation involving fusion of morphemes and loss of semantic compositionality. After the univerbation of preverbs with simple verbs, in some cases preverbs underwent a phonological fusion: cf. e.g. *affero* 'bring to' <*ad-fero*. Scholars generally agree that some Latin PVs lost their semantic relation to the original verb so that their etymological meaning tended to weaken. This process led some preverbs to take a "more grammatical" role (distinct from that of prepositions), such as intensive, attenuative, iterative, or aspectual. For example, Cuzzolin (1995) proposes an evolution of some preverbs to aspectual markers with no lexical content: cf. *com-edo* (lit. 'eat with') which means 'eat up', and not 'eat with someone'. As suggested by Hewson and Bubenik (2006, 255), this phenomenon can be identified as an instance of *semantic bleaching*, which implies a replacement of a "lexical content meaning" with a "new, more abstract, grammatical meaning" (Brinton and Traugott, 2005, 29), as in the typical example of the English grammaticalized form *going to* from the motion sense to the future marker.

Certain other Latin preverbs did not acquire an aspectual sense. For these preverbs scholars have claimed a development towards a different, but still non-compositional meaning of the PVs (López Moreda, 1998). For example, the etymological sense 'bind around' of *ob-ligo* is rarer than the sense 'oblige, make liable', where the prefix does not hold an explicit semantic content. Likewise, *permitto* originally meant 'send through', but by the first century BC it had acquired the meaning 'allow', cf. French *permettre* and Italian *permettere* (Vincent, 1999).

Studies on the origin of verbal prefixes in Romance languages have claimed that Latin preverbs underwent a lexicalization process within the PV they were prefixed to, and have connected this with a gradual loss of transparency of Latin preverbs (Tekavčić 1972, § 948.3–1345, Salvi and Vanelli 1992, 206, Crocco Galèas and Iacobini 1992, 172, Vicario 1997, 129, Haverling 2000, 458–460, Dufresne et al. 2003, 40). This phenomenon did not affect all preverbs in the same way and was more pronounced for some preverbs (such as *ad-* 'to', *in-* 'in, to') and less for others (such as *de-* 'from'). Allen (1981, 84) connected this with the phonological combination between preverb and verb stem. For example, consonantal assimilation and loss of final consonants in prepositions caused verbs prefixed with the preverbs *ab-* 'from' and *ad-* 'to' to converge into the same class.

Specific interwoven phenomena attest a lexicalization process, which has been related with the gradual loss of Latin case system and the subsequent increase of analytic forms with prepositions in neo-Latin languages (Iacobini and Masini, 2007). First, the productivity of some Latin locative preverbs contrasts with their low productivity or non-productivity in Romance languages. Certain Latin preverbs (e.g. *ad-* vs. *in-*) indicated different spatial directions; for instance the difference between *ad-* and *in-* had to do with the opposition between approaching and entering a limit. In the Romance languages this functional distinction is almost never present any longer: cf. French *attendre* 'wait' vs. *entendre* 'hear' (Iacobini, 2005). Second, Durante (1981, 66) connected the loss of productivity of some Latin preverbs with the switch to SVO word order that caused their replacement by analytic forms: cf. *subire*>*ire susu(m)* 'go from below upwards'. The use of such postverbal particles instead of preverbs is connected with the later rise of phrasal verbs in some Italian dialects (Simone, 1997; Vicario, 1997; Masini, 2005).

In conclusion, it seems reasonable to hypothesize a connection between the gradual lexicalization of Latin preverbs—already attested in the Classical era—and an increasing use of analytic forms such as prepositions and adverbial elements to express directional meanings, which finally led, among other things, to the emergence of Italian phrasal verbs. As I will show in section 6.3, my interest is in detecting with quantitative means the extent to which this evolution affected the argument structure of Latin PVs, with particular reference to the use of PPs as spatial complements.

6.2.2 *Spatial Preverbs and Motion Events*

Being my interest on PVs that are prefixed with spatial preverbs and whose semantics is related to motion events, I will briefly summarize some theories proposed on this topic. This overview aims to give a theoretical introduction to this topic, and prepares the ground for the empirical investigations.

In Talmy (2000)'s theorization of spatial schemas, motion events consist of a Figure and a Ground. The Figure follows a Path with respect to the Ground and the Motion "refers to the presence per se of motion or locatedness in the event" (Talmy, 2000, 25). For example, consider the following sentences:

(2) The boy is in the room.
(3) The boy is going into the room.
(4) The boy runs out of the room.

In (2), *the boy* is the Figure, *is* is Location, and *the room* is the Ground. In (3), *is going* is a Translational Motion, *into* is the Path, and *the room* is the Ground. We can also find a conflation of a Co-event (for example Manner) and a translational motion, as in (4) (Translational Motion+Manner), where *out of* is the Path and *the room* is the Ground. Path expressions can be of three types:

- FROM paths
- TO paths
- VIA paths

FROM paths refer to the Source from which the Figure moves, while TO paths refer to its Goal. In the previous sentences the Path component is encoded outside the verbal root in the prepositions *in*, *into*, and *out of*, which are the heads of the PPs *in the room*, *into the room*, and *out of the room*. This is not the only possibility. For example, in (5), the particle *out* relates to the verb *run* and contains the Path of the motion event.

(5) The boy ran out.

Talmy (1991, 486) defines particles like *out* in the English phrasal verb *run out* as *satellites*, i.e. "a grammatical category of any constituent other than nominal complement that is in sister relation to the verb root". Satellites complement the content of the verb from a lexical and semantic point of view, and (unlike adpositions) do not govern an NP. In spite of this categorization, particles in phrasal verbs bear an "ambiguous categorical status" between prepositions and adverbs, and the resulting multi-word expressions may assume a metaphorical non-compositional meaning (Masini, 2005, 155). Satellites, in fact, may lexicalize with the verb and lose their spatial meaning, as in the sentence *We ran out of sugar*.

Talmy (2000) presents a semantic typology based on the different ways languages morphologically encode the Path component of motion events. According to his typology, most languages belong to one of the two following groups:

- verb-framed languages
- satellite-framed languages

In verb-framed languages the Path component is in the verb root, while in satellite-framed languages languages the Path component is in the satellite and/or preposition. The first category of languages includes Romance languages as well as Semitic, Japanese, Tamil, Polynesian languages, and others. The second category includes Germanic, Finno-Ugric, and Chinese languages, among others.

A sentence like (5) displays a Path component in the particle *out* and Motion +Manner is encoded at the same time in the verb *run*. On the other hand, sentence (6), Motion and Path are fused into the verbs *exit*.

(6) The boy exited (running).

Several scholars have shown that Talmy's categorization is too strict: a language can in fact perform more than one strategy for encoding the Path component (Wälchli, 2000; Slobin, 2004). Both Italian and English, for example, allow the two encodings. Examples of satellite-framed features are the so-called *verbi sintagmatici* in Italian (Rohlfs, 1970; Simone, 2008) and phrasal verbs in English: cf. English *go out* and Italian *andare fuori* 'go out', or *buttare via*, which means 'throw away' but also 'waste'. Examples of verb-framed features are the Italian verbs *discendere* and *uscire*, and the English verbs *descend* and *exit*.

6.2.3 *Classifying Latin*

Where does Latin place itself in Talmy's classification and how does this affect spatial preverbs and PVs? A strict interpretation of Talmy's classification implies that Latin belongs to the satellite-framed class, due to its category of preverbs. However, Romance languages are generally said to be verb-framed languages because they mostly encode Path inside the verb: cf. for example French *sortir*, Italian *uscire* 'exit'.

Some Romance descendants of Latin PVs have kept a spatial meaning, although preverbs may not be recognisable any longer as satellites. In her study on Late Latin PVs, Stolova (2008) states that the Romance verbs *entrar* (Spanish), *entrer* (French), *entrare* (Italian), *entrar* (Portuguese), *a intra* (Rumanian), and *entrar* (Catalan), derived from Latin *intrare* 'enter, go in' (with preverb *intro-* 'inside'), were etymologically compounds but perceived as simple forms. The same argument holds for the Latin verbs *ascendo* 'ascend, go up', *descendo* 'descend, go down', *exeo* 'exit, go out', and *pervenio* 'arrive'. The preverbs of these verbs became "non-transparent" and they survived in the Romance languages just as simple verbs (like *venio* 'come') did.

Therefore, although Talmy defines Latin preverbs as satellites, some Romance verbs from Latin PVs do not compositionally show the presence of the same preverbs as satellites. Hence, we can hypothesize a development that turned some Latin preverbs functioning as satellites into Romance verbal prefixes that still encode Path but do not hold the satellite function any more. See Brucale et al. (2011) and Brucale (2011) for a discussion of factors involved in this typological shift and a study of manner of motion verbs in Latin, showing that "Latin, unlike prototypically satellite-framed languages, does not assign a great salience to the information concerning the manner in which a motion is performed" (Brucale, 2011, 8).

All these facts help frame the typological shift from Latin to Romance as a lexicalization process. I will now examine how this lexicalization can be partially identified by some properties of the argument structure of Latin PVs, and which differences among Latin preverbs can help understand their problematic definition as satellites.

6.3 Argument Structure of Latin Prefixed Verbs

I will now concentrate on the argument structure of Latin PVs. In particular, I will consider verbs of motion and verbs of rest, and the realization of their spatial preverbs' *relata*, i.e. the morpho-syntactic expressions of the Path components corresponding to the preverbs.

There has been a discussion in linguistics about whether or not to consider the status of Path expressions within the verbs' argument structure. For example, Jackendoff (1990) does not consider Path as a part of the argument structure of Manner of Motion verbs. Nevertheless, other verbs like *buy*, *sell*, or *give* do require the Path component in their semantics and syntax. Since these specific Path expressions are annotated as verb arguments in the treebanks I use, I will consider the preverbs' *relata* as part of the argument structure of Latin verbs of motion and verbs of rest.

6.3.1 *Synchronic Overview*

Latin PVs exhibit a variety of constructions in the realization of their *relata*. The following examples illustrate the syntactic construction of the verb *adeo* 'go to, reach' with an accusative expressing the spatial complement (7), contrasted with the intransitivity of the simple verb *eo* 'go' occurring with a spatial complement introduced by *ad* (8):

(7) patrios-que AD-IT inpiger
fatherly:ACC.M.PL-and to-go:IND.PRS.3SG quick:NOM.M.SG
ORTUS
sunrise:ACC.M.PL
'he rushed to his father's orient' (Ov., *Met.*, I, 779)

(8) IBAT res AD summam NAUSEAM
go:IND.IMPF.3SG thing:NOM.F.SG to highest:ACC.F.SG nausea:ACC.F.SG
'The thing was becoming extremely sickening' (Petron., *Sat.*, 78)

In (7) the preverb corresponds to a preposition governing the accusative case (*ad*). In such cases, the valency of the PV seems to be somehow affected by the valency of the preverb, which causes an apparent "transitivization" of the verb. As a matter of fact, we can establish a relation between the argument structure of a PV and the argument structure of the corresponding simple (i.e. non-prefixed) verb, via the role played by the argument structure of the preverb. In other words, if we limit the analysis to those PVs whose semantics can be predicted from that of the simple verb, like *ab-eo* 'come from', we may analyse their argument structure in relation with that of the simple verbs (*eo*) and of the preverbs (*ab-*) itself. This also leads us to concentrate on preverbs with a spatial sense, on PVs with compositional meaning and, therefore, on spatial complements occurring as arguments of these PVs.

In the terminology adopted by Lehmann (1983, 146–147) *locatum* is "something whose position in space or time is described by the construction", while *relatum* is "the item with respect to which the locatum is localized. It is an animate, lifeless or abstract object, a nominal concept which serves as a point of reference for the localization". From a syntactic point of view, the *locatum* of the preverb is the subject of the PV if the corresponding simple verb is intransitive, and is its direct object if the simple verb is transitive. In sentence (8), the *locatum* coincides with the subject of the verb; in sentence (7), *ortus* is the *relatum* of the preverb *ad.*

Analogously to sentence (7), double accusatives expressing *relata* and *locata* are attested with PVs originating from transitive verbs prefixed with preverbs/prepositions requiring the accusative case, mostly *circum-* and *trans-*. Sentence (9) shows an example of this construction, where the second accusative *exercitum* (*locatum*) is the direct object of the verb *traducere* and the first accusative *flumen* (*relatum*) can be seen as governed by the preverb.

(9) FLUMEN Axonam [...] EXERCITUM TRA-ducere
river:ACC.N.SG Axona:ACC.M.SG [...] army:ACC.M.SG lead over:INF.PRS
maturavit
hasten:IND.PPF.3SG
'he hastened to lead his army over the river Aisne' (Caes., *B. G.*, II, 5)

Moreover, when the preposition corresponding to the preverb requires an indirect case, like *ab* with the ablative, the *relatum* can be expressed as the respective bare case, as exemplified in (10).

(10) DOMINA cogis AB-ire mea?
mistress:ABL.F.SG urge:IND.PRS.2SG from-go:INF.PRS my:ABL.F.SG
'Do you urge me to leave my mistress?' (Prop., I, IV, 2)

All the examples presented so far show morpho-syntactic realizations of *relata* as NPs with the case required by the preposition corresponding to the preverb; in these cases the preverb seems to act as an adposition.[1] The morpho-syntactic realizations of a preverb's *relatum* can thus manifest themselves in the following constructions:

1. (CasePrev) as an NP, whose case is that governed by the preposition corresponding to the preverb:

(11) patrios-que AD-it inpiger
fatherly:ACC.M.PL-and to-go:IND.PRS.3SG quick:NOM.M.SG
ORTUS
sunrise:ACC.M.PL
'he rushed to his father's orient' (Ov., *Met.*, I, 779)

(12) CASTRIS E-gressi
camp:ABL.N.PL from-go:PTCP.NOM.M.PL
'having marched out of the camp' (Caes., *B. G.*, II, 11, 1)

2. (CaseNonPrev) as an NP, whose case is not the one governed by the preposition corresponding to the preverb:[2]

(13) num TIBI aut stultitia AC-cessit aut
perhaps you:DAT.SG or folly:NOM.F.SG to-go:IND.PF.3SG or
superat superbia?
overcome:IND.PF.3SG pride:NOM.F.SG
'is it folly that has come to you, or does pride overcome you?' (Plaut., *Amph.*, 709)

---

1 Oniga (2005, 218–219) associates these phenomena to the syntactic valency of the corresponding preposition rather than to the semantics of the preverb only, since he observes that these constructions do not occur with preverbs that do not formally correspond to prepositions, like *dis-* 'un-' (cf. *dissuadeo* 'dissuade'). Conversely, while discussing the prevalence of these phenomena with the simple *ablativus separativus* (with *ab-*, *de-*, *ex-* and *pro-*) over the *ablativus locativus* (with *in-*), Lehmann (1983, 153) claims that this may be (at least partially) based on the meaning of the ablative rather than on the preverb itself.

2 *Accessit* is a form of the verb *accedo*<*ad-cedo* by assimilation.

(14) FONTESque A-vertitur
and spring:ACC.M.PL from-turn:IND.PRS.3SG.PASS
'he turns away from the springs' (Verg., *Georg.*, 499)

3. (PrepPrev) as a PP, whose preposition corresponds to the preverb:[3]

(15) canem istam A foribus ⟨aliquis⟩
dog:ACC.F.SG this:ACC.F.SG from door:ABL.F.PL somebody:NOM.SG
AB-ducat face
from-take:SBJV.PRS.3SG make:IMP.PRS.2SG
'make somebody move the dog away from the door' (Plaut., *Mostell.*, 853)

(16) E castris Helvetiorum E-gressi
from camp:ABL.N.PL Helventian:GEN.M.PL from-go:PTCP.NOM.M.PL
'having marched out of the Helvetians' camp' (Caes., *B. G.*, I, 27, 4)

4. (PrepNonPrev) as a PP, whose preposition does not correspond to the preverb:

(17) AB-i-n E conspectu meo?
from-go:IND.FUT.2SG-INTERR.PART. from sight:ABL.M.SG my:ABL.M.SG
'will you be away from my sight?' (Plaut., *Amph.*, 518)

(18) IN cuius participationem nullo modo
to who:GEN.SG participation:ACC.F.SG any:ABL.M.SG way:ABL.M.SG
corpus AD-duci potest
body:NOM.N.SG to-take:INF.PRS.PASS can:IND.PRS.3SG
'to whose participation the body cannot be drawn in any way' (Th., *Sent. P. L.*, II)

Connecting to the typology of space introduced earlier, these syntactically different behaviours of PVs can be diachronically mirrored in the different statuses of the preverbs themselves, i.e. as adpositions or as satellites.

3 *A* and *ab* are different forms of the same preposition; the former is usually found before words beginning with a consonant, while the latter with words beginning with a vowel.

6.3.2 *Diachronic Hypotheses*

The distributions of the four constructions exhibited by PVs and described in section 6.3.1 have been diachronically investigated in the literature.

6.3.2.1 Construction 1 (CasePrev)

As described in Latin grammars (see, for example, Ernout and Thomas (1972); Traina and Bertotti (1993)), spatial complements containing names of cities and small islands are often found without spatial prepositions, just like the nouns *domus* 'home', *rus* 'country', *locus* 'place', *pars* 'part', *litus* 'sea-shore', *regio* 'region', *cornu* 'horn', and adjectives like *medius* 'middle', *imus* 'lowest', *summus* 'highest'.[4] In addition, special idioms show the same behaviour: *ire malam crucem* 'go to hell', *exsequias ire* 'go to a funeral', *alicui suppetias ire/(ad-)venire/proficisci* 'go/come help someone'.

Some scholars have used these facts to hypothesize a connection between the use of construction 1 (CasePrev) with verbs prefixed with spatial preverbs and "a grammaticalization of the *accusativus directionis* commonly taken by such verbs" (Lehmann, 1983, 156). Along this reasoning, they have considered construction 1 (CasePrev) as a result of some specific stylistic choices such as archaisms, Hellenisms, and the poetic genre (Ernout and Thomas, 1972; Janssen, 1988; López Moreda, 1998). They have also diachronically framed it into a more general archaic tendency by simple verbs and PVs to encode spatial complements with bare cases; in other words, they have seen construction 1 (CasePrev) as a relic of an older stage of Latin, when preverbs still kept some semantic and syntactic autonomy from the verb.

According to these premises, I would expect to find this construction significantly more often in archaic writers and authors (particularly in poets) who make use of archaisms, which leads me to formulate the following hypothesis:

Hypothesis 6.3.2.1.1. *Construction 1 (CasePrev) is significantly more frequent in the archaic age and in works by poets than in the later ages and in prose writers.*

6.3.2.2 Construction 2 (CaseNonPrev)

Accusative. The instances of construction 2 (CaseNonPrev) contain some "transitivization" cases: in such cases an accusative NP occurs as the spatial argument of a PV, while the simple verb is intransitive and the preposition corre-

4 However, some of these nouns (including names of cities and small islands) may feature a dedicated locative case, depending on their inflectional class.

sponding to the preverb does not govern the accusative case (Coleman, 1991, 335). For instance, *evado* 'come out' is prefixed with *ex-* 'from' which requires the ablative case, but *evado* can occur with the accusative.

The following sentence shows an example with the verb *averto* 'turn away' < *ab+verto* followed by the accusative *fontes* 'springs'.

(19) fontes-que A-vertitur
spring:ACC.F.PL-and from-turn:IND.PRS.3SG.PASS
'he turns away from the springs'. (Vergil, *Geor.* 3, 499)

I have presented some diachronic hypotheses which assigned construction 1 (CasePrev) to archaic and poetic language. The use in the poetic language applies to construction 2 (CaseNonPrev) as well, if we limit the analysis to these "transitivization" cases, where the accusative is the bare case used for expressing the preverb's *relatum* (Rosén, 1999).

Dative. A special remark should be devoted to the dative case. According to many scholars (cf. e.g. Sweetser 1988, 395, Coleman 1991, 335, Bortolussi 2005), in several languages, among which Latin, a spatial metaphor drives the choice between dative and ablative in local complements, according to which dative is employed for Goal expressions and ablative for Source. Regarding the evolution of the constructions involving the dative, Rohlfs (1970, 6–7) notices that in Latin (and later in Romance languages), *ad* 'to' + accusative can be used to replace the dative case, and Vincent (1999, 1115–1116, 1130–1131) distinguishes this case-marking use of *ad* from a prepositional use of *ad*. This fact should be taken into account while considering construction 2 (CaseNonPrev), since a motion PV prefixed with *ad-* can appear with the bare dative case to express direction. Furthermore, Rosén (1999, 146) argues that Augustan poets prefer the so-called "dative of direction" to a PP, and Janssen (1988, 105–108) labels this as an archaism feature in poetry, supported by Greek models and its affinity with *dativus commodi* and *dativus incommodi* (Leumann et al., 1965; Löfstedt, 1956). In addition, Longrée (2005) considers the use of the dative as opposed to a PP to be more frequent when the verb has a figurative sense and the complement position is lexically filled by an animate entity, especially when the subject is inanimate. He also notices that some idiomatic expressions (like *timor/terror in-cessit*+dative 'fear/terror struck'+NP) might have favoured analogical constructions, such as *terror in-cidit*+dative 'terror fell upon'+NP. Finally, Pinkster (2010) analyses some PVs occurring with dative complements and finds that this construction "can be explained by referring to one or more (classes of) verbs with a similar meaning, or especially in creative texts by assuming a more complicated bridge, which is none the less semantic". It is thus realistic to assume that semantic factors may explain the use of construction 2 (CaseNonPrev) with dative.

In conclusion, the examples of construction 2 (CaseNonPrev) are difficult to categorize from a diachronic point of view, given that different hypotheses have been proposed depending on the specific case involved (accusative or dative). Since a specific analysis on these constructions falls outside the scope of my work, in my corpus investigations I will aim at testing a general preference for this construction in poets.

Relational preverbs. While analyzing preverbs in Homeric Greek, Imbert (2008) distinguishes between *incorporated relational preverbs* and *lexicalized relational preverbs*. Both these classes syntactically occur with the accusative case even if the corresponding prepositions do not govern this case. Incorporated relational preverbs are not semantically lexicalized within the PV: cf. *ekdiabaínō* 'go through from' followed by an accusative NP, although *ek-* 'from' governs the genitive case. Imbert also argues that lexicalized relational preverbs have undergone some degree of lexicalization and loss of semantic compositionality. An example is the Ancient Greek verb *apanaínomai* 'deny', prefixed with *apó-* 'off' (relational preverb, requiring the genitive) and occurring with an accusative object. According to Imbert's categorization, Goal preverbs almost never lexicalize in Homeric Greek, while Source preverbs tend to become lexicalized relational preverbs more easily. If I extend her definition of incorporated and lexicalized relational preverbs to PVs occurring with bare cases different from the accusative, construction 2 (CaseNonPrev) corresponds to these groups of preverbs.

6.3.2.3 Constructions 3 (PrepPrev) and 4 (PrepNonPrev)

Scholars have generally recognized construction 1 (CasePrev) involving the bare case as being less innovative than constructions 3 (PrepPrev) and 4 (PrepNonPrev), which involve the presence of a preposition (Coleman 1991, 332, Rosén 1999, 37). One could interpret this appearance of innovative constructions co-existing with older ones in the light of the diachronic development of preverbs from an adpositional-like behaviour to a progressive lexicalization. Indeed, one may view construction 1 (CasePrev) as an instance of the more "original" situation, where preverbs acted as adpositions, thus syntactically governing the case of the NP expressing their *relata*. Conversely, one could connect the presence of the preposition in constructions 3 (PrepPrev) and 4 (PrepNonPrev) with an innovative situation, where the gradual lexicalization of preverbs and the increasing degree of semantic non-compositionality of the PVs might have favoured the use of PPs for expressing spatial complements. The decreasing proportion of construction 1 (CasePrev) and the increasing proportion of constructions 3 (PrepPrev) and 4 (PrepNonPrev) with time would thus be in accordance with this evolution. This is, of course, one of the possible perspectives from which one can examine the distribution of these constructions. It is also possible that stylistic and pragmatic factors drove the author's syntactic choices. However, if we only focus on a diachronic perspective, we can formulate the following hypothesis:

Hypothesis 6.3.2.3.1. *The frequency of construction 1 (CasePrev) with respect to constructions 3 (PrepPrev) and 4 (PrepNonPrev) tends to decrease with time.*

If we consider the literary genre rather than chronology only, we can formulate some additional hypotheses. López Moreda (1998, 964) claims that construction 3 (PrepPrev) is more frequent in the dramatic genre and in the familiar and colloquial register. Rosén (1999, 148–149) identifies stylistic criteria affecting the choice between the different constructions in the later Republican and early Imperial age, associating the use of PPs with the familiar register and the use of bare case to a more elaborated style. Summing up, I will hypothesize a general preference for construction 3 (PrepPrev) in dramatic writers and authors whose style contains some features from the spoken language.

In constructions 3 (PrepPrev) and 4 (PrepNonPrev) we may have instances of redundancy (Sinha and Kuteva, 1995), because the Path component may be at the same time expressed by the preverb and by the preposition.

(20) E castris [...] E-gressi
from camp:ABL.N.PL from-go:PTCP.NOM.M.PL
PATH GROUND TRANSLATIONAL MOTION + PATH
'having marched out of the Helvetians camp' (Caes., *B. G.*, I, 27, 4)

(21) AB-i-n E conspectu [...]?
from-go:IND.FUT.2SG-INTERR.PART from sight:ABL.M.SG
TRANSLATIONAL MOTION+PATH PATH GROUND
'will you be away from my sight?' (Plaut., *Amph.*, 518)

Lexicalization. As a matter of fact, it is difficult to detect a weakened transparency of the preverb in the verb's semantics and decide whether the Path component is actually expressed in the preverb or not. In sentence (21), for example, the verb *ab-eo* could have either kept the compositional meaning 'go from', or lost it, simply meaning 'go, leave'. Although the verb's semantics is subject to interpretation, I can nevertheless hypothesize that the presence of the prepositions *e* 'from' in (20) and (21) is related to the fact that the preverb played a role which is different from the adpositional one. Imbert (2008) calls these preverbs *satellite preverbs* and claims that they represent the end of a grammaticalization process that started from relational preverbs.

Moreover, Imbert refers to the semantic-conceptual criterion of the Goal/Source asymmetry, which has been investigated in several subfields of linguistics, including cognitive linguistics and typology. Among the typological studies on syntax, Ikegami (1987) analyses the asymmetric way in which languages express Source and Goal, showing psychological reasons for the so-called 'goal-over-source principle'. According to this principle, the expressions of Goal are predominant in languages if they are compared with expressions of Source; evidence for this can be found in the possibility of replacing the Source marker with the Goal marker, and in the markedness of Source expressions. Among psycholinguistic studies, Lakusta and Landau (2005) show that there is a non-linguistic and linguistic bias towards Goal in encoding paths; this bias applies to all event types and is evident in both children and adults. Imbert claims that the Goal/Source asymmetry partially drove the process of grammaticalization for Ancient Greek and Old English preverbs: Goal preverbs tended to hold an adpositional role (relational preverbs), while Source preverbs tended to lexicalize (satellite preverbs). In my analyses I will investigate to what extent the Goal/Source nature of preverbs affects the type of constructions occurring with their PVs.

The general trend which took place throughout the history of Latin from the Indo-European origins to Romance languages and which led to lexicalization of certain Latin preverbs can only be detected over a large time span. Consequently, the effects of this trend are not necessarily "measurable" at each point of this process. Put in other words, the developments described in the previous sections do not seem to explain the whole story about the interplay of synchronic and diachronic factors governing the expression of *locata* and *relata* of Latin preverbs. As a matter of fact, it is possible to find both the presence and the absence of prepositional constructions in the same author, already in the archaic age (Oniga, 2005); this is sometimes justified by certain stylistic choices (Ernout and Thomas, 1972, 33) and by the principle of *variatio* (Longrée, 2005, 302), or even by pragmatic factors. In addition, the lexicalization of preverbs is not only a chronological feature relative to a particular historical age, but is attested since early Latin. The situation is in fact more complex than a general trend would suggest, since the preference towards a particular construction is prone to influence of additional criteria, involving for example the animacy and lexical properties of the *locatum* and *relatum*, as well as the particular (concrete or figurative) sense of the verb (Longrée, 2005; Viti, 2008).

In my corpus-based investigations I will focus on the four constructions occurring with Latin PVs, aiming at finding the conditions under which one construction is preferred over the others. My general assumption is that there is a connection between a more advanced degree of lexicalization of the preverbs within the PVs and a preference for prepositional constructions such as construction 3 (PrepPrev) and 4 (PrepNoPrev). In particular, I will test whether this can be associated with a general diachronic trend and how it can be detected in corpus data; I will also show how variables other than the chronological one should be taken into account in the analysis.

6.4 Research Design

The linguistic goal of this research is to carry out corpus-based quantitative analyses on the argument structure of Latin PVs. In addition to producing corpus results, I aim at proposing a more general empirical approach, which constitutes the methodological goal of this work.

6.4.1 *The Example-Based Approach*

No study that can be defined corpus-based in the modern sense exists on Latin preverbs and their interaction with the argument structure of PVs. All previous studies are qualitative, and quote example data. In some cases, the examples are numerous, especially considering the manual effort that went into collecting them. However, the lack of adequate statistical techniques to handle the examples makes it impossible to derive quantitative generalizations from them, and justifies the name 'qualitative' for this kind of research.

I do not aim to give a systematic survey of such studies here, since the main focus is on the original contribution of my work; I will however, take the opportunity to explain the value of my approach by comparing it to one previous study, which is particularly interesting because it could incorrectly be considered a data-driven/quantitative study.

In the preface to the second of his two volumes on the syntax of early Latin, Bennett (1914), introduces the reader to his methodological choices (Bennett, 1914, iii–iv).

> My task in the preparation of this second volume has been much more difficult than I had anticipated. Barring a few of the more recent monographs, I soon found that the treatises on which I had hoped largely to depend, were extremely defective, not only lacking a large proportion of the important material, but being based, in great measure, on conjectural

> readings of the past generation. Not infrequently false interpretations added to the confusion. Under these circumstances, it became necessary to make my own special collections to supplement the obvious lacunae encountered at almost every turn. The expenditure of time and labor thus caused have unquestionably been greater than if I had made independent collections of the entire material from the beginning. Nevertheless I believe that substantial completeness has been achieved in the material here presented. Wherever possible, I have given the exact number of instances of the occurrence of a usage. When a usage is found ten or more times, I have marked it "frequent".

The labour that went into collecting such material from primary text sources must have certainly been impressive. The data are presented in the book in the form of lists of Latin verbs, categorized according to the case they occur with (with a particular attention to Early authors), followed by quotations.

As you can see from the previous quote, in the preface the author defines as "substantial" the completeness of the material. Unfortunately this completeness was not recorded in the book, given both its size and probably the impossibility for the author (and any human being) to present a huge amount of data in a manageable format without turning to statistical tools. Instead, the author employs the term 'frequent' whenever he found an instance more than ten times in his dataset. The consequence of this methodological choice is that, for those cases where ten or fewer instances were found, the reader can check the quotations and be reassured; for the other cases, a summary is offered by the author to help the reader understand what are the "frequent" patterns.

This attitude towards recording infrequent behaviours systematically, and leaving the frequent ones specified under a generic label 'frequent' has some similarities with the way traditional dictionaries address valency properties, which I discussed in section 3.2.

Let me start with some illustrative examples from Bennett (1914). Prefixed verbs occurring with the dative case are grouped into three sets, depending on whether "both a simple verb [...] and the compound [...] appear with the dative in substantially the same value" (as *dico*/*indico*/*praedico* 'say') ('Simple Indirect Object'), or "in a compound of *ad*, *ante*, *con*, *in*, *inter*, etc., the prepositional force has disappeared (as in *convenit*, 'it suits', 'pleases')" ('Verbs with Special Meanings'), or the meaning is compositional ('Prepositional Compounds'). While talking about the last group, the author summarizes (Bennett, 1914, 122–123):

> It not infrequently happens that a simple intransitive verb which does not take the dative may, when combined with a preposition, form a compound which takes a dative of indirect object. Less often a transitive verb, when compounded with a preposition, loses its transitive character and governs the dative instead of the accusative e.g. *obsequor*. In addition to the foregoing, we find certain transitive verbs which, when compounded with prepositions, become capable of taking a dative in addition to an accusative of direct object, as *inicite huic manicas mastigiae*! The prepositions involved in the phenomena here mentioned are: *ad*, *ante*, *com-*, *in*, *inter*, *ob*, *prae*, *pro*, *sub*, *super*. Yet by no means all verbs compounded with these prepositions exhibit the property referred to. Furthermore, many compounds which take the dative appear either occasionally or frequently with the accusative or with prepositional phrases (introduced especially by *ad* or *in*).

Then, follows a review of previous views on this topic, concerning the appropriateness of this category as semantically independent from the group of corresponding simple (i.e. non-prefixed) verbs. The author then motivates his categorization (Bennett, 1914, 123):

> It certainly is not unworthy of note that a large number of simple verbs which take a prepositional phrase may, when compounded with certain prepositions, take the dative. It is perfectly true that some of these compound verbs approach in signification other uncompounded verbs which are construed with the dative; but that seems to me to be by no means true of the bulk of the verbs in my list. [...] No one ever claimed that *all* compounds, or *most* compounds, but merely *many* compounds, of the prepositions enumerated, were construed with the dative. Such compounds as do take the dative, take it because their meaning is naturally adapted to construction with an indirect object. Yet I hold that this adaptation is a result of the composition.

An example of a verb prefixed with *ad-* and occurring with the dative is given below, with the author's comments on the statistical relevance of this construction (Bennett, 1914, 124).

> accedo (only in figurative sense): Amph. 709, num tibi aut stultitia accessit? Epid. 474; Merc. 24; Hec. 506. The accusative occurs: Epid. 149, ego istuc accedam periclum; Most. 446; 689; Enn. Ann. 537 (V), accedit muros Romana iuventus; Lucil. 112 (Mx). As these examples show, with the accu-

> sative, *accedo* is used in either the literal or figurative sense. More frequent than either the dative or the accusative is the construction with prepositions (*ad*, and occasionally *in*), in both the literal and figurative senses, e.g. Men. 82, si ad malum accedit malum; Rud. 787, ad te accedent.

Bennett gives a large list of such verbs, with a few quotations from each, and concludes it with the following remark (Bennett, 1914, 131–132).

> Of the foregoing prepositional compounds governing the dative, those with *ante*, *inter*, *ob*, *prae*, *sub*, and *super* are used with the dative almost exclusively. They rarely take the accusative or prepositional phrases as alternative constructions. Of the other compounds, those with *com-* show greater hospitality toward the admission of alternative constructions, especially prepositional compounds; while those with *ad* and *in* exhibit the greatest tendency in this direction.
>
> A general tendency is exhibited in all the compounds to employ the dative rather in figurative relations than in literal ones, though examples of the latter are not especially rare. Literal relations are expressed more usually by the accusative or prepositional phrases; yet we frequently find figurative relations also expressed by these same means.

It is clear that this remark is meant to summarize the material previously presented, and aims at giving some kind of guidance on the frequency of each construction. However, it is impossible to derive falsifiable hypotheses from such statements, because they do not contain a properly quantitative account of the phenomenon, but rather express its complexity by stressing how different constructions are found, none of which is very infrequent.

In the study presented in this chapter, I show that a more advanced approach is needed in order to give an accurate, quantitative account of the phenomenon at hand.

6.4.2 *The Data-Driven Approach*

In contrast with previous work, here I take a data-driven approach to investigate the behaviour of Latin PVs. As a basis for my investigations, I use the valency lexicon described in chapter 3, enriched with the SP information acquired by the model described in chapter 4. One advantage that follows from this methodological decision concerns the research design.

All the previous studies on Latin preverbs make claims about the preverbs' linguistic properties supported by sets of examples. As I showed in section 6.4.1, even authors like Bennett, who manually collected large samples of textual materials, presented them as limited lists of quotations. In order to give a summary for the statistical trend found in the data, such studies have to resort to human judgements about what is frequent and what is not. As showed in the quotation on page 144, probably for reasons of space, whenever a construction was found more than ten times, Bennett claimed it as simply "frequent". This, however, would not be satisfactory by the standards of today's quantitative research, given the ambiguity of the word 'frequent' and the extent to which it depends on its terms of comparison and its context.

Thanks to the statistical and computational tools available today, in this study I aim at an exhaustive analysis of the entire corpus material at my disposal. The approach I choose is quantitative, because I employ statistical techniques to make sense of the corpus data. This is the original contribution of this work, as I said, since no quantitative study exists on Latin preverbs whose methodology goes beyond manual inspection and simple comparisons of frequency counts.

The relatively large annotated corpora I use (and the valency lexicon extracted from them) were created before this study on preverbs was designed, which reduces potential biases. Further, using an existing annotation schema, like the one adopted for the treebanks I refer to, leads to replicable and more transparent results, which adds to the systematicity of the study.

I do not refer to the corpora in order to provide a set of examples displaying the evidence for theoretical statements, as in qualitative approaches; instead, I systematically analyse the corpus data through specific statistical techniques. My procedure starts from collecting the data with relevant linguistic information (which I will call 'variables') in the form of corpus instances of PVs ('observations'). Part of this information is originally present in the annotated corpora (morphological and syntactic features), and the rest has been added manually (verb sense, verb class, and animacy annotation). On the one hand I follow the deductive reasoning typical of confirmatory data analysis and inferential statistics, on the other hand I employ an exploratory approach.

Confirmatory data analysis. The deductive reasoning behind confirmatory data analysis (also known as hypothesis testing) starts from a theory in the form of a hypothesis (model): for instance the freer word order in archaic Latin as opposed to a more fixed order in Classical Latin. The next step involves developing an appropriate methodology that produces quantitative data. Typically, the data in hypothesis testing are so that there is one variable under investigation (e.g. some index of word order) and the procedure functions as a controlled experiment, where all the other factors are kept constant in order to detect a possible change in that single variable. Then, the aim of the research is to prove or disprove the hypothesis by drawing inferences from the sample (corpus data) to the population (a definition of the sublanguage we want to model) in an inferential perspective. Adopting this approach requires a clearly stated hypothesis to test. In my case some general hypotheses can be formulated (section 6.3.2) and tested. However, the complexity of the phenomenon is so great that there are several variables contributing to it and it is not always possible to formulate theoretical hypotheses in advance. For this reason, I will also employ an exploratory approach.

Exploratory data analysis. Tukey (1977) coined the term 'exploratory data analysis', which indicates an approach to data analysis aiming at uncovering the underlying structure of the data. Unlike confirmatory data analysis, this view requires the researcher to explore the data, open to gain new insight into it. The model then "emerges" from the data rather than being confirmed or not by them. This view is very suitable when a high degree of variability is present in the data and the researcher does not have pre-defined theoretical hypotheses in mind.

After a first deductive investigation, I will adopt an exploratory approach in order to fully account for the variability in my corpora. This way, I will let the analysis produce the best model to fit the evidence at hand, thus allowing relevant interactions between the variables to emerge from the data. For most statistical analyses, I will make use of the interactive programming environment R (R Development Core Team, 2008) and the *ca* package in R for Correspondence Analysis.

6.4.3 *Preliminary Steps*

In accordance with the collaborative research paradigm I introduced in section 1.4, for my research I have decided to use the corpora that are as extensive as possible, while at the same time requiring as little manual pre-processing as possible. For this, the valency lexicon described in chapter 3 proves to be the optimal choice: it is the only corpus-driven lexicon for Latin containing information on verbal arguments and their morphological, syntactic, and lexical realizations. Being corpus-based, it contains the frequency information necessary for my analysis.

In order to broaden the chronological and genre range of the authors considered, I have also planned to manually analyse two plays by Plautus. Therefore, the basis for my empirical research consists of three datasets:

- Plautus: *Amphitruo* and *Mostellaria* (edition used in the Perseus Digital Library)

- Latin Dependency Treebank (LDT): Caesar (selections from book II of *De bello gallico*), Cicero (*In Catilinam*, 1.1–2.11), Sallust (*Catilina*), Ovid (*Metamorphoses*, book I), Propertius (*Elegies*, book I), Vergil (*Aeneid*, selections from book VI), Petronius (*Satyricon* 26–78), Jerome (*Apocalypse* from *Vulgate*)
- *Index Thomisticus* Treebank (IT-TB): selections from *Scriptum super Sententiis Magistri Petri Lombardi* and *Summa contra Gentiles* by Thomas Aquinas

Starting from the above corpora, I will focus on the following list of preverbs which have a spatial meaning:

- *ab-* 'away from'
- *ad-* 'to, toward; at, by, on'
- *ante-* 'before, in front of, forwards'
- *circum-* 'around'
- *de-* 'from, down from, off'
- *ex-* 'out of'
- *in-* 'in within, on, into, to'
- *inter-* 'between, among, through'
- *intro-* 'within, inside of'
- *ob-* 'towards, against; before'
- *per-* 'through'
- *prae-* 'before', 'in front of'
- *pro-* 'before', 'in front of'
- *sub-* 'under'
- *trans-* 'across, through, over'

Most Latin preverbs are polysemic. About this issue, García-Hernández (2005, 230–235) notices the semantic evolution of spatial preverbs from a concrete to a more abstract meaning. For example the allative preverbs *ad-* and *in-* originally indicated a direction in space and then gained an abstract meaning: cf. the two verbs *adeo* 'go to, approach' and *in-eo* 'go into, enter', which also acquired the ingressive metaphorical senses of 'undertake something' and 'start something', respectively. Moreover, ablative preverbs that indicate the direction from a place (like *ab-*, *ex-* and *de-*) had an "aspectual evolution towards resultative": cf. *sumo* 'take' vs. *ab-sumo* 'take away, consume' and *bibo* 'drink' vs. *e-bibo* 'drink up'. Finally, the preverbs *per-* (longitudinal direction) and *trans-* (transversal direction) had "an evolution toward progressive aspect": cf. the verbs *per-ago* and *trans-igo* which mean 'accomplish' vs. *ago* 'put, lead'.

In the analysis I will only focus on the cases where these preverbs have a spatial meaning. Consequently, I will leave out those preverbs that have an aspectual or intensive meaning rather than a spatial one, such as *per-* in *per-venio* 'arrive at', which is telic unlike *venio*, and does not compositionally mean 'go through'.

In what follows I will go through the steps to take in order to prepare the data for the analysis.

1. The starting point of the analysis is the set of all verb lemmas in the valency lexicon: this is made possible by the information on part-of-speech and lemma contained in the treebanks.
2. Select those PVs occurring in the corpora and prefixed with the previously listed preverbs.
3. From the two plays by Plautus, manually extract all occurrences of PVs whose preverbs belong to the previous list of spatial preverbs.
4. Further select those PVs occurring in the corpora that meet some additional requirements.
   (a) First, the PVs semantically belong into one of the following three classes:
   - verbs of motion: e.g. *adeo* 'go to', 'reach'
   - verbs of rest: e.g. *adsum* 'be present'
   - verbs of transport: e.g. *adduco* 'lead to'

   The last class also includes verbs that imply a movement, but are not motion verbs, for example *circumdo* 'put around'.

   (b) Second, the relation between the semantics of the PV, the semantics of the preverb, and the semantics of the simple verb is such that the meaning of the PV is compositional: e.g. *in-sum* 'be in'. Analyse the semantics of the PVs by inspecting the verbal occurrences in context and the verb senses listed in the entries from the Perseus Latin dictionary Online (Lewis and Short, 1879). Then categorize the verbs on the basis of the following criteria:
   - the PV has a concrete locative sense (*abducere aliquem in agros* 'lead somebody into the fields', *abire in terras* 'go towards the countries');
   - the PV has a figurative (metaphorically locative) sense (*abire in villos* 'be transformed in a tuft of hair', *absolvere de coniuratio* 'loosen from the conspiracy');
   - the PV has an abstract non-locative sense (*promittere alicui aliquid* 'promise something to somebody').

   Distinguish the second category from the first one by the label 'figurative', and exclude the last one.

(c) Third, set a frequency threshold of 2 for the type frequencies of PVs, in order to exclude idiosyncratic usages that may not reflect a reliable evidence for the analysis, or simple annotation errors.

5. The goal of this study concerns the morpho-syntactic realizations of the arguments of PVs. More specifically, since the selected preverbs have a spatial meaning, I am interested in the realization of spatial arguments of PVs in terms of *relatum* and *locatum* of the preverb, and other locative complements, such as Goal or Source expressions. As Brachet (2000, 10–11) points out, the phenomenon of preverbation turns adjuncts into arguments. Therefore, the next step consists in collecting both the instances of case-assigning preverbs and PPs occurring with PVs and expressing the preverbs' *locata*; such complements are annotated as arguments in the treebanks and hence appear in the valency lexicon; consequently, they are considered as part of the PVs' argument structure. For each relevant argument position (*relatum*, *locatum*, Goal, Source), calculate the LWN node with the highest SP probability assigned by my model (or the first one alphabetically in case there are more than one).
6. Since a manual inspection of the single selected occurrences is necessary in order to annotate the semantic features of the verb and the arguments, this also allows me to correct some errors present in the lemmatization, as well as in the morphological and syntactic annotation.

Table 6.1 displays the composition of the corpora in terms of the number of verb tokens per author and the number of PVs observed in each author: the last figures correspond to the actual size of my dataset. The number of verbal tokens for Plautus is not displayed, since I extracted the PVs by manual inspection. For the next studies, I will refer to several subsets taken from these data.

6.5 Detecting a Diachronic Trend

In this section I report on a first corpus-based analysis aiming to test the hypotheses formulated in section 6.3.2. In this first exploration I will focus on the realization of preverbs' *relata*, that is on the realization of the portion of motion events represented by the preverbs. For example, when a preverb expressed the Source of a motion event (like *ab-eo* 'go from'), I collect the Source complements occurring with that verb, as in sentences (22), (23), and (24).

TABLE 6.1 *Number of word tokens, verb tokens and PV tokens by author in the data. The number of verb tokens for Plautus is not recorded because the original data are not tagged by part of speech.*

Corpus	Author	Verb tokens	PV tokens
Plautus	Plautus	–	114
LDT	Cicero	1283	30
↓	Caesar	295	13
	Sallust	2295	52
	Vergil	511	27
	Propertius	1039	21
	Ovid	1092	23
	Petronius	2901	67
	Jerome	1770	48
IT	Thomas Aquinas	9072	150
	TOTAL		545

(22) AB-eo domo
from-go:IND.PRS.1SG home:ABL.F.SG
'I leave home'

(23) AB-eo A te
from-go:IND.PRS.1SG from:PREP you:ABL.SG
'I go away from you'

(24) AB-eo E conspectu
from-go:IND.PRS.1SG from:PREP sight:ABL.M.SG
'I go away from the sight'

I am looking for a diachronic trend (if it exists) in the opposition between some of the constructions illustrated on page 137. In Meini and McGillivray (2010) and McGillivray (2012) I discuss a similar analysis on a smaller dataset. In the present study I focus on the alternation between construction 1 (CasePrev) on the one hand, and constructions 3 (PrepPrev) and 4 (PrepNoPrev) on the other, i.e. between the presence of a PP vs. the presence of an NP governed by the preverb in the realization of the *relatum* of the preverb. Consequently, I will limit the dataset to the instances where the *relatum* of the preverb falls into one of the following cases:

– Construction 1 (CasePrev): an NP whose case coincides with that governed by the preverb, as in (25).

(25) Exercitum Ligerim TRA-ducit
army:ACC.M.SG Loire:ACC.M.SG across-lead:IND.PRS.3SG
'He leads his army across the Loire'. (Caes., *B. G.* 7, 11, 9)

– Construction 3 (PrepPrev): a PP whose preposition corresponds to the preverb, as in (26).

(26) INTER me atque te murus
Between:PREP I:ACC.SG and you:ACC.SG wall:NOM.M.SG
INTER-sit
between-be:IND.PRS.3SG
'There is a wall between me and you' (Cic., *Cat.* I, 5)

– Construction 4 (PrepNoPrev): a PP whose preposition does not correspond to the preverb, as in (27).

(27) Et AD-ferent gloriam et honorem
And to-bring:IND.FUT.3PL glory:ACC.F.SG and honour:ACC.M.SG
gentium IN illam
nation:GEN.F.PL into that:ACC.F.SG
'And they shall bring the glory and honour of the nations into it' (Jer., *Vulg., Ap.* 21)

In order to represent the preposition vs. bare case alternation, I set a binary variable called 'construction'; this allows me to identify construction 1 (CasePrev) in a univocal way by the value 'CasePrev' of this variable, while constructions 3 (PrepPrev) and 4 (PrepNoPrev) correspond to the value 'Preposition'. With these selection criteria I can extract 237 verbal tokens, which constitute the first dataset.

First, I want to look for a general trend for what concerns the distribution of the binary variable 'construction'. The most fine-grained diachronic categorization in my data is by author; hence, I choose 'author' as the second variable under study. Table 6.2 contains the distribution of 'construction' in the different authors attested in the dataset; the following examples display the two constructions 'CasePrev' and 'Preposition' in different authors.

- CasePrev
  - Plautus

(28) Is AD-it me
He:NOM.M.SG to-go:IND.PRS.3SG I:ACC.SG
'He came to me' (Plaut., *Most.*, 1155)

- Cicero

(29) vitam istam multis suppliciis
life:ACC.F.SG that:ACC.F.SG many:ABL.N.PL punishment:ABL.N.PL
iustis debitis-que E-reptam
fair:ABL.N.PL due:ABL.N.PL-and deprive:PTCP.PF.ACC.F.SG
'Your life, deprived of many fair and due punishments' (Cic., *Cat.*, I, 8)

- Caesar

(30) Hanc si nostri TRANS-irent
that:ACC.F.SG if:CONJ our:NOM.M.PL across-go:SBJV.IMP.3PL
'If our men should cross this (swamp)' (Caes., *B. G.*, II, 9)

- Sallust

(31) Laetabatur intelligens [...] civitatem
delight:IND.IMPF.3SG.PASS realize:PTCP.PRS.NOM.SG [...] city:ACC.F.SG
periculis E-reptam esse
danger:ABL.N.PL from-pull:PTCP.PF.ACC.F.SG be:INF.PRS
'He was delighted to see that the city had been liberated from danger' (Sall., *De Catilinae coniuratione*, 46)

- Vergil

(32) Vagina E-ripe ferrum
scabbard:ABL.F.SG from-draw:IMP.PRS.2SG sword:ACC.N.SG
'Draw your sword from its scabbard' (Verg., *Aen.*, 260)

– Propertius

(33) ferunt olim Pagasae navalibus Argon
say:IND.PRS.3PL once:ADV Pagasa:GEN.F.SG port:ABL.N.PL Argo:ACC.F.SG
E-gressam
from-go:PTCP.PF.ACC.F.SG
'They say that once the Argo set off from Pagasa's port' (Prop., I, 20, 17–18)

– Ovid

(34) Maenala TRANS-ieram latebris horrenda
Maenala:ACC.N.PL across-go:IND.PPF.1SG den:ABL.F.PL frightful:ACC.N.PL
ferarum (Ov., *Met.*, I, 216)
beast:GEN.F.PL
'I had gone across Menala, frightful for the beasts' dens'

– Petronius

(35) Sine dubio paulisper trepidavimus,
Without:PREP doubt:ABL.N.SG for a little while:ADV fear:IND.PF.1PL
ne contra praeceptum aliquis
that:CONJ against:PREP rule:ACC.N.SG somebody:NOM.M.SG
nostrum limen TRANS-iret
we:GEN.PL threshold:ACC.N.SG across-go:SBJV.IMPF.3SG
'Without a doubt for a little while we were afraid that one of us might cross the threshold against the rules' (Petron., *Sat.*, 30)

– Preposition
  – Plautus

(36) E-gredere [...] EX aedibus
from-go:IMP.PRS.2SG.DEP [...] from:PREP house:ABL.F.PL
'Get out of the house' (Plaut., *Most.*, 3)

– Cicero

(37) ut abs te non E-missus
so that:CONJ by:PREP you:ABL.SG not:NEG from-send:PTCP.PF.NOM.M.SG
ex urbe, sed IM-missus
from:PREP city:ABL.F.SG but:CONJ to-send:PTCP.PF.NOM.M.SG
IN urbem esse videatur?
against:PREP city:ACC.F.SG be:INF.PRS see:SBJV.PRS.3SG
'So that it seems that he was not expelled by you from the city, but he was sent against the city?' (Cic., *Cat.*, I, 11)

– Caesar

(38) milites EX oppido EX-ire
soldier:ACC.M.PL from:PREP fortified city:ABL.N.SG from-go:INF.PRS
iussit
order:IND.PF.3SG
'He orders the soldiers to go out of the city' (Caes., *B. G.*, II, 32)

– Sallust

(39) qui Catilinae nuntiaret [...]
who:NOM.M.SG Catilina:DAT.M.SG announce:SBJV.IMPF.3SG [...]
properaret AD urbem AC-cedere
hasten:SBJV.IMPF.3SG to:PREP city:ACC.F.SG go:INF.PRS
'So that he could tell Catilina that he should hasten to gain access to the city' (Sall., *De Catilinae coniuratione*, 48)

– Propertius

(40) clausis EX-pulit E foribus?
shut:ABL.F.PL from-drive:IND.PF.3SG from:PREP door:ABL.F.PL
'Has it driven (you) out of shut doors?' (Prop., I, 3)

– Ovid

(41) per quae Peneus AB imo
through:PREP this:ACC.N.PL Peneus:NOM.M.SG from:PREP low:ABL.M.SG
E-ffusus Pindo spumosis
from-gush:PTCP.PF.NOM.M.SG Pindus:ABL.M.SG foaming:ABL.F.PL
volvitur undis
flow:IND.PRS.3SG.PASS wave:ABL.F.PL
'The foaming waters of Peneus flow through this (grove), gushing out from the bottom of Pindus' range' (Ov., *Met.*, 546–547)

– Petronius

(42) AD caput eius symphoniacus cum
to:PREP head:ACC.N.SG he:GEN.M.SG musician:NOM.M.SG with:PREP
minimis tibiis AC-cessit
tiny:ABL.F.PL flute:ABL.F.PL to-go:IND.PF.3SG
'A musician with a tiny flute approaches his head' (Petron., *Sat.*, 28)

– Jerome

(43) DE fumo EX-ierunt lucustae
from:PREP smoke:ABL.M.SG from-go:IND.PF.3PL locust:NOM.F.PL
in terram
on:PREP earth:ACC.F.SG
'From the smoke locusts came on the earth' (Jer., *Vulg.*, *Ap.*, 9)

– Thomas

(44) Unde etiam AC-cedit AD similitudinem
So:ADV also:CONJ to-go:IND.PRS.3SG to:PREP similarity:ACC.F.SG
secundum materiam
according to:PREP matter:ACC.F.SG
'So it also comes close to similarity according to the matter' (Th., *Sent. P. L.*, I, Q. 2, Art. 1)

Figure 6.1 plots the relative frequencies, from which we can see a general trend for the presence of prepositions with respect to their absence. The dotted line ('CasePrev') remains under the solid line ('Preposition') in all authors except for the poets (Vergil, Propertius, Ovid). Moreover, the proportion for

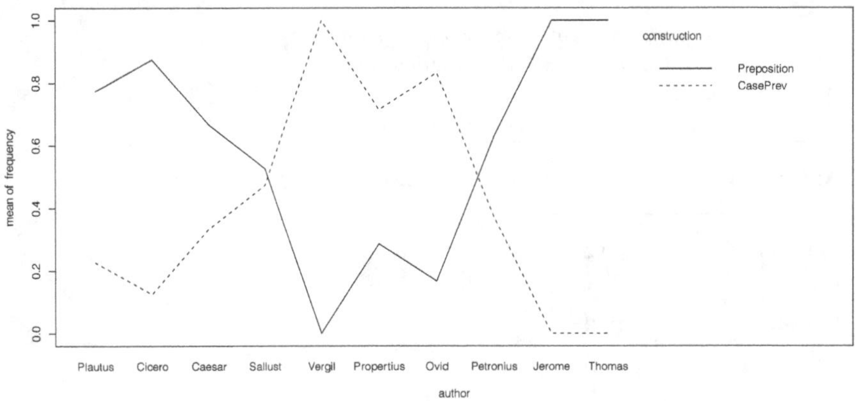

FIG. 6.1 *The variables 'author' and 'construction' plotted against each other in the first dataset. The proportions of the two values of 'construction' in each author are displayed.*

Plautus, Cicero, Caesar are similar to the proportions for Jerome and Thomas.

However, a simple comparison of relative frequencies may lead to misinterpretations, especially when dealing with low figures. For this reason, I want to investigate the data from a statistical point of view, in order to detect a significant difference appearing in the distribution of these frequencies.

The questions are then:

- Is there a significant pattern in how the two constructions are distributed among the authors?
- If so, do chronological or genre-related groups emerge?

In statistical terms, this corresponds to investigating the interaction between the two variables 'author' and 'construction'. I will do that by testing Hypothesis 6.3.2.1.1 on page 139 and Hypothesis 6.3.2.3.1 on page 142 against this Null Hypothesis:

Null Hypothesis 6.5.0.0.2. *In the first dataset the variables 'author' and 'construction' are independent of each other.*

Pearson's chi-square tests. I use Pearson's chi-square test for independence illustrated in section 7.1, which allows me to decide whether or not I am able to reject this null hypothesis, given the data at hand. A chi-square test works by comparing the actual frequencies observed in the data with the expected frequencies we would get from a random distribution. This test gives the level

TABLE 6.2 *Frequency counts of 'CasePrev' and 'Preposition' ('PrepPrev' and 'PrepNonPrev') by author in the first dataset*

Author	CasePrev	Preposition
Plautus	12	41
Cicero	1	7
Caesar	2	4
Sallust	9	10
Vergil	7	0
Propertius	5	2
Ovid	5	1
Petronius	10	17
Jerome	0	29
Thomas	0	74

of significance as output, which states whether the result is significant or not, i.e. whether the two variables are significantly independent or not. In addition, it is important to calculate the effect size, which accounts for the size of the detected dependence. The results from the independence test on the data from Table 6.2 reveal that the variable 'author' and the variable 'construction' are not independent at the 0.01 level of significance ($p < 0.01, \chi^2_{(df=9)} = 89.68$), so I can reject the null hypothesis 6.5.0.0.2. The strength of this association is large ($V = 0.62$) according to the classification in Cohen (1988, 224).

I now know that *somewhere* in my data there is a significant difference in the distribution of the two constructions 'CasePrev' and 'Preposition'. If I want to see *where* this difference is concentrated, I can inspect an association plot. Figure 6.2 is a Cohen-Friendly association plot and shows the contribution made by each author-construction pair (i.e. each cell of Table 6.2) to the total chi-square statistic. In this plot the area of the each rectangle is proportional to the difference between observed and expected frequencies, where the dotted lines refer to expected frequencies. The height of the rectangles is related to the significance and the width to the amount of data that support the result.

From Figure 6.2 we notice that in the data from Thomas and Jerome the construction 'CasePrev' occurs significantly less frequently than expected, whereas construction 'Preposition' occurs more frequently than expected; on the other hand, Sallust, Petronius and the poets (Ovid, Propertius and Vergil) display the opposite behaviour. Note that a simple inspection of the barplot in Fig-

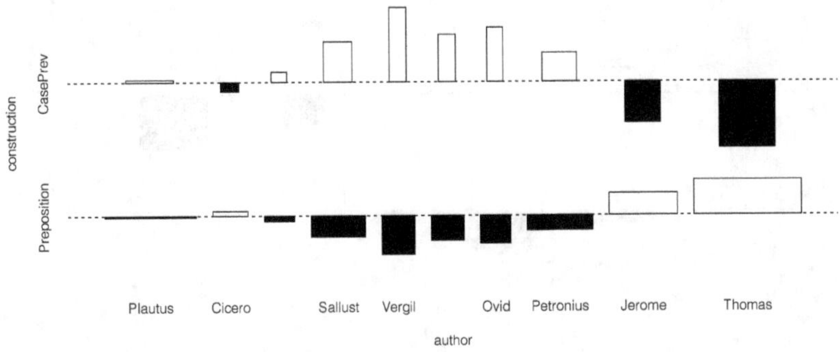

FIG. 6.2 *Association plot for the chi-square statistics on the two values for the variable 'construction' by author in the first dataset*

ure 6.1 for Sallust and Petronius would have erroneously implied the contrary. In the case of Plautus' plays, I seem to have a rather large data evidence, but the deviation of the frequencies of the two constructions from the expected frequencies is small. This may imply that the variability in these data can be captured by a different and more complex combination of variables, as shown by the study reported in section 6.5.1. Due to the low frequencies for Caesar and Cicero, these authors contribute very little to the overall association between the two variables, which makes it difficult to generalize from the data from these authors.

As a matter of fact, the chi-square test gives unreliable results when applied to a table whose expected frequencies are lower than 5. Table 6.2 produces 8 out of 20 expected cell frequencies below this recommended threshold, as shown in Table 7.3 on page 181. For this reason, I will try merge together the frequencies for the poets (Ovid, Propertius and Vergil) on the one hand, and the frequencies for the late republic authors (Caesar, Cicero and Sallust) on the other hand. This way, only one cell (corresponding to the construction 'CasePrev' for the poets) of the 20 expected frequencies is lower than 5. A chi-square test performed on these data still results in a significantly large association between 'author' and 'construction' ($p < 0.01, \chi_{(5)} = 83.90, V = 0.60$), although this procedure causes a loss of information during the interpretation of the results, because it obviously does not allow to make distinctions between the single authors merged.

Figure 6.3 represents the association plot for the merged data. These preliminary results confirm the claims given in section 6.3.2 on the preference of poets and the earliest author in my corpus (Plautus) for construction CasePrev (Hypothesis 6.3.2.1.1 on page 139).

If we look for a progression in time, we realize that there is no one-way pattern emerging from the data. Figure 6.3 shows a decrease in the distribution

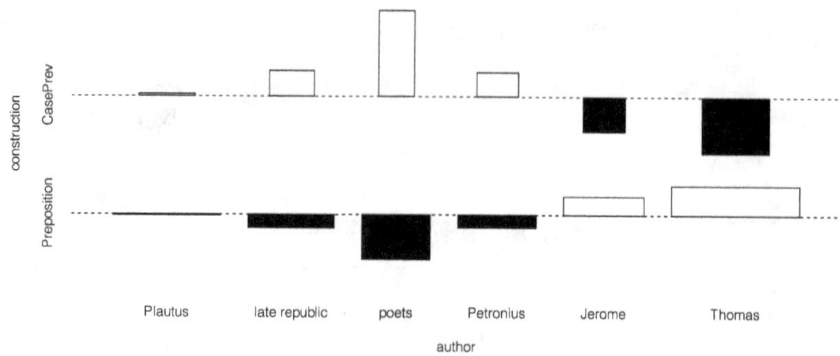

FIG. 6.3 *Association plot for the chi-square statistics on the two values for the variable 'construction' by author in the first dataset. I merged the data from Caesar, Cicero and Sallust under the label 'late republic', and the data from Ovid, Propertius and Vergil under the label 'poets'.*

of 'CasePrev' (and a symmetrical increase for 'Preposition') from the poets to Petronius and, later, Jerome and Thomas. However, the late republic authors do not fit into this trend. One of the reasons for this may be a "structural" feature of the data, namely the fact that the chronological variable in this case is not distinguishable from the genre variable, as attested by Table 1.1 on page 12. This places the late republic authors among the prose writers and the Augustan writers among the poets; I would need data from late republic poets and Augustan prose writers to see whether the detected trend is a chronological one, or it is instead related to genre. In a similar vein, the data from the late imperial age (Jerome) and middle ages (Thomas) overlap with the data from two kinds of religious texts.

Since there is no way to solve this variable overlap, I will try to achieve the most informative results from the data at hand. If I group the authors in two main eras—'early' (Plautus, Cicero, Caesar, Sallust, Vergil, Propertius, Ovid and Petronius) and 'late' (Jerome and Thomas)—I obtain a statistically significant, medium-to-large difference in the distribution of the two constructions 'CasePrev' and 'Preposition' ($p < 0.01, \chi^2_{(1)} = 48.15, V = 0.46$). This results in a clear trend, which contrasts the early age and CasePrev on the one hand, and the Late age and Preposition on the other, thus corroborating Hypothesis 6.3.2.3.1.

6.5.1 *A Multivariate Investigation*

The first investigation I reported on in section 6.5 could only account for the interaction between a diachronic variable ('author') and the "target" variable, i.e. the syntactic realization of the preverb's *relatum*. In this context, a chi-square test was able to detect some differences in the use of one construction

(CasePrev) over another (Preposition) by certain authors. In some respects, this result shows a partially diachronic trend in the data. However, my aim is not only to verify whether the two alternative constructions are used in a significantly different way among the authors, but also to detect the relevant variables that influence this difference, such as preverb, verb semantics, SP of the arguments, etc.

I start with carrying out a chi-square test for the association between the target variable 'construction' and the variable 'preverb'. The result is a significant medium-to-large association ($p < 0.01, \chi_{(8)} = 49.33, V = 0.46$), slightly lower than the effect size found for 'construction' vs. 'author' ($V = 0.62$), but still considerable. This shows that both the variables 'author' and 'preverb' are relevant for this study, since they both affect the realization of the preverb's *relatum* as encoded by the variable 'construction'. Consequently, if I want to explore the correlation between the target variable and more than one variable (for example the type of preverb, as well as the author), I need more advanced techniques. Ideally, I would like to use techniques that allow me to pinpoint or exclude interactions and effects ascribable to each variable.

The solution is *regression modeling*, illustrated in section 7.2. Linear regression models aim at quantifying the relationship between a specific variable (called *response*) and a set of independent variables (called *predictors*). Here I make use of a particular type of linear regression models: the *generalized mixed-effect models*, illustrated in section 7.2.4. My dataset has an uneven composition as far as chronological ages and genres are concerned (see the discussion in section 1.5); this reflects the selection of authors and cannot be eliminated if not at cost of considerably decreasing its size. However, the peculiarity of mixed-effect models consists in the *random effects* they contain. The random effects make it possible to (at least partially) compensate for biases in the data that may make the sample not representative of the population. So, I consider 'author' as one of the random effects: this way, I assume that the dataset consists of a collection of random samples from an unknown, potentially infinite population of authors, instead of a single sample from one population of authors.

I want to quantify the relationship between 'construction' (the response) and three variables (predictors): the type of preverb the PV is prefixed with (variable 'preverb'), a diachronic variable for the literary age ('era', taking the values 'early_republican', 'late_republican', 'Augustan', 'imperial', 'late_imperial' and 'medieval'), and a classification of the preverbs based on the case required by the corresponding preposition (variable 'case', values 'accusative' and 'ablative'). The random effects are 'author' and 'class', i.e. the verb class of the PV, which is either 'motion' (e.g. *abeo* 'leave'), 'rest' (e.g. *adeo* 'be present'), or 'transport' (e.g. *abduco* 'lead from'). The model is hence:

construction ~ preverb + era + case + (class | author)

where I indicated the response, followed by the predictors and the random effects.

Below you can find some examples showing the values for the predictors and the random effects in different authors.

- construction='Preposition', preverb='ad-', case='accusative', class='transport', author='Caesar'

(45)

vererentur	ne	[...]	AD	eos
fear:SBJV.IMPF.3PL.DEP	that:CONJ	[...]	to:PREP	he:ACC.M.PL

exercitus	noster	AD-duceretur
army:NOM.M.SG	our:NOM.M.SG	to-lead:SBJV.IMP.3SG.PASS

'They feared that our army would be pushed against them' (Caes., *B. G.*, II, 1)

- construction='Preposition', preverb='ex-', case='ablative', class='motion', author='Jerome'

(46)

DE	ore	eius	gladius
from:PREP	mouth:ABL.F.SG	he:GEN.M.SG	sword:NOM.M.SG

utraque	parte	acutus	EX-iebat
both:ABL.F.SG	side:ABL.F.SG	sharp:NOM.M.SG	from-go:IND.IMPF.3SG

'out of his mouth came a sharp twoedged sword' (Jer., *Vulg.*, *Ap.*, I)

- construction='Preposition', preverb='ad-', case='accusative', class='rest', author='Plautus'

(47)

Sed	ubi	summus	imperator
but:CONJ	when:CONJ	supreme:NOM.M.SG	commander:NOM.M.SG

non	AD-est	AD	exercitum
not:PREP	by-be:IND.PRS.3SG	by:PREP	army:ACC.M.SG

'But when the Supreme commander is not with his army' (Plaut., *Amph.*, 504)

- construction='Preposition', preverb='ad-', case='accusative', class='transport', author='Caesar'

(48) principum liberos obsides AD
leader:GEN.M.PL child:ACC.M.PL hostage:ACC.M.PL to:PREP
se AD-duci iussit
oneself:ACC.SG to-lead:INF.PRS.PASS order:IND.PF.3SG
'He ordered that the leaders' children were taken to him' (Caes., *B. G.*, II, 5)

- construction='Preposition', preverb='in-', case='accusative', class='motion', author='Thomas'

(49) per illam actionem non tantum
through:PREP that:ACC.F.SG action:ACC.F.SG not:NEG just:ADV
IN-ducitur materia IN actum
to-take:IND.PRS.3SG.PASS matter:NOM.F.SG to:PREP act:ACC.M.SG
formae accidentalis, sed etiam IN
form:GEN.F.SG accidental:GEN.F.SG but:CONJ etiam:CONJ to:PREP
actum formae substantialis
act:ACC.M.SG form:GEN.F.SG substantial:GEN.F.SG
'Hence, through such action, the matter is not only brought to the act of the accidental form, but also to the act of the substantial form' (Th., *Sent. P. L.*, II, Q. 1, Art. 4)

- construction='Preposition', preverb='ab-', case='accusative', class='motion', author='Thomas'

(50) et A-scendit fumus incensorum
and:CONJ from-go:IND.PRS.3SG smoke:NOM.M.SG incense:GEN.N.PL
DE manu angeli coram
from:PREP hand:ABL.F.SG angel:GEN.M.SG before:PREP
Deo de orationibus sanctorum
God:DAT.M.SG from:PREP prayer:ABL.F.PL saint:GEN.M.P
'And the smoke of the incense of the prayers of the saints ascended up before God from the angel's hand' (Jer., *Vulg.*, *Ap.*, 8)

Among several models involving different combinations of the variables, this model is the best one for predicting the values of 'construction' in my dataset. This means that the value of 'construction' can be best predicted as a linear function of the type of preverb, the literary age, and the case governed by the preposition corresponding to the preverb. Section 7.2.5 reports the details of this model and its diagnostics.

The model estimates the probabilities that the construction is 'preposition' while switching from the reference level (early republican era, preverb *ab*-, ablative case) to the value of each predictor, as shown in Table 7.5 on page 193. On the whole, the preverbs have a small (negative with respect to the reference level) effect on the type of construction: the probability of 'construction' having the value 'preposition' is 11% (if the preverb is *ad*- 'to'), 69% (*de* 'down from'), 0% (*sub* 'under'), and 30% (*ob*- 'towards'). Another linguistic effect is represented by case (the accusative has a noticeable positive effect on the presence of preposition, probability =96%). Finally, the Augustan era has a negative effect and a probability of 20%. This effect for 'era' is present even after factoring out the differences between the single authors through the random effects: this means that the probability of finding a preposition does not only depend on the specific author, but also on the diachronic age.

In conclusion, hypothesis testing and regression modeling have enabled me to discover relevant associations between the main variable of interest (presence vs. absence of preposition in the expression of the *relatum* of preverbs), specific chronological variables ('era' and 'author'), and two morphological ones ('preverb' and 'case'). In particular, the multivariate analysis has highlighted the role played by non-diachronic variables in the choice of the syntactic constructions for the PVs, which contributes to showing the complexity of this phenomenon.

The question now arises as to whether the partial diachronic trend detected in the first chi-square analysis is eventually confirmed or not. I will look for an answer to this by having recourse to a different technique and by extending the dataset.

6.6 Further Explorations

So far, I have focussed on the alternation between construction 1 (CasePrev) and constructions 3 and 4 (Prep), which can be encoded as the opposition between presence and absence of the preposition in the realization of the *relatum* of the preverb. This is because I modelled the alternation with a binary variable, which allowed us to make use of binomial distributions and logistic regression models. These models gave me some information about the data, by showing the effects of specific linguistic variables. However, they impose strict constraints on the input (see section 7.2.2), which are not necessarily met by the dataset.

Now I will make use of a different technique which does not impose strict constraints on the input data, while at the same time allowing me to focus on all four constructions for the morpho-syntactic expression of the *relatum* of a preverb (see section 6.3.1 on page 137):

1. (CasePrev): NP whose case is required by the preposition corresponding to the preverb, as in (51);

(51) HANC ego [...] conor AD-ire
that:ACC.F.SG I:NOM.SG [...] try:IND.PRS.1SG.DEP to-go:INF.PRS
'I set out to approach her' (Prop., I, 3)

2. (CaseNonPrev): NP whose case is different from the one required by the preposition corresponding to the preverb, as in (52) (*ad* 'to' requires the accusative);

(52) TIBI AD-duxi hominem
you:DAT.SG to-bring:IND.PF.1SG man:ACC.M.SG
'I have brought the man to you' (Plaut., *Most.*, 804)

3. (PrepPrev): PP whose preposition corresponds to the preverb, cf. (53) (preposition/preverb *ab* 'from');

(53) vereor ne te [...] AB-strahat
fear:IND.PRS.1SG.DEP that:CONJ you:ACC.SG from-tear:SBJV.PRS.3SG
A nostro pulvere iniquus
from our:ABL.M.SG ash:ABL.M.SG iniquitus:NOM.M.SG
Amor
Cupid:NOM.M.SG
'I fear that iniquitus Cupid will move you away from my ashes' (Prop., I, 19)

4. (PrepNoPrev): PP whose preposition does not correspond to the preverb, cf.(54) (preposition *in* 'to', preverb *ad* 'to').

(54) tres albi sues IN
three:NOM.PL white:NOM.M.PL pig:NOM.M.PL to:PREP
triclinium AD-ducti sunt
triclinium:ACC.N.SG lead:IND.PF.3PL.PASS
'Three white pigs are led into the triclinium' (Petron., *Sat.*, 47)

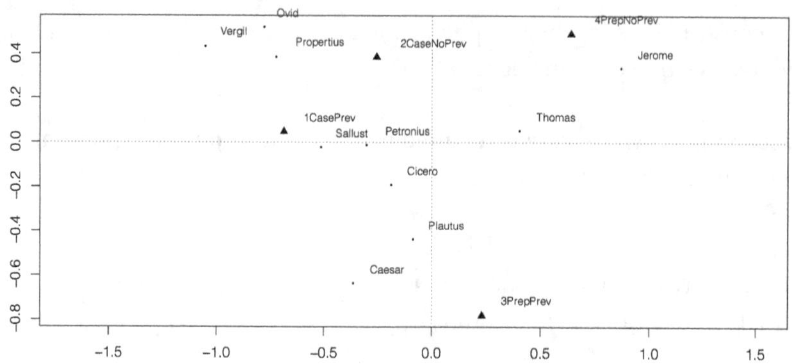

FIG. 6.4 *Plot from CA on the variables 'construction' and 'author'. The first axis accounts for 67.6 % of the explained inertia, the second axis for 21.9 %.*

I want to collect the occurrences of all four constructions in the dataset and look at the interaction between specific variables affecting them. This is the dataset for the second investigation, consisting of 353 observations.

6.6.1 *Correspondence Analysis*

For this investigation, I will opt for an exploratory approach using Simple Correspondence Analysis (CA; Benzécri 1973) and Multiple Correspondence Analysis (MCA), a data-analysis technique widely used in social sciences and described in section 7.3. The main reason for this methodological choice is that, unlike confirmatory data analysis, exploratory techniques do not require *a priori* theoretical hypotheses to be tested. Instead, they start by observing the dynamics taking place between the variables in the data; then, they propose a model for the account of the data evidence, as exemplified by the famous quote by Benzécri: "the model should follow the data. The data should not follow the model" (Benzécri, 1973).

Starting from a multi-dimensional representation of the dataset, CA and MCA produce low-dimensional plots that describe the essential structure of the data. The accuracy of this approximation is measured by the so-called percentage of explained inertia, which is the proportion of the variability present in the data that is captured by my analysis. Hence, I describe the linguistic phenomenon by using several sets of variables and comparing the percentages of inertia explained by the relative analyses: the higher the percentage of inertia, the best choice of variables. I will focus on two-dimensional plots, because they are easier to interpret and reproduce on paper.

I will start from a very simple model, with the two variables 'construction' and 'author'. If I run a CA on the dataset classified by these two variables, I obtain a faithful representation of the original space (for the details of the output see in section 7.3.0.1). Figure 6.4 displays the two-dimensional plot of the CA, accounting for 89.4% of the total inertia.

In a CA plot, the points far from the origin are the most interesting ones, because they are associated with the least expected behaviour, so I will concentrate on those. Moreover, I can detect correlations between variables by looking at the angles between the corresponding vectors: small angles correspond to positive correlations, angles close to 180° correspond to negative correlations, angles close to 90° to no correlation.

By looking at the strongest positive correlations in Figure 6.4, it is possible to associate specific constructions to different authors: construction 4 (PrepNoPrev) and Late era authors (Jerome and Thomas), construction 3 (PrepPrev) and the early author (Plautus), and finally constructions 1 (CasePrev) and 2 (CaseNonPrev) and the Classical authors, with a particular preference for construction 2 (CaseNonPrev) by the poets.

Overall, this corroborates the main diachronic result from the regression analysis described in section 6.5.1, since the poets seem to prefer the constructions with no preposition: 1 (CasePrev) and 2 (CaseNonPrev). The behaviour of the prose writers (especially Petronius, Sallust and Cicero) is close to expected. Additionally, this technique allows me to detect a stronger preference of poets for the first construction (CasePrev) than for the second one (CaseNonPrev), which is, again, in accordance with what I hypothesized in section 6.3.2. In addition, I am able to differentiate the behaviour of the Late era authors (Jerome and Thomas)—who prefer the fourth construction (PrepNoPrev)—from the early author (Plautus), who prefers the third construction (PrepPrev). Again, this is in accordance with what was stated in section 6.3.2. Finally, the analysis for Sallust, Petronius, Cicero and Caesar shows that these authors' behaviour is close to the expected one.

From a methodological point of view, this exploration gives a preliminary picture of the distribution of the four constructions: unlike a one-dimensional representation, the two-dimensional plot allows to display a wider range of possibilities for the position of the points corresponding to the variables of interest. For example, I can see that Thomas, while preferring construction 4 (PrepNoPrev), behaves closer to expected than Jerome; on the other hand, Caesar and Cicero prefer construction 3 (PrepPrev) but show also some preference for construction 1 (CasePrev). Now I will show how this picture can be enriched.

6.6.1.1 More Variables

CA has allowed me to get a more detailed picture of the preferences of single authors for particular constructions. What happens if I take more variables into account? What is the interaction between semantic variables and the morpho-syntactic realization of the arguments of PVs? When dealing with more than two variables, CA is not sufficient and we need to resort to Multiple CA (MCA; see section 7.3.1 for an illustration of this technique). I will now run an MCA on the following variables:

- 'construction', values from 1 to 4: 'CasePrev', 'CaseNonPrev', 'PrepPrev', 'PrepNoPrev';
- 'era', a broad chronological classification of the authors of my dataset: 'early' (Plautus), 'classical' (Caesar, Cicero, Ovid, Petronius, Propertius, Sallust, Vergil) and 'late' (Jerome and Thomas);
- 'case', the case required by the preposition corresponding to the preverb (ablative or accusative);
- 'sp_relatum', the LWN node with the highest probability assigned by my SP model (see chapter 4) to the argument slot corresponding to the *relatum*; this variable projects the lexical-semantic properties of the verbal arguments on the arguments' lexical fillers.
- 'class', the semantic class of the verb: values 'motion', 'rest' and 'transport'.

In the following examples you can find some instances of the values of these variables in different authors.

- construction='PrepPrev', era='archaic', case='ablative', sp_relatum='entity, something', class='motion'

(55) AB-scede AB aedibus
from-go:IMP.PRS.2SG from:PREP house:ABL.F.PL
'Move away from this house' (Plaut., *Most.*, 460)

- construction='PrepPrev', era='medieval', case='accusative', sp_relatum= 'abstraction', class='transport'

(56) Unum quo vult formam
One:ACC.M.SG which:ABL.M.SG want:IND.PRS.3SG form:ACC.F.SG
domus IN-ducere IN materiam
house:GEN.F.PL in-lead:INF.PRS in:PREP matter:ACC.F.SG
'One with which he wants to introduce the form of the house in the matter' (Th., *Sent. P. L.*, I, Q. I, Art. 3)

- construction='CaseNonPrev', era='Augustan', case='dative', sp_relatum='entity,something', class='transport'

(57) fluminibus vestris totas IN-mittite
river:DAT.M.PL your:DAT.M.PL all:ACC.F.PL to-send:IMP.PRS.2PL
habenas!
restraint:ACC.F.PL
'Give fill rein to all your rivers!' (Ov., *Met.*, 280)

- construction='CaseNonPrev', era='late_republican', case='dative', sp_relatum ='actio,actus,res', class='rest'

(58) cui PRAE-erat Q.
who:DAT.M.SG before-be:IND.IMPF.3SG Quintus:NOM.M.SG
Titurius legatus
Titurius:NOM.M.SG messenger:NOM.M.SG
'Whose leader was the messenger Quintus Titurius' (Caes., *B. G.*, II, 9)

- construction='prepNonPrev', era='late_imperial', case='accusative', sp_relatum='affectus, civitas, classis, detentatio, detentio, entity, instrumentality, instrumentation, location,natural_object, object, part, physical_object, possessio, res, something', class='rest'

(59) qui IN-habitant SUPER terram
who:NOM.M.PL in-live:IND.PRS.3PL on:PREP earth:ACC.F.SG
'Those who live on the earth' (Jer., *Vulg.*, *Ap.*, XI, 10)

I present the output of the analysis in section 7.3.1 and the two-dimensional plot of the MCA on this dataset in Figure 6.5. The percentage of inertia explained by the first two axes of an MCA on the dataset described by all these variables is 53.0%. This figure is lower than that of the previous CA analysis (81.4%), which should not surprise since the complexity of the model is higher. However, the main pattern is the same; this means that the presence of these new variables does not change the basic structure of the data. In fact, the following associations are as before: between constructions 4 (PrepNoPrev) and 3 (PrepPrev) and the Late era authors (Jerome and Thomas) and between construction 1 (CasePrev) and the Classical authors. The early era author (Plautus) is now closer to the origin.

At the same time, this analysis allows me to obtain a geometrical picture of the interaction between new variables. For what concerns verb classes, motion verbs seem to be more strongly associated with the Classical authors, construction 1 (casePrev) and verbs which prefer the class 'artefact' for the position filled by the *relatum*. On the other hand, the verbs of transport are associated with the Late era, construction 3 (PrepPrev), and the class 'abstraction'.

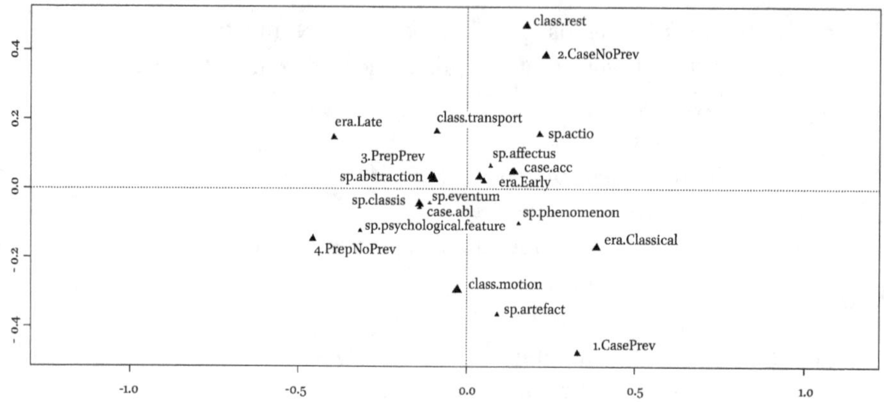

FIG. 6.5 *Plot of the MCA for the interaction between 'construction', 'era', 'preverb', 'sp_relatum' (the LWN node with the highest SP probability for the syntactic position of the relatum), and 'class'. Percentages of explained inertia: 34.6 (first axis), and 18.5 (second axis).*

If the points of an MCA plot correspond to binary variables, I can inspect the vectors through the origin defined by joining the pairs of variables' values. In this case, 'case' is a binary variable, which defines a vector through the origin. On the upper right hand side, 'acc' (corresponding to the PVs whose preverb is *ad-*, *circum-*, *in-*, or *trans-*) is positively associated with CaseNonPrev and with the classes 'actio' and 'affectus' for the position of the *relatum*. On the lower left hand side I find the ablative-case PVs (prefixed with *ab-*, *de-*, *ex-*, *in-*, *prae-*, and *sub-*), positively associated with PrepNoPrev and the classes *eventum* and *psychological feature*.

According to this description, I can say that my result is generally in accordance with Imbert (2008)'s hypothesis illustrated in sections 6.3.2.3 and 6.3.2.2. Her hypothesis is based on the Source-Goal asymmetry, a topic which has been widely discussed in typology, syntax and psycholinguistics (cf. e.g. Ikegami 1987; Stefanowitsch and Rohde 2004; Lakusta and Landau 2005). Imbert (2008) employs the argument of the Source-Goal asymmetry in her explanation of the grammaticalization/lexicalization of Homeric and Old English preverbs. According to her proposal, Source preverbs (requiring the ablative case) have a higher tendency towards lexicalization—thus behaving as satellite preverbs—unlike Goal preverbs (requiring the accusative case), which more frequently hold an adpositional role (relational preverbs). If I assume a correspondence between the satellite role of preverbs and their occurrence in constructions involving prepositions, and between the adpositional role and the occurrence in constructions involving the bare case, I can say that this statement is overall confirmed by my data, although further specifications are in order, due to the complex nature of the phenomenon.

The MCA analysis has allowed me to proceed further in the investigation of the data by building on the results from the chi-square test and the regression model (section 6.5). The chi-square test has highlighted a partial diachronic trend, while the regression analysis has shown that the detected trend is not only due to the author-specific differences (i.e. stylistic choices and genre), but to more general chronological groups. Moreover, the regression analysis has identified other relevant variables affecting the syntactic constructions for the PVs. In particular, it has shown that some preverbs (*ab-* in particular) have a strong effect on the presence of the preposition. As to relating these preverbs with constructions, MCA has detected a correlation between preverbs requiring the ablative case and the fourth construction (PrepNoPrev), and between preverbs requiring the accusative case and the second construction (CaseNonPrev).

6.6.2 *A Wider Picture*

So far, I have considered the morpho-syntactic realizations of the preverbs' *relata*. For the next investigation, I will focus on all spatial complements occurring with PVs (e.g. *advenio* 'go from' + a goal complement), thus containing not only the preverbs' *relata* (e.g. *advenio* + a source complement). The reason for this is that I want to investigate the type of spatial expressions occurring with PVs and their relation to diachronic and semantic factors. Therefore, I will use a larger dataset, to see if this allows me to capture a higher degree of variability for the complex phenomenon under investigation.

I collect all instances of the selected PVs containing an expression of either the *relatum* of the preverb—constructions 1 (CasePrev), 2 (CaseNonPrev), 3 (PrepPrev), and 4 (PrepNoPrev)—or another spatial argument of the type Goal or Source. For the latter case I define a positive occurrence of construction 5 (PrepOther) if it is a PP, and a positive occurrence of construction 6 (CaseOther) if it is an NP. These instances add up to 398. Examples of the fifth construction are in sentences (60) and (61).

(60)	IN	villos	AB-eunt	vestes
	Into	hair:ACC.M.PL	from-go:IND.PRS.3PL	garment:NOM.F.PL

'The garments change to hair'. (Ov., *Met.*, 1, 236)

(61)	Et	AB-ii	AD	angelum
	And	from-go:IND.PF.1SG	towards	angel:ACC.M.SG

'And I went towards the angel'. (Jer., *Vulg.*, *Ap.*, 10)

An example of the sixth construction is in sentence (62).

(62) aramque sepulcri congerere
altar:ACC.F.SG-and sepulchre:GEN.N.SG accumulate:INF.PRS
arboribus caeloque E-ducere certant
tree:ABL.F.PL sky:DAT.N.SG-and raise:INF.PRS compete:IND.PRS.3PL
'And they compete in covering the altar of the sepulchre with trees and raising it to the sky'. (Verg., *Aen.* VI, 177–178)

I am interested in finding whether the expression of a spatial complement of a PV depend on some specific chronological, morphological, lexical, syntactic and semantic factors. I then consider the following variables:

- 'preposition', distinguishing the prepositional constructions (PrepPrev, PrepNoPrev and PrepOther) from the NP ones (CasePrev, CaseNonPrev and CaseOther);
- 'era': Early, Classical, Late;
- 'complement': type of spatial complement, either G (goal) or S (source)
- 'animacy' of the lexical filler of the verb's complement: values 'animate' and 'non.animate'.

The following sentences show some examples of occurrences of those variables in the corpora.

- preposition='yes', era='Late', complement='Goal', animacy='inanimate'

(63) omnis operatio propria alicujus
every:NOM.F.SG operation:NOM.F.SG typical:NOM.F.SG some:GEN.F.SG
rei E-greditur A forma
thing:GEN.F.SG from-go:IND.PRS.3SG.DEP from:PREP form:ABL.F.SG
propria ejusdem
typical:ABL.F.SG same:GEN.F.SG
'Every operation typical of some thing moves from the form typical of the same thing' (Th., *Sent. P. L.*, I, Q. 1, Arg. 2)

- preposition='no', era='Classical', complement='Goal', animacy='inanimate'

(64) animas formatae IN-fundere terrae!
soul:ACC.F.PL form:PTCP.PF.DAT.F.SG in-pour:INF.PRS earth:DAT.F.SG
'Mould the earth and blow the souls into it!' (Ov., *Met.*, 364)

– preposition='yes', era='Classical', complement='Source', animacy= 'inanimate'[5]

(65) apes AB Athenis iussit
bee:ACC.F.PL from:PREP Athens:ABL.F.PL order:IND.PF.3SG
AF-ferri
in-bring:INF.PRS.PASS
'He had bees brought from Athens' (Petron., *Sat.*, 38)

I aim to perform an MCA to explore the relation between these variables in my data, and report the details of the output in section 7.3.1. Figure 6.6 shows the plot from the analysis, which is a simplified 2-dimensional representation of the data, accounting for 83.7% of the total variance. The first axis accounts for most of the inertia (80.9%). This axis is defined by the opposition between the presence and the absence of preposition with the PV: 'no.preposition' to the right and 'preposition' to the left, respectively associated with animate and inanimate fillers of the spatial complements. The opposition between Goal complements and Source complements is transversal with respect to the animacy opposition, showing a positive association between Source complements and presence of the preposition on the one hand, and between Goal complements and absence of preposition on the other. The second axis constrasts the chronological distinctions by era: at the bottom we find the early era, associated with both 'preposition' and 'no.preposition'; at the top we find the Classical and the Late eras, respectively associated with 'no.preposition' and with 'preposition'. In addition, I see that the Late era authors use a higher proportion of inanimate fillers than expected (which is compatible with the religious and philosophical topic of their works), the opposite holding for the Classical authors.

Summing up, this investigation confirms a general statement about the presence of the preposition in the Late era and its absence in the Classical era, the exception being the early author, who uses both. In addition, the analysis has allowed me to detect the correlation between Source complements and the use of the prepositions on the one hand, and between Goal complements and the use of bare cases on the other. This shows evidence for the Goal/Source asymmetry (section 6.6).

Plautus. The result for Plautus is in partial contrast with the previous analysis reported on in section 6.6, where I detected a preference of Plautus for

5 *Afferri* is a form of the verb *affero* <*ab+fero* 'bring'.

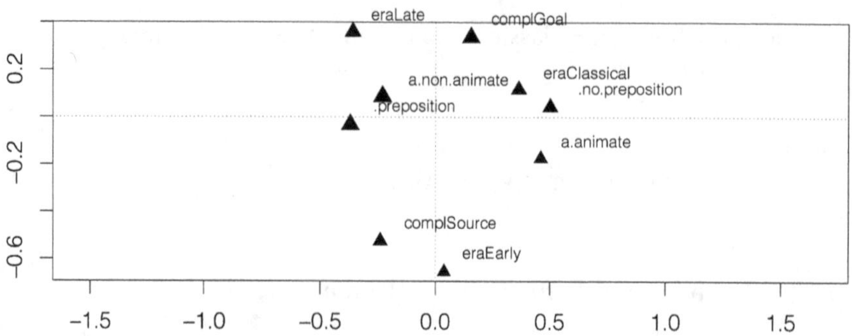

FIG. 6.6 *Plot of the MCA for the third investigation. The first axis accounts for 80.9 % of the explained inertia, while the second axis accounts for 2.7 %.*

construction 3 (PrepPrev), a prepositional construction. Thus, if we consider the sixth construction (CaseOther) as well, Plautus suddenly appears to share a comparable preference for constructions with and without preposition. This shows that his preference for prepositions is related with the preverb's *relatum*, while he prefers the bare case to express a different complement. Plautus' status as a literary author coexists with the presence of elements from the spoken language in his works: cf., among others, Fischer (1971) and Hofmann (1980). De Vivo (1994) underlines the communicative nature of Plautus' language, aimed at addressing the large audience of his comedies; at the same time, he acknowledges the literary function of Plautus' style, and stresses the importance of sound effects in the performance on stage. This explains the frequent alliterations, parallelises, repetitions and rhymes. As noted by Traina (1999, 55 ff.), the prepositional construction PrepPrev can be considered among those figures of speech, because it involves some kind of repetition between the preverb and the preposition. Therefore, the particular position of Plautus in the detected diachronic trend should be assessed in light of the features of this author's style, which help understand the high degree of variability in the constructions he uses.

López Moreda (1998, 964) argues that a higher frequency of construction 3 (PrepPrev) is more common in the dramatic genre and the colloquial register (see section 6.3.2.3). The present analysis allowed me to acquire more information about this correlation in my corpora. Here I consider the author from the dramatic genre recorded in the corpora (Plautus) and assume the generally recognized presence of colloquial features in his style (cf. e.g. Väänänen 1971; Poccetti et al. 1999; Rosén 1999). Then, in the data Plautus' preference for construction 3 (PrepPrev) is not associated with all verb classes and preverbs, but it is especially related with verbs of transport and with the Source preverb *ab-* 'from'.

6.7 Main Findings

The main aim of this chapter has been to show the potential of advanced statistical techniques for investigating a diachronic phenomenon. This section will summarize the linguistic findings that resulted from this methodological approach.

The corpus-based quantitative analysis I carried out in this chapter allowed me to tackle a complex linguistic phenomenon, for which different theoretical hypotheses have been proposed in the literature. I have found partial evidence for a general diachronic trend which has been stated in Latin Linguistics studies and in grammaticalization theory, namely the increasing prevalence of prepositional constructions to express spatial complements of PVs. This is compatible with the more general evolution from the synthetic features of Latin towards the analytical systems of Romance languages. My conclusion is also in agreement with previous theories on the development of preverbs which frame it as a grammaticalization/lexicalization process involving Path expressions (Imbert, 2008). These theories are based on the assumption that the presence of a preposition (PrepPrev or PrepNoPrev) could indicate a more advanced degree of lexicalization of preverbs, which is opposite to their original adpositional behaviour. This assumption focusses on syntactic evidence for a process which involves the semantics of the PV, thus acting at the syntax-semantics interface.

This broad tendency has been stated in many places, including standard handbooks of Latin like Bennett (1914), Leumann et al. (1965), Löfstedt (1956); however, it was not my aim here to carry out a systematic survey of those handbooks, but to show how some known facts can be corroborated by corpus-based studies like the present one.

In addition to confirming the general tendency towards more frequent prepositional constructions, my approach has an important merit in that it gives *quantitative* evidence supporting both known facts and new specific results. In fact, the multivariate techniques I used (regression modeling and correspondence analysis) have made it possible to conduct advanced investigations, which led me to more detailed conclusions. I further specified the general trend by recognizing that the Late era authors of my corpus prefer the use of prepositions that are different from the ones corresponding to the preverb of the PV (PrepNoPrev). On the other hand, based on the two plays analysed here, the Early author (Plautus) prefers the same preposition as the preverb (PrepPrev) when expressing the preverb's *relatum*, and a bare noun phrase for other complements. These findings confirm the issues related to a strictly unidirectional interpretation of the trend from Latin synthetic case-based morpho-syntax to the analytic syntax of the Romance languages, which have been discussed in the diachronic literature (see Schwegler (1990); Vincent (1997) for Romance and Barðdal (2009) for Germanic). Finally, I found some evidence supporting the Goal/Source asymmetry, associating the presence of prepositions with Source complements and its absence with Goal complements.

These results refer to single authors as representatives of chronological eras. This is a tricky question, given the fact that we cannot disregard stylistic factors affecting the authors' choices, as well as metric constraints in poetic texts (see for example Janssen (1988, 83–84)), not to mention the peculiarities of the dramatic genre. The case of Plautus—the only Early Era author in the corpus—is particularly indicative of this. His choice of which constructions to use is also driven by stylistic factors, which have the effect of introducing expressive repetitions and sound effects. In addition, I have found that poets in my corpora tend to avoid the use of prepositions in the realization of the preverbs' *relata*, while Plautus shows an opposite behaviour, although with some restrictions. This result could be viewed in light of Jakobson's studies (Jacobson, 1966), according to which the poetic function focusses on the linguistic form; see also Janssen (1988, 127). In my case, the emphasis on the preverb within the PV (and therefore on the constructions with the bare case) is more expected in poetry and less expected in spoken language and my findings seem to confirm these expectations.

CHAPTER 7

Statistical Background to the Investigation on Preverbs

This chapter illustrates the statistical techniques employed in chapter 6 and gives details of the case studies. This overview covers the chi-square test (section 7.1), linear models (section 7.2), and Correspondence Analysis (section 7.3). The goal here is to allow the reader to familiarize with these notions of advanced statistics thanks to a simplified explanation supported by linguistic examples taken from the corpus analyses of the case studies. For more in-depth discussions of these topics, I will refer to other specific works.

7.1 Pearson's Chi-Square Test of Independence

In this section I will briefly describe Pearson's chi-square test of independence and discuss its use in the first study on Latin preverbs reported on in section 6.5. For a more in-depth description and mathematical details on this test, see Hinton (2004, 248–259).

Pearson's chi-square test is one of the techniques used in hypothesis testing, aiming at testing a formal hypothesis by attempting to reject it. Research questions often involve decisions about *populations* and their distributions, for example the frequencies of word order patterns in Classical and Late Latin. The populations are in most cases not available for direct study; however, hypothesis testing makes it possible to compare *samples* from the populations, based on which it is possible to decide whether or not the populations differ significantly.

Hypothesis testing works by setting up a *null hypothesis* (H_0), and comparing it with an *alternative hypothesis* (H_1). H_0 can be formulated in a number of ways; however, it always specifies the most conservative scenario such as 'no difference' or 'no effect'. In the word order example mentioned above, I can formulate the null hypothesis that the two samples (frequencies of word order patterns from Classical and Late Latin, respectively) are drawn from the same population. The analysis proceeds by *a priori* deciding on a *significance level* (commonly 0.05 or 5% in the humanities and social sciences), which is the threshold under which we reject H_0; then either we reject or we do not reject the null hypothesis. Put differently, we only reject the null

 | DOI: 10.1163/9789004260122_008

TABLE 7.1 *Frequency counts of two constructions in Plautus and Thomas in the corpora*

Author	Construction A	Construction B	Row totals
Plautus	15	24	39
Thomas	2	53	55
column totals	17	77	94

hypothesis when the data seem extremely unlikely in the light of the assumptions of H_0, so that the probability of making the right decision is at least 95%.

Pearson's chi-square test works on frequency data in the form of a table, where two variables are assigned to rows and columns, respectively. I will illustrate the case of two-by-two tables, where two variables are divided into two categories; however, the discussion applies to a higher number of categories as well. As an example, Table 7.1 gives the frequencies of two syntactic constructions (A and B) in two authors (Plautus and Thomas), taken from the dataset of the first study on preverbs described in section 6.5. In this case, I categorized the data in terms of the two variables 'construction' and 'author'.

Observed frequencies and expected frequencies. A Pearson chi-square test for independence formally tests the null hypothesis that rows and columns are independent of each other, i.e. the observations in the table follow a random uniform discrete distribution. In the current example, the null hypothesis states that the frequencies of constructions A and B do not depend on the particular author they occur in. The total number of observations is 39 for Plautus and 55 for Thomas, so even under the null hypothesis I do not expect the same observed frequencies for the two constructions in the two authors; rather, I expect the same *proportion* of each construction in each author. For example, the 24 occurrences of construction B in Plautus correspond to $\frac{24}{15+24} = 0.62$ or 62% of the total frequency in Plautus. If there were no difference between the two authors in terms of the constructions used, then the 17 total occurrences of construction B should be distributed between Plautus and Thomas in proportion to the authors' frequencies. The proportion for Plautus is $\frac{39}{94} = 0.41$, so I would expect $0.41 * 17 = 7.07$ instances of construction A in Plautus, as shown by the first cell of Table 7.2.

TABLE 7.2 *Expected frequency counts from Table 7.1*

Author	Construction A	Construction B
Plautus	7.07	31.57
Thomas	9.95	45.05

TABLE 7.3 *Expected frequencies corresponding to the observed frequencies in Table 6.2*

Author	CasePrev	Preposition
Plautus	10.51	42.49
Cicero	1.59	6.41
Caesar	1.19	4.81
Sallust	3.97	16.03
Vergil	1.39	5.61
Propertius	1.39	5.61
Ovid	1.19	4.81
Petronius	5.35	21.65
Jerome	5.75	23.25
Thomas	14.68	59.32

In general, the expected value of each cell (i,j) ($i = 1, \ldots, nr$ =number of rows and $j = 1, \ldots, nc$=number of columns) in the table is calculated as follows:

$$expected_{i,j} = \frac{\text{row } i \text{ total} * \text{column } j \text{ total}}{\text{overall total}}$$

For example, Table 7.3 contains the expected frequencies relative to Table 6.2 on page 160.

The assumption of a Pearson's chi-square test for independence is that the observations are independent and randomly extracted from the population, and that their expected frequencies are higher than 5 (Hinton, 2004, 258), as in this example. Under the null hypothesis, the observed values are very close to the expected values, although they may not coincide with them due to random variation. The deviation from the expected behaviour is measured by the chi-square statistic:

$$\chi^2 = \sum_{i=1,\ldots,nr;j=1,\ldots,nc} \frac{(O-E)^2}{E}$$

where O refers to the observed value in a cell and E to its expected value. In the previous example, $\chi^2 = \frac{(15-7.07)^2}{7.07} + \frac{(24-31.57)^2}{31.57} + \frac{(2-9.95)^2}{9.95} + \frac{(53-45.05)^2}{45.05} = 18.45$. 15, 24, 2, and 53 are the observed frequencies (see Table 7.1) and 7.07, 31.57, 9.95, and 45.05 are the expected frequencies (see Table 7.2).

A decision on the statistical significance of this value is taken by comparing it with its table of critical values.[1] For example, given the chi-square statistic just calculated and the number of rows and columns in the input table, I find a critical value of 3.84: since the calculated value (18.45) is greater than this critical value, I can reject the null hypothesis with a probability of 5.117e-05. This is the *p*-value given by the test; if it is lower than the predefined level of significance (0.05), then the probability of finding those observed values under the assumption that the two variables are independent is less than 5%. Therefore, the two authors use the two constructions in ways which are significantly different at the 0.05 level.

Effect size. In addition to the *p*-value, which states whether the result is significant or not, i.e. whether the two variables are significantly independent or not, it is important to consider the *effect size*, which accounts for the size of the detected independence. The effect size is an indicator of the size of the sample: in fact, high frequencies—as well as a large number of categories, i.e. columns in the input table—tend to magnify small deviations, as pointed out in Mosteller (1968, 2). The effect size factors out the sample size, and provides a standardized measure of how large the difference is. A measure of effect size for 2 × 2 tables is ϕ: $\phi = \sqrt{\frac{\chi^2}{n}}$ where n is the total sum of the cell frequencies, so ϕ varies between 0 and 1. In this example, $\phi = 0.42$. For larger tables, *Cramér V* is used, which approximately varies between 0 and 1: $V = \sqrt{\frac{\chi^2}{n*(min\{nr,nc\}-1)}}$. $min\{nr, nc\}$ is the smallest value between nr (number of rows) and nc (number of columns). According to Cohen (1988, 222–227), values of ϕ (or V) around 0.10

1 The input of a chi-square test is identified by the number of *degrees of freedom*, calculated as $(nr-1)(nc-1) = 1$ in the previous example. The degrees of freedom count how many values in the table we need to know to infer the values of the whole table, given the row and column totals. Once we know the number of degrees of freedom and a significance level, we can calculate the corresponding critical value for the chi-square statistic: if this value is greater than the value we calculated, then we can reject the null hypothesis at the decided level of significance, e.g. 0.05. Tables of critical values are usually recorded in statistics manuals. Here, I use the table contained in Hinton (2004, 370).

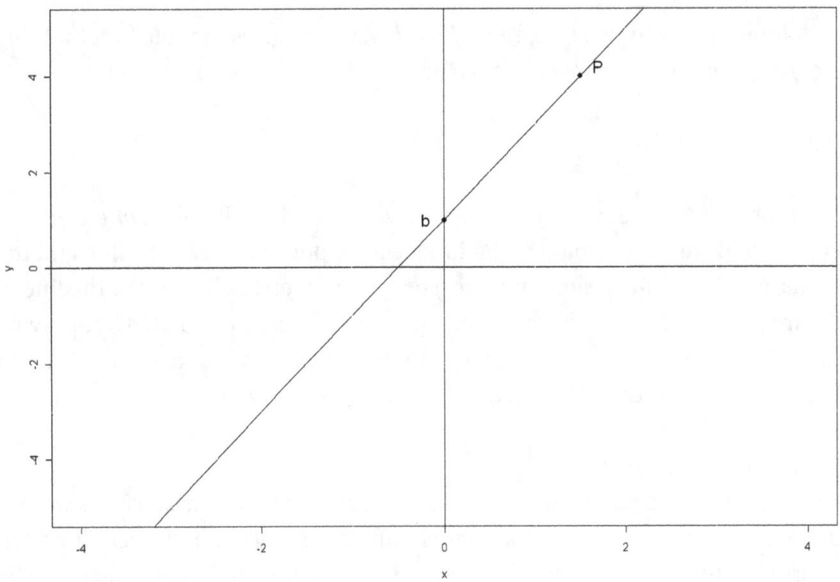

FIG. 7.1 *Example of the line with equation* $y = 2x + 1$ *and intercept* $b = 1$*; the point* $P = (1.5, 4)$ *is also represented.*

are to be considered a small effect, values around 0.30 a medium effect, and values around and above 0.50 a large effect. In the previous example, we get a medium-to-high effect (0.42).

7.2 Linear Regression Models

This section provides an overview of linear regression models, which are a more advanced (and powerful) statistical technique than the chi-square test. Linear regression models have been studied recently in statistics and are employed in the second study on Latin preverbs I reported on in section 6.5.1. I refer to Gorard (2003, 202–226) and Hinton (2004, 262–281, 284–294) for a more detailed discussion on linear regression models.

Linear regression models work on linear spaces on the kind defined in section 5.2. I will hence start by defining linear functions.

7.2.1 *Linear Functions*

Let us consider a two-dimensional space, identified by the x and y axes, and suppose the data consist of a set of points, each of which is uniquely associated with a pair of coordinates (x, y). I will focus on the particular case when the points lie along a *line*, as in Figure 7.1.

A line can be defined by a *linear function*, which gives the rule for obtaining a corresponding y from each x: this function has a simple expression:

$$y = ax + b \tag{7.1}$$

So, in order to obtain y, we multiply x by a and add b. b is called *intercept* and corresponds to the ordinate of the intersection point between the line and the y axis, while a is called *slope* and measures how steep the line is. For the line in Figure 7.1, $b = 1$ and $a = 2$. Note that, for each x, y can be calculated by applying formula (7.1): for example, if $x = 1.5$, then $y = 2 * 1.5 + 1 = 4$, so point P in Figure 7.1 has coordinates $(1.5, 4)$.

7.2.2 *Linear Regression*

Given a set of data (which we can imagine as a set of points in space), as we saw in section 7.2.1, linear regression models aim at finding the best linear function approximating these points. Because linear functions allow to calculate the y values based on the x values, linear regression models make it possible to *predict* one variable (called 'response') as a linear function of the other(s) (called 'predictors'). Since the linear function is an approximation for the observed data, we want this function to be reasonably similar to the data, so that the error is minimized. In other words, in a good model the predictors explain most of the variability observed in the response.

The assumptions of a regression analysis are numerous (see, for example, Gorard (2003, 213)) and they require, among other things, that the data come from a random sample, the response is approximately linearly related to the predictors, the differences between calculated and observed scores are approximately normally distributed,[2] and the predictors are uncorrelated.

Finding a regression model for the data at hand is equivalent to finding a *correlation* between the variables. For example, I may find that the average length of the utterances spoken by babies and their age in months are correlated (or linearly related), since the length of the utterances increases by progressing in time (positive slope). However, it should be pointed out that correlation is distinguished from causality. As Gorard (2003, 205) notes, finding that children

2 The *normal distribution* or *Gaussian function* is a probability distribution represented by the well-known bell shape and characterized by the fact that most of its values tend to cluster around the mean (the peak of the bell). Its wide use is also explained by the fact that the frequency distribution of the means of a large number of equally-sized samples tends to a normal distribution (central limit theorem). For a more in-depth illustration of the normal distribution, see e.g. Hinton (2004, 28–33).

TABLE 7.4 *Example containing values for car speed and distance to stop*

Observation	Speed	Distance
P_1	4	2
P_2	7	4
P_3	9	10
P_4	11	17
P_5	12	20
P_6	13	26

with bigger feet also tend to spell better does not explain why this is the case, and may be due to a third variable affecting the two previous ones, such as age.

7.2.2.1 Simple Linear Regression

Let us suppose that the data consist of sets of scores, i.e. vectors: X and Y. For example, X may represent the measured speed of cars, (second column of Table 7.4) and Y their distance to stop (third column of Table 7.4). X is thus the vector

$$(x_1, x_2, x_3, x_4, x_5, x_6) = (4, 7, 9, 11, 12, 13)$$

and Y is

$$(y_1, y_2, y_3, y_4, y_5, y_6) = (2, 4, 10, 17, 20, 26)$$

First, I need to set which variable to predict (i.e. the response, say Y, the cars' distance to stop in the example of Table 7.4) and which variable to use as predictor, X (say the cars' speed). I want to find the linear function L such that the Y scores can be obtained by applying L to the X scores, except for some random variation.

$$Y = L(X) + E$$

or

$$Y = Y' + E$$

where Y' is a straight line and E is the error which causes the data points to deviate from the line. $Y' = a + bX$ is the *regression line*. The best regression line

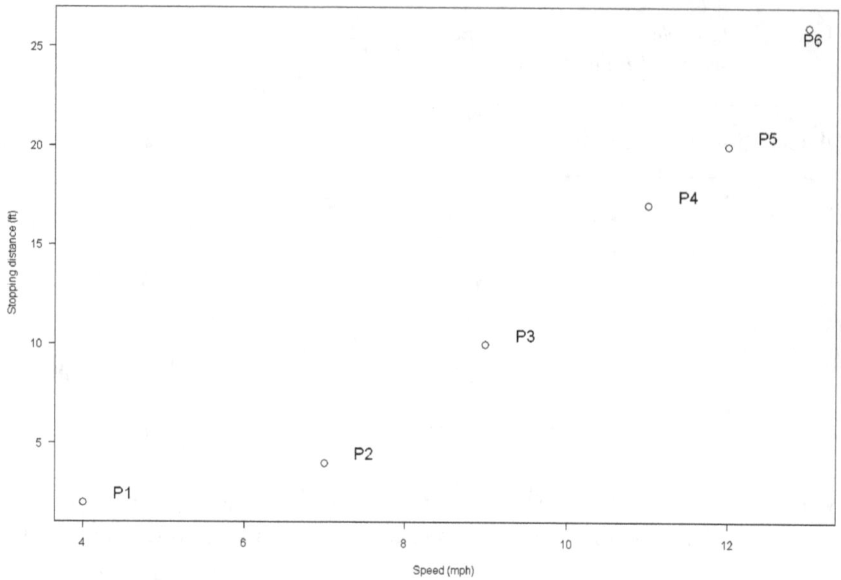

FIG. 7.2 *Data points from Table 7.4 relative to speed of cars and their distance to stop*

is considered to be the line that gives the best fit to the data, i.e. the line that minimizes the error E. A regression analysis tests if the corresponding linear model is a good model for the data at hand.

$E = Y - Y'$ can be seen as the deviation between the data points and the regression line. E is found through the procedure of *least squares*, i. e. by trying to minimize the sum of the squared signed vertical distances between the data points and the regression line (called *residuals*). This procedure finds the constants a and b defining Y':

$$b = \frac{SP}{SS_X}$$

and

$$a = \bar{Y} - b\bar{X}$$

where $\bar{X}$ and $\bar{Y}$ are the means of the values of X and Y.

$$SP = \sum (X - \bar{X})(Y - \bar{Y})$$

and

$$SS_X = \sum (X - \bar{X})^2.$$

Going back to the cars example, consider the points in Figure 7.2, which are a subset of the 'cars' dataset contained in the R manual (R Development Core Team, 2008) and representing the speed of cars on the x axis and the corresponding distance to stop on the y axis. The points' coordinates are displayed in Table 7.4.

As shown in Figure 7.2, the points are scattered in the space, but a linear pattern can be detected. If we apply the least square method to this example, we get

$$\bar{X} = \frac{4+7+9+11+12+13}{6} = \frac{79}{6} = 9.33$$

$$\bar{Y} = \frac{2+4+10+17+20+26}{6} = \frac{79}{6} = 13.17$$

We thus obtain:

$$\begin{aligned} SP &= (x_1 - 9.33)(y_1 - 13.16) + (x_2 - 9.33)(y_2 - 13.16) + \\ &\quad + (x_3 - 9.33)(y_3 - 13.16) + (x_4 - 9.33)(y_4 - 13.17) + \\ &\quad + (x_5 - 9.33)(y_5 - 13.17) + (x_6 - 9.33)(y_6 - 13.17) = \\ &= (4 - 9.33)(2 - 13.16) + (7 - 9.33)(4 - 13.16) + \\ &\quad + (9 - 9.33)(10 - 13.16) + (11 - 9.33)(17 - 13.17) + \\ &\quad + (12 - 9.33)(20 - 13.17) + (13 - 9.33)(26 - 13.17) = \\ &= (-5.33)(-11.16) + (-2.33)(-9.16) + (-0.33)(-3.16) + \\ &\quad + (1.67)(3.83) + (2.67)(6.83) + (3.67)(12.83) = 153.59 \end{aligned}$$

and

$$\begin{aligned} SS_X &= (x_1 - 9.33)^2 + (x_2 - 9.33)^2 + (x_3 - 9.33)^2 (x_4 - 9.33)^2 + \\ &\quad + (x_5 - 9.33)^2 + (x_6 - 9.33)^2 = (4 - 9.33)^2 + (7 - 9.33)^2 + \\ &\quad + (9 - 9.33)^2 + (11 - 9.33)^2 + (12 - 9.33)^2 + (13 - 9.33)^2 = \\ &= (-5.33)^2 + (-2.33)^2 + (-0.33)^2 + (1.67)^2 + (2.67)^2 + (3.67)^2 = \\ &= 28.41 + 5.43 + 0.11 + 2.79 + 7.13 + 13.47 = 57.33 \end{aligned}$$

Thus $a = (13.16 - 2.68) * 9.33 = -11.85$ and $b = \frac{153.59}{57.33} = 2.68$. The regression line is then defined by $Y' = 2.68X - 11.85$ and represented in Figure 7.3.

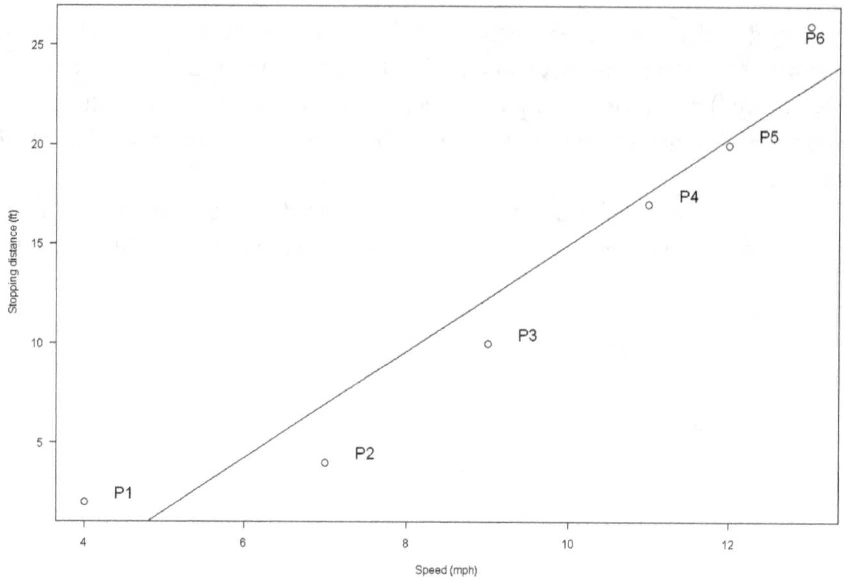

FIG. 7.3 *Regression line of the data points plotted in Figure 7.2*

7.2.2.2 Multiple Linear Regression

Multiple linear regression is the generalization of simple linear regression to the case where more than two variables are involved. As in simple regression, one variable must be chosen as the response Y and will be predicted by other k variables, i.e. the predictors $X_1, \ldots, X_k$. Then, I aim at solving the linear equation:

(7.2) $$Y = a + b_1X_1 + b_2X_2 + \ldots + b_kX_k.$$

If n is the number of observations, both the response and the predictors are n-dimensional vectors: $Y = (y_1, y_2, \ldots, y_n)$, $X_1 = (x_{1,1}, x_{1,2}, \ldots, x_{1,n})$, …, …, $X_k = (x_{k,1}, x_{k,2}, \ldots, x_{k,n})$. Equation (7.2) translates into a system of n equations: $y_i = a + b_1x_{1,i} + b_2x_{2,i} + \ldots + b_kx_{k,i}$ For each $i = 1, \ldots, n$. For example, I may be interested in predicting the salary of people based on two predictors: years of education and age; that is, I want to express the salary (Y) in my dataset (D) as linearly depending on the length of the education (X_1) and the age (X_2) of a person. In this example, the linear equation to be solved is:

(7.3) $$Y = a + b_1X_1 + b_2X_2$$

or

(7.4) $$salary = a + b_{education} * education + b_{age} * age$$

Explaining the way equations (7.2) and (7.3) are solved falls outside the scope of this chapter. Instead, I will illustrate the way this problem is formulated in R and the kind of generated output, since this is how I used multiple regression models in the study on preverbs presented in section 6.5.1, whose results are reported on in section 7.2.5.

The function `lm()` in R fits a linear model to a dataset in the form `response ~ predictors`, where the predictors are listed with the '+' sign; thus the model represented by equation (7.4) (where predictors are education and age) is calculated as follows:

```
lm(salary ~ education + age, data =D)
```

R produces an output summary containing the distribution of residuals (which are assumed to follow a random distribution), a coefficient for the intercept (a) and a coefficient for the slope (b_i) of each predictor. These coefficients are followed by numbers attesting the statistical significance and the reliability of the estimated coefficients. In addition to inspecting the model's summary, an appropriate model diagnostic should be carried out that checks the model's fit to the data by plotting its residuals. I will examine the output summary and the diagnostic plots more in detail case by case in section 7.2.5, after outlining the main subtypes of models I used in sections 7.2.3 and 7.2.4.

7.2.3 *Generalized Linear Models*

A *Generalized Linear Model* (GLM) is a generalization of a linear regression model that deals with a wider range of cases. A GLM is specified by a family distribution for the residuals. A particular class of GLMs are *logistic models*, which are used when the response is a binary variable (i.e. it takes only two values, 0 and 1, failure and success), for example a construction with or without a preposition. In addition, a logistic model requires the response to have a binomial error distribution, which describes the distribution of a number of independent experiments yielding only two possible outcomes. In logistic models the goal is to estimate the probability of one of the two possible outcomes (e.g. absence or presence of preposition), given the predictors (e.g. author and verb). Instead of being modelled directly, the probabilities are modelled through a so-called *link function*, which is the *logit* transformation of the probability x:

$$logit(x) = ln(\frac{x}{1-x})$$

The logit function maps the range [0,1] to the range $[-\infty, +\infty]$. Once the logit coefficients are produced by the model, it is necessary to back-transform them with the inverse of the logit function to interpret them as probabilities.

The R syntax for a logistic GLM modelling the binary variable 'preposition' (taking two values) on the predictors 'author' and 'verb' is:

```
glm(preposition ~ author + verb, data =D, family =binomial)
```

7.2.4 *Mixed-Effect Models*

Mixed-effect models are an expansion of classical linear regression involving *fixed effects* (i.e. predictors) and *random effects*. The combination of fixed and random effects allows us to account for both individual and group-level variation in a model. This turns out particularly useful when the data have been collected from various groups. Unlike classical regression, which tries to fit a unique model for the whole dataset, a mixed-effect model lets the regression intercepts vary group by group.

I will use mixed-effect models to neutralize the effect of non-independent data, a situation that typically arises with diachronic linguistic data: I will thus set the random effect as a diachronic variable, such as 'author'.

In R a mixed-effect model for the response 'construction', predictors 'verb' and 'preposition', and random effect for 'author' is formulated as:

```
lmer(construction ~ verb + preposition + (1 |author), data =D, family
=binomial)
```

In the case of a binary response, if I specify the binomial family, the default link function used is the logit (see section 7.2.3).

7.2.5 *The Model for Prefixed Verbs*

The investigation on Latin preverbs described in section 6.5.1 involves the use of mixed-effect models to predict the value of the binary variable 'construction' based on the values of certain other variables. In this model I model the response 'construction' (taking the two values 'CasePrev' and 'Preposition') on the following variables:

- 'preverb' (values 'ab', 'ad', 'circum', 'de', 'ex', 'in', 'intro', 'ob', 'prae', 'sub', 'trans')
- 'era' (values 'Augustan', 'early_republic', 'imperial', 'late_imperial', 'late_republic' and 'medieval')
- 'case' ('accusative' and 'ablative')

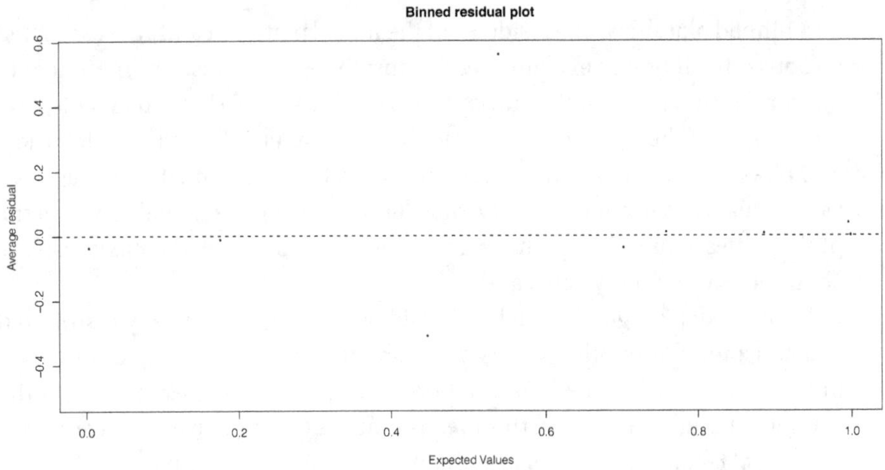

FIG. 7.4 *Binned plot of the residuals against fitted values of the linear model*

Random effects are:

- 'author' (values 'Caesar', 'Cicero', 'Jerome', 'Ovid', 'Petronius', 'Plautus', 'Propertius', 'Sallust', 'Thomas', and 'Vergil')
- 'class' (values 'motion', 'rest', and 'transport')

Note that the response is binary and that I choose the binomial distribution as the family distribution for the residuals (see section 7.2.4). The syntax for the random effects shows that I allow the slope to vary by the verb class and the intercept to vary by the author. In other words, instead of fitting a single model for the whole dataset by producing one intercept and one slope, I want to obtain different slopes and different intercepts for the different authors and verb classes.

Before showing the details of the model, it is important to evaluate its fit to the data. The so-called Nagelkerke R^2 compares the fitted model with null models from the point of view of data coverage. For example, if I compare the full model with a null model which has the same random effects but no predictors, the improvement is of 45%; if I compare the model with a null model that has the same predictors but no random effects, the improvement is of 71%; finally, going form a model with just the model's random effects to a model with just its predictors causes an improvement of 48%. In all cases, the improvements are quite good, showing that the model's parameters improve upon the predictions of the null models.

A complementary measure of goodness of fit is by means of diagnostic plots. Figure 7.4 is the binned plot for the model (Gelman et al., 2009).

A binned plot shows the residuals of the model plotted against the estimated response. I will briefly explain these terms; for a fuller illustration on how to interpret residuals plots, cf. Faraway (2006). The x axis of a binned plot displays the values for the response ('construction') as predicted by the model; the y axis plots the corresponding average residuals from the model. The response, as it appears in the data, is binary, thus discrete, while the model provides the probabilities of the response having the value '0':[3] this is why the x axis displays continuous values between 0 and 1.

If the model is a good model, the residuals should be normally distributed and constant; put in other words, there should not be ascending or descending patterns in the binned plot. In addition, in a good regression model the variance should be constant; this means that the grey line (which corresponds to the 95%-confidence interval) should be as constant as possible. Finally, the points that fall inside the area delimited by the grey line are correctly assigned by the model, so it is desirable that most points fall into this area. Since good estimates are difficult with small datasets, in this case the number of points falling outside the area (3 out of 9) may be due to the small size of the dataset (containing 236 observations). Given the fact that this is the model that gives the best fit to the data (based on the diagnostic plot in Figure 7.4 and Nagelkerke R^2), I consider it to be an acceptable model for the data at hand.

Table 7.5 summarizes the output details for each predictor value which deviates from the reference level, represented by the early republican era, the preverb *ab-*, and the ablative case. I will focus on the first two columns of Table 7.5, giving the estimated coefficient for each predictor's value and the standard error of this estimate. It is important that the error is smaller than the absolute value of the coefficient, otherwise the estimate is not reliable, as for 'preverb.de', 'preverb.ex', 'preverb.intro', 'preverb.in', 'preverb.trans', 'era.imperial', 'era.medieval', 'era.late_imperial', and 'era.late_republican'. I will thus focus on the rows whose names are in small caps in Table 7.5.

3 This is the standard R notation for binary variables, for which the values are defined as '0' and '1'. For sake of clarity, in this book I will assign more meaningful names to the values. For 'construction', for example, I named the values as 'CasePrev' and 'Preposition'.

TABLE 7.5 *Estimated coefficient, standard error, probability of 'construction', and effect size of each predictor in the model*

Fixed effect	Est. coef.	Std. Error	Pr(construction)	Effect size
(Intercept)	1.14	0.55	0.76	0.76
PREVERB.AD	-3.18	1.55	0.11	0.04
preverb.de	-0.35	1.37	0.69	0.41
preverb.ex	-0.04	0.91	0.75	0.49
preverb.in	-1.20	1.31	0.48	0.23
preverb.intro	16.80	12160.00	1.00	1.00
PREVERB.OB	-7.13	6.86	0.00	0.00
PREVERB.SUB	-1.97	1.42	0.30	0.12
preverb.trans	-23.75	14110.00	0.00	0.00
ERA.AUGUSTAN	-2.54	0.93	0.20	0.07
era.imperial	0.12	0.79	0.78	0.53
era.medieval	19.34	2804.00	1.00	1.00
era.late_imperial	19.73	4454.00	1.00	1.00
era.late_republican	-0.30	0.74	0.70	0.42
CASE.ACC	1.97	1.33	0.96	0.88

The estimated intercept is 1.14 (first row, first column in Table 7.5). Since this is a mixed-effect model on a binary response and since I have specified in the model that the residuals follow a binomial distribution, the default link function is the logit (cf. section 7.2.3). Therefore, if I consider a coefficient (for example the estimated intercept 1.14) and calculate its value by the Inverse-logit function (0.76, first row and third column of Table 7.5), this figure corresponds to the probability of 'construction' at the reference level. Among the preverbs, *ad-*, *sub-*, and *ob-* have a negative effect on 'construction' with respect to the reference level represented by *ab-*, which means that the probability of finding a preposition in the expression of *relatum* decreases if the preverb is one of those ones, compared with the probability of finding a preposition if the preverb is *ab-*. The effect for the Augustan era is invlogit(-2.54)=0.07, which means that switching from the reference level given by the early republican era to the Augustan era causes a decrease (due to the minus sign in the coefficient) by 7% in the probability of 'construction' being 'preposition'; this probability is invlogit(-2.54+1.14)=0.20 when the era is Augustan. Finally, the accusative case governed by the preposition corresponding to the preverb causes an increase of 88% in the probability of finding a preposition.

7.3 Correspondence Analysis

In this section I introduce Correspondence Analysis (CA), a data analysis technique I used in the study on Latin preverbs described in section 6.6.2.

CA is a technique in exploratory data analysis. It analyses tables of positive integer numbers (typically frequencies) to detect the correspondence between the rows (observations or individuals) and the columns (variables or characteristics). Unlike traditional hypothesis testing techniques which aim at verifying hypotheses about relations between variables, exploratory data analysis aims at identifying systematic relations between variables and observations in the data without *a priori* expectations on these relations.

CA can also be defined as a *multivariate* descriptive technique for data analysis, like clustering (see section 5.2.2), which allows to visualize either the relation between individuals or that between characteristics. It works on multidimensional data, i.e. sets of observations in the form of vectors in multidimensional spaces (see section 5.2.2). Starting from such complex data, CA reduces the number of dimensions of the space: the output is a minimal space displaying the underlying structure of the data and providing a simplified version of the original input. As a matter of fact, CA allows to study individuals (rows) and their characteristics (columns) in a unified representation (the so-called *biplot*). In addition, CA is a projection technique in that it projects the data points into a lower-dimensional space while preserving certain properties of the structure of the dataset as faithfully as possible. Finally, CA is a graphical method, which displays row and column points onto a common space (biplot); this helps detect structural relationships between rows and columns in the data.

As we saw in section 7.1, the chi-square test is able to detect an association between the rows and the columns of a matrix. However, it does not tell us *where* this association is concentrated, i.e. which are the significant individual associations between row-column pairs of the matrix. CA, on the other hand, provides a picture of these individual associations through a common representation in the biplot.

The modern formulation of CA was coined by Benzécri (1973) with reference to philological models regarding Chinese consonants and vowels. Later on, other scholars followed Benzécri's idea and applied it to different fields: sociology, marketing, archeology, political sciences, linguistics, and others. The main idea behind CA is to represent the data K as the "sum" of a reduced model K', a residual unexplained variance R, and an error E: $K = K' + R + E$

This resembles the approximation pursued by linear regression models (see section 7.2). However, Greenacre (2007, 47) points out that regression requires

TABLE 7.6 *Frequency table of a constructed dataset with verbal tokens counted by verb lemma and author*

Author	Verb			TOTAL
	Dico	*Do*	*Eo*	
Caesar	2	7	0	9
Cicero	3	1	0	4
Petronius	2	0	11	13
Plautus	2	1	6	9
Sallust	10	2	0	12
TOTAL	19	11	17	47

one of the variables to be considered as response; in contrast, CA does not require a response variable and treats all the variables at the same level. Now I will briefly outline the procedure common to all CA analyses; for a more in-depth discussion of each step, see Greenacre (2007).

Dataset. In section 5.2 I showed the data format usually dealt with in empirical linguistic analysis and how it can be turned into a frequency table. This table, or matrix, has in turn a geometrical interpretation if we consider its rows as vectors in the space defined by the number of columns. For example, imagine we want to investigate the occurrences of Latin verbs in certain authors: we have a number of observations, corresponding to the verbal tokens, and two variables: 'author' and, say, 'verb'. Table 7.6 shows constructed frequencies for this case: rows correspond to authors and columns to verbal lemmas. CA can be applied to larger tables, but here I will make use of this toy example for the sake of clarity.

Profiles. CA interprets the rows of the input table as points (called *row profiles*) in a multidimensional space defined by the columns, and it interprets the columns as points (called *column profiles*) in the space defined by the rows. In the example above, this means considering the row points—'Caesar', 'Cicero', 'Petronius', 'Plautus', and 'Sallust'—in the 3-dimensional space defined by the three verbs *dico, do,* and *eo*; in addition, the three verbs are points in a 5-dimensional space defined by the five author names.

Row and column profiles are calculated as the relative row and column frequencies, respectively. For example, the sum of the forth row in Table 7.6 is

TABLE 7.7 *The first 5 rows of this table represent matrix R of row profiles from Table 7.6. The last row represents the average row profile.*

Author	Verb			Row masses
	Dico	*Do*	*Eo*	
Caesar	0.22	0.78	0	0.19
Cicero	0.75	0.25	0	0.09
Petronius	0.15	0	0.85	0.28
Plautus	0.22	0.11	0.67	0.19
Sallust	0.83	0.17	0	0.26
average row profile	0.40	0.23	0.36	1

2+1+6=9; hence, 'Plautus' corresponds to the row profile $(2,1,6)/9 = (0.22, 0.11, 0.67)$; similarly, the profile for *dico* is $(2,3,2,2,10)/19 = (0.10, 0.16, 0.10, 0.10, 0.05)$. I will call the matrix of row profiles R and represent it in Table 7.7; for example, $R(1,1)$ is the cell corresponding to the first row and first column of R.

I calculate the *average row profile* as the row sums divided by the total sum. In other words, the average profile corresponds to the most expected behaviour. In the example, this is given by dividing the last row of Table 7.6 by the grand total 47: $(19,11,17)/47 = (0.40, 0.23, 0.36)$, which is the profile of all authors put together.

Masses. The *mass* of a row i is defined as the ith row total divided by the grand total; likewise for a column. For example, the mass of the first row in Table 7.6 is $\frac{9}{47} = 0.19$; row masses are displayed in the last column of Table 7.7.

The concept of mass helps us imagine the row and column profiles as *weighted* points in space: the *profile space*. In the example above, the total frequency of the fourth row ('Plautus') is distributed among the verbs with the following weights: 0.22 (*dico*), 0.11 (*do*), and 0.67 (*eo*). In other words, the weighted average or *barycentre* for 'Plautus' can be calculated by assigning the weights $\frac{2}{9} = 0.22$ to *dico*, $\frac{1}{9} = 0.11$ to *do*, and $\frac{6}{9} = 0.67$ to *eo*.

If I associate the three verbs to the vertices of a triangle as in Figure 7.5, I can imagine that two cases (*dico*) are situated in the first vertex, one in the second (*do*) and six in the third one (*eo*). Since *eo* has more cases, the average position of 'Plautus' is closer to the third vertex. In the same way, each row profile (author) is placed within the triangle as an average point, and the

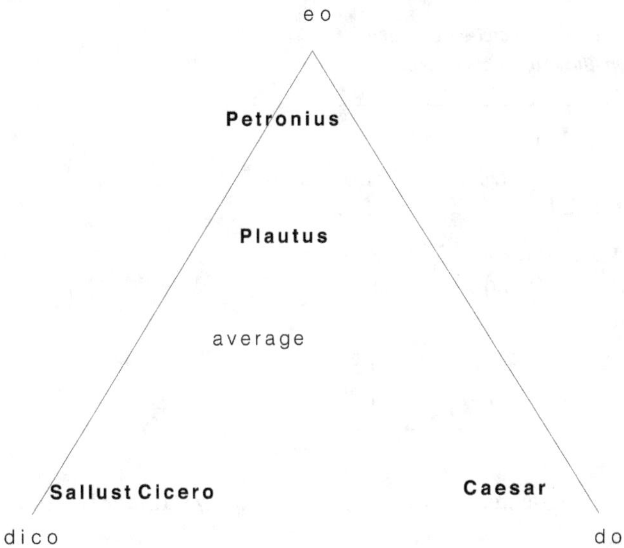

FIG. 7.5 *Geometrical visualization of the row profiles from Table 7.7, including the average profile*

profile values (i.e. the relative frequencies) correspond to weights associated to the vertices; these weights are the masses of the profiles. In addition, the average row profile is the barycentre of the five row profiles, as shown in Figure 7.5: it is centrally positioned among the row profiles, but more attracted to the higher-frequency ones. For this reason, if the row profile points are close to the average row profile, it means that there is little variation in the table.

All I have said about row profiles holds for column profiles as well, and the average column profile is the weighted average of the column profiles. In general, the average column profile coincides with the set of row masses, and the column masses are the elements of the average row profile.

Inertia and chi-square distance. The hypothesis of independence in statistics assumes that there is no significant difference between the rows (or the columns) of a frequency table. Let us consider the example of Table 7.6 and assume that there is no preference in the way the authors used the verbs *dico*, *do* and *eo*: in other words, the variables 'author' and 'verb' are independent. Since there are 9 occurrences of these verbs in Plautus and *dico* takes 40% of the total occurrences (see Table 7.7), I would expect 40% of the 9 occurrences in Plautus (i.e. $0.40 * 9 = 3.6$) to be for *dico*. Similarly, I would expect $0.23 * 9 = 2.07$ occurrences for *do* and $0.36 * 9 = 3.24$ for *eo* in Plautus.

TABLE 7.8 *Matrix of expected frequencies from Table 7.6 under the hypothesis of independence*

Author	Verb		
	Dico	*Do*	*Eo*
Caesar	3.60	2.07	3.24
Cicero	1.60	0.92	1.44
Petronius	5.20	2.99	4.68
Plautus	3.60	2.07	3.24
Sallust	4.80	2.76	4.32

Table 7.8 displays the expected frequencies from Table 7.6 under the independence hypothesis.

If I calculate the relative expected frequencies, I get: $(3.6, 2.07, 3.24)/9 = (0.4, 0.23, 0.36)$ for Plautus and Caesar, $(1.60, 0.92, 1.44)/4 = (0.40, 0.23, 0.36)$ for Cicero, and the same for the other authors. The relative expected frequencies coincide with the average row profile (last row of Table 7.7). The relative observed frequencies coincide with the row profiles (first 5 rows of Table 7.7).

I may then ask the following question: is the difference between expected and observed relative frequencies significant or not? In other words, is it likely that this difference arose by chance? Calculating the chi-square statistics answers this question. From section 7.1:

$$(7.5)\quad \chi^2 = \sum_{i=1}^{i=nr} * \frac{(\text{observed } row_i\text{profile-expected } row_i\text{profile})^2}{\text{expected } row_i\text{profile}} =$$

The (*total*) *inertia* is defined as

$$(7.6)\quad inertia = \frac{\chi^2}{N}$$

where N is the grand total of the table. In the example, $inertia = \frac{45.92}{47} = 0.97$. The total inertia measures how the individual profiles are spread around the weighted average profile, i.e. how much variance is in the table.

We can define a distance that measures how far each profile is from the average profile, thus accounting for how expected the behaviour of the profiles is. The *chi-square distance* between two row profiles i_1 and i_2 is:

$$(7.7)\quad \chi^2(i_1, i_2) = \sum_{j=1}^{c} \frac{(R(i_1,j)-R(i_2,j))^2}{A(j)}$$

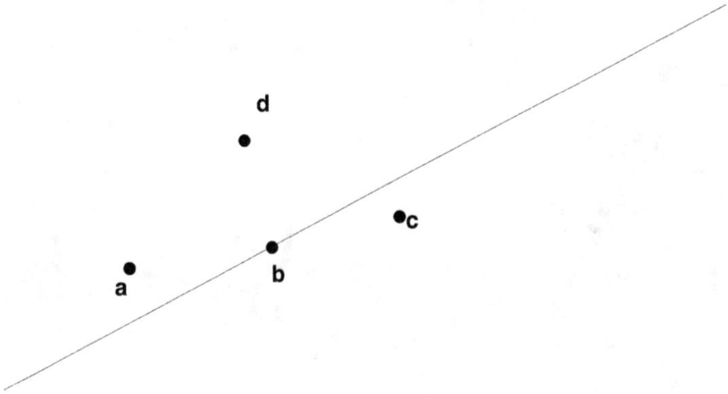

FIG. 7.6 *Four points in a two-dimensional space*

where $A(j)$ is the jth coordinate of the average row profile and $R(i,j)$ is the (i,j)th row profile. In the example, the chi-square distance between 'Plautus' and the barycentre is:

$$(7.8) \quad \sqrt{\frac{(0.22-0.40)^2}{0.40} + \frac{(0.11-0.23)^2}{0.23} + \frac{(0.67-0.36)^2}{0.36}} = 0.64.$$

The corresponding Euclidean distance would be:

$$(7.9) \quad \sqrt{(0.22 - 0.40)^2 + (0.11 - 0.23)^2 + (0.67 - 0.36)^2} = 0.38.$$

The inertia is given by the sum of the mass of each profile multiplied by the chi-square distance between the profile and the barycentre:

$$inertia = \sum_{i=1}^{r} (i\text{-th mass}) * (\chi^2 \text{distance from } i\text{-th profile to barycentre})^2$$

We can obtain an analogous formula for the column profiles. A high inertia corresponds to large deviations of row profiles from the barycentre; the maximal inertia is reached when all the profiles lie at the vertices of the profile space.

Dimensionality reduction. The example in Table 7.6 corresponds to a 3-dimensional space, which can be visualized. More often matrices for CA come with a higher number of columns (i.e. dimensions) so that it is necessary to reduce their dimensionality in order to get a manageable plot. This reduction happens at the expense of a loss of information: CA aims at limiting this loss as much as possible. For this purpose, CA looks for the optimal subspace S that

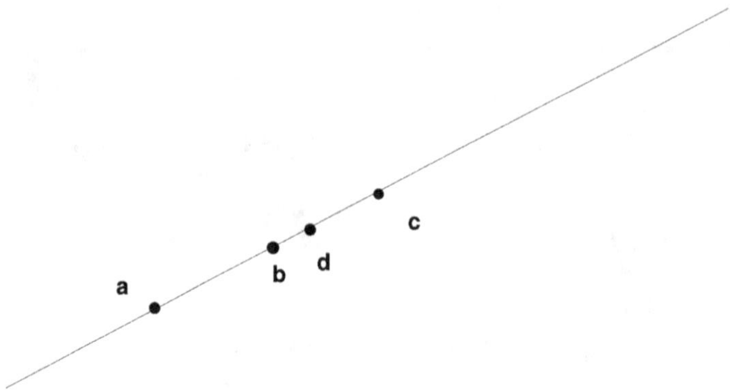

FIG. 7.7 *One-dimensional projection from Figure 7.6*

minimizes the chi-square distance from the profile points. The idea behind this can be visualized with a simple example.

Figure 7.6 shows a two-dimensional space, i.e. a plane, with a line and four points: *a*, *b*, *c*, and *d*. Figure 7.7 shows a one-dimensional space, i.e. a line, with the projections of *a*, *b*, *c*, and *d*. The line covers most of the total variation of the points, thus it is a good representation of the original plane. However, not all the points are equally well projected: for instance, *b* is an optimally represented point, since its projection in Figure 7.7 coincides with its original position in Figure 7.6; *d*, instead, has the least accurate projection.

The optimal subspace *S* is obtained by using the Singular Value Decomposition (SVD), which finds the most "important" components of a matrix. More specifically, a matrix *A* with *r* rows and *c* columns is decomposed by SVD into the product $A = UDV^T$, where *D* is a diagonal matrix with the decreasing positive numbers $\lambda_1, \lambda_2, \ldots, \lambda_k$ in its diagonal and 0 everywhere else. *k* is the rank of *A*.[4] V^T indicates the transpose of *V*[5] and *U* and *V* are so-called orthonormal matrices, i.e. $UU^T = I$ and $VV^T = I$, where *I* is the identity matrix.[6] $\lambda_1, \lambda_2, \ldots, \lambda_k$ are called *singular values*. If we define a matrix *R* as the original matrix *M* divided by the grand total *N*, then SVD is applied to the matrix $R - IB$, since we centre the space on the barycentre *B*. SVD decomposes this matrix as the product UDV^T, where *D* is a diagonal matrix with positive coefficients $\lambda_1 \geq \lambda_2 \geq \ldots \geq \lambda_k$ (singular values) and *U* and *V* are orthonormal matrices.

4 The *rank* of a matrix is the maximal number of linearly independent rows (or equivalently columns) of *A*.

5 The transpose of *V* is the matrix whose rows are the columns of *V*: that is, its (i,j)-th element is $V(j,i)$.

6 The identity matrix is the matrix that has 1 along its diagonal and 0 everywhere else.

The columns of V are the orthonormal basis vectors that define S and are called *principal axes of inertia*; the rows of matrix $F = N * D$ are the projections of the row profiles onto S. SVD, hence, gives all the relevant information to project the original space into the optimal subspace.

Decomposition of inertia. The total inertia of the matrix is decomposed into the direction of the principal axes of inertia. The first axis represents the direction where the inertia of the original cloud of points is maximal; the second axis maximizes the inertia among all the directions orthogonal to the first axis, and so on. Geometrically, rows that contribute highly to a principal axis largely determine it. It can be proven that the reduction of dimensionality of the row profiles and the reduction of dimensionality of the column profiles are solved by the SVD of the same matrix. In addition, the row analysis and the column analysis give the same decomposition of inertia into the principal axes. This explains the French name 'analyse des correspondances' given to CA.

In the previous example, a CA on the data from Table 7.6 gives a decomposition of inertia into 0.67 (70.4%) and 0.28 (29.6%) respectively for the two principal axes. This shows that, together, the two axes account for the whole inertia contained in the data.[7]

Biplot. For $k = 2$ or 3, finding the optimal subspace S allows us to plot the new coordinates in a two or three-dimensional space and get the CA of the row profiles. Then, the points are projected onto this subspace, which constitutes the final plot of the analysis. Since both the row and the column analyses decompose the inertia into the same system of principal axes, I can merge the two representations into one single geometric display which shows at the same time the projections of row and column points in the subspace. Nevertheless, although it is in general possible to interpret the distances between points in the same cloud (either row or column points), the interpretation of distances between points belonging to different clouds is more actively discussed.

Figure 7.8 displays the plot of the CA for Table 7.6. Circles correspond to row points and triangles to column points. This plot is another version of Figure 7.5, since in this case the subspace coincides with the original space. Figure 7.8 shows three clear clusters of points and the similarity between the profiles for Plautus and Petronius on the one hand, and Cicero and Sallust on the other.

---

7 In fact, this case is particularly simple, since the rank k of the matrix is 2, given that the number of columns is 3. In general, the number of principal axes cannot be larger than the rank of the matrix $k \leq min(r-1, c-1)$.

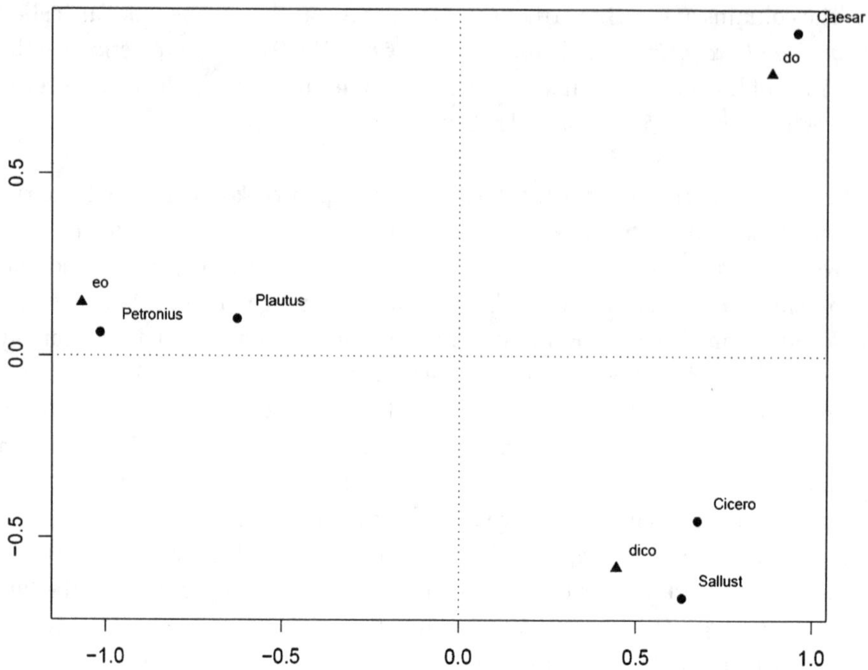

FIG. 7.8 *CA plot for the Table 7.6*

Diagnostics. CA is able to diagnose how faithful this new representation is with respect to the original profile space. In addition, it identifies which points contribute the most to this representation. CA provides a system of diagnostic measures for each of the two dual spaces:

- contributions of the rows (and columns) to the axes, i. e. the inertia of the points projected onto the axes, which contributes to the principal inertia;
- contributions of the axes to the row (and column) points;
- quality of representation (cumulative sum of contributions of the axes for each point); this highlights well represented points.

7.3.0 *Construction and Author*

The investigation on Latin preverbs described in section 6.6 consists of a CA on the dataset collecting all four constructions for the realization of the preverb's *relatum*; this analysis aims at showing the interaction between the variable 'construction' and other relevant variables.

At first, I considered the diachronic variable 'author'. The singular values of a CA on this dataset are reported in Table 7.9, from which we can see that the first two axes account for 89.4% of the total variance in the data.

TABLE 7.9 *Singular values of the CA and percentages of explained inertia for the investigation on the interaction between 'construction' and 'author'*

Axis number	Percentage	Cumulated percentage
1	67.6	67.6
2	21.9	89.4
3	10.6	100.0

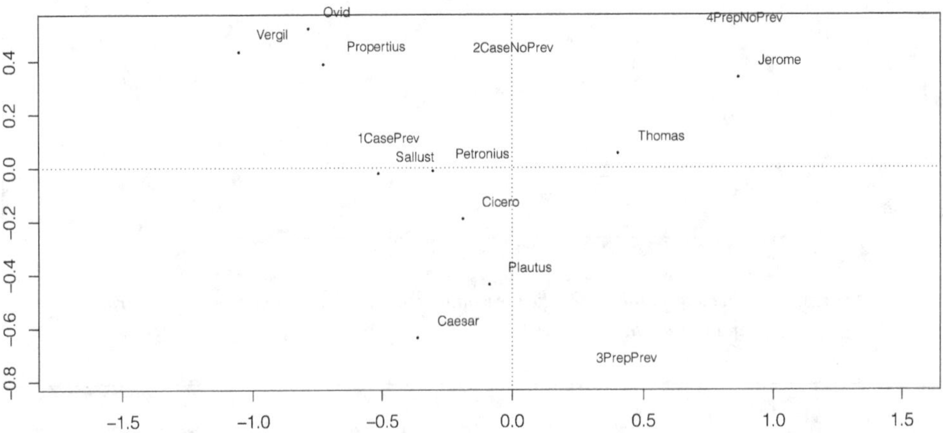

FIG. 7.9 *Plot of the CA for the investigation on the interaction between 'construction' and 'era' in the dataset*

Figure 7.9 shows the two-dimensional plot of the analysis: the points are identified with triangles whose size is proportional to their mass and whose colour intensity is proportional to their quality of representation.

The first axis accounts for most of the inertia (0.26, equal to 67.6% of the total inertia); therefore, I will now concentrate on the horizontal layout of the plot. If I project the points corresponding to the four constructions (as displayed in Figure 7.10, where the diagonal vector corresponds to the first axis), I get, from top right to bottom left, constructions 4 (PrepNoPrev) and 3 (PrepPrev) and then construction 2 (CaseNonPrev) and 1 (CasePrev). Constructions 3 (PrepPrev) and 4 (PrepNoPrev) are strongly associated with the Late era authors (Jerome and Thomas), construction 1 (CasePrev) is strongly associated with Vergil, and construction 2 is somehow shared by the other two poets (Ovid and Propertius), Petronius and Sallust, although the latter ones behave close to expected, as Cicero and Plautus. If I now focus on the vertical

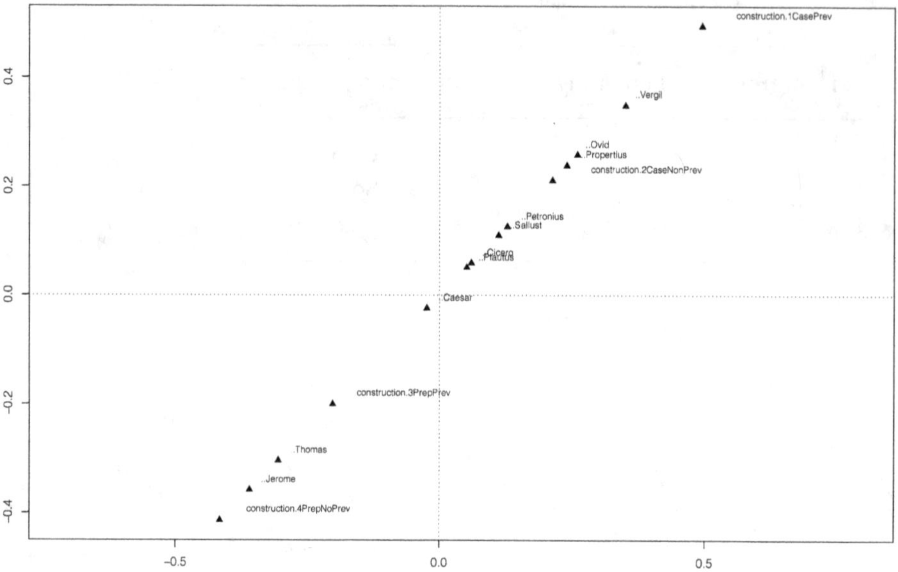

FIG. 7.10 *First axis of the CA for the investigation on the interaction between 'construction' and 'author' in the dataset*

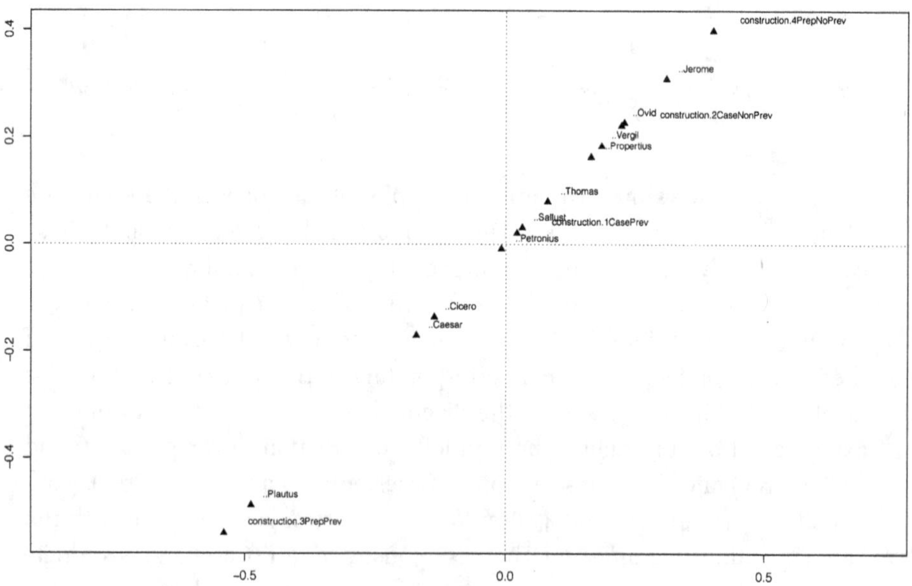

FIG. 7.11 *Second axis of the CA for the investigation on the interaction between 'construction' and 'author'*

TABLE 7.10 *CA diagnostics of the row points for the investigation on the interaction between 'construction' and 'author'. For each profile, the table contains its mass (second column), the quality of its display in the subspace (third column), its inertia in permills of the total inertia (fourth column), its coordinates in each dimension (fifth and eight columns), the (relative) contribution of the principal axes to the point's inertia (sixth and ninth columns), and the (absolute) contribution of the point to the inertia of the axes in permills of the principal inertia (seventh and tenth columns).*

Name	Mass	Qlt	Inr	K=1	Cor	Ctr	K=2	Cor	Ctr
Caesar	20	888	31	-354	211	10	-635	678	95
Cicero	48	184	47	-179	86	6	-191	98	21
Jerome	96	887	248	875	772	283	338	115	130
Ovid	42	989	97	-774	681	98	520	308	136
Petronius	113	853	30	-294	851	38	-11	1	0
Plautus	190	956	101	-78	29	4	-437	927	430
Propertius	42	999	73	-717	775	84	386	224	75
Sallust	82	923	59	-505	921	80	-22	2	0
Thomas	320	868	164	411	854	208	53	14	11
Vergil	45	998	150	-1044	852	190	433	146	101

TABLE 7.11 *CA diagnostics of the column points for the investigation on the interaction between 'construction' and 'author'*

Name	Mass	Qlt	Inr	K=1	Cor	Ctr	K=2	Cor	Ctr
1.CasePrev	144	889	361	-925	887	474	37	1	2
2.CaseNonPrev	331	616	125	-228	357	66	195	260	149
3.PrepPrev	337	999	169	203	213	53	-390	786	608
4.PrepNoPrev	187	949	345	752	796	406	329	153	241

axis (also displayed in Figure 7.11 in the form of a diagonal vector), I see that this axis isolates Plautus, strongly associated with construction 3 (PrepPrev), from the others.

Tables 7.10 and 7.11 show the diagnostics of the analysis: for each profile point (first column), they contain its mass (second column), the quality of its display in the subspace (third column), its inertia in permills of the total inertia (fourth column), its coordinates in each dimension (fifth and eight columns), the (relative) contribution of the principal axes to the point's inertia (sixth and ninth columns), and the (absolute) contribution of the point to the inertia of the axes in permills of the principal inertia (seventh and tenth columns). The values displayed in this table confirm the high mass and low inertia of the third construction and the Late era.

7.3.1 *Multiple Correspondence Analysis*

MCA is a generalized extension of CA that can handle more than two variables. The input to an MCA is a matrix whose rows correspond to observations and whose columns correspond to the values of the variables; the cell values of this matrix are ones or zeros, depending on whether the observations appear with the variable values or not.

The interpretation of an MCA plot is similar to the one of a simple CA. I performed an MCA by using the *mjca* function of the *ca* package in R (R Development Core Team, 2008) and setting the parameter lambda="adjusted". As pointed out by the authors in the package's manual (Greenacre and Nenadic, 2009), this means that the MCA is performed so that "the optimal scaling properties of MCA are conserved while raising the percentages of inertia". I plotted the results of the MCA analyses by setting the 'map' parameter to 'symmetric', which plots the row and column points in principal coordinates. I performed an MCA on the same dataset used in section 7.3.0.1, but encoded with a higher number of variables, as illustrated in section 6.6:

- 'construction'
- 'era'
- 'preverb'
- 'sp_relatum'
- 'class'
- 'case'

Table 7.12 contains the singular values, the explained inertia, the percentage of inertia, and the cumulated percentage of inertia of this analysis; Figure 7.12 shows the plot and Table 7.13 displays the diagnostics.

TABLE 7.12 *Singular values and inertia explained from the MCA for the investigation on the interaction between 'construction,' 'era,' 'case,' 'sp_relatum,' and 'class'*

Axis number	Inertia	Percentage	Cumulated Percentage
1	0.0348	34.6	34.6
2	0.018	18.5	53.0
3	0.011	11.0	64.0
4	0.004	4.0	68.1
5	<0.001	0.4	68.5
6	<0.001	0.1	68.6
7	<0.001	0.0	68.6
	Total: 0.099		

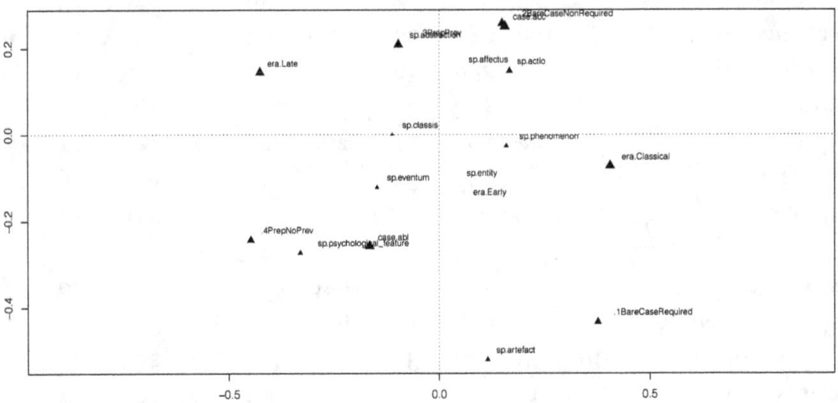

FIG. 7.12 *Plot of the MCA for the investigation on the interaction between 'construction,' 'era,' 'case,' 'sp_relatum,' and 'class.' N.B.: The labels for 'sp.abstraction' and '3PrepPrev' partially overlap.*

TABLE 7.13 *MCA diagnostics of the column points for the investigation on the interaction between 'construction', 'era', 'case', 'sp_relatum', and 'class'. For each profile, the table contains its mass (second column), the quality of its display in the subspace (third column), its inertia in permills of the total inertia (fourth column), its coordinates in each dimension (fifth and eight columns), the (relative) contribution of the principal axes to the point's inertia (sixth and ninth columns), and the (absolute) contribution of the point to the inertia of the axes in permills of the principal inertia (seventh and tenth columns).*

Name	Mass	Qlt	Inr	K=1	Cor	Ctr	K=2	Cor	Ctr
1CasePrev	29	563	113	357	267	20	-376	295	31
2CaseNonPrev	67	434	86	166	176	10	202	258	20
3PrepPrev	65	75	45	-78	71	2	19	4	0
4PrepNoPrev	39	545	112	-431	517	39	-100	28	3
era.Classical	85	566	80	245	513	28	-79	53	4
era.Early	23	20	39	61	18	0	20	2	0
era.Late	92	563	83	-241	523	29	67	40	3
case.abl	93	272	22	-87	259	4	-20	13	0
case.acc	106	281	20	78	263	4	21	18	0
sp.abstraction	91	258	12	-62	247	2	13	11	0
sp.actio	16	433	37	315	339	8	165	93	3
sp.affectus	4	183	11	206	122	1	146	61	1
sp.artefact	6	397	55	213	41	2	-625	356	18
sp.classis	1	349	11	-823	326	2	-219	23	0
sp.entity	77	39	14	24	26	0	17	14	0
sp.eventum	1	546	11	-1046	506	4	-294	40	0
sp.phenomenon	2	572	14	653	467	4	-310	105	1
sp.psychological_feature	3	546	56	-1046	506	19	-294	40	2
class.motion	141	484	27	-15	9	0	-106	474	12
class.rest	25	401	107	196	74	5	413	328	32
class.transport	34	140	45	-92	51	2	122	89	4

Then, I worked on the following variables, as illustrated on page 174:

- 'preposition'
- 'era'
- type of complement ('compl')
- animacy of the lexical filler of the verb's complement ('a')

TABLE 7.14 *Singular values of the MCA for the investigation on the interaction between 'preposition', 'era', type of complement ('compl'), and animacy of the lexical filler of the verb's complement ('a')*

Nr	Value	Percentage	Cumulated Percentage
1	0.036	80.9	79.5
2	0.001	2.7	83.7
	Total: 0.099		

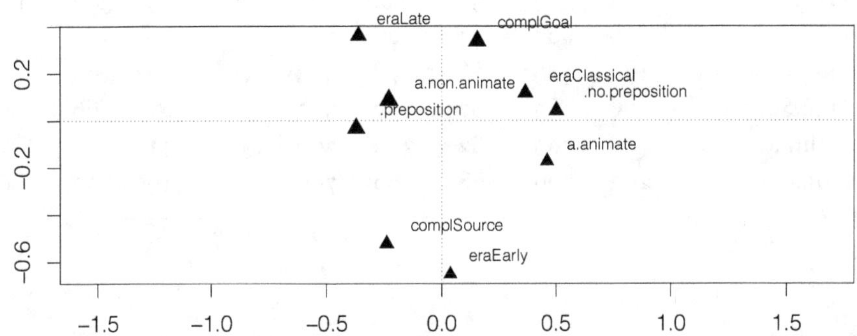

FIG. 7.13 *Plot of the MCA for the investigation on the interaction between 'preposition', 'era', type of complement ('compl'), and animacy of the lexical filler of the verb's complement ('a')*

Table 7.14 contains the singular values of the MCA on this dataset, from which we can see that the first two axes account for 83.7 % of the total variance in the data.

Figure 7.13 shows the two-dimensional plot and Table 7.15 displays the diagnostics of the analysis.

TABLE 7.15 *MCA diagnostics of the column points for the investigation on 'preposition', 'era', type of complement ('compl'), and animacy of the lexical filler of the verb's complement ('a'). For each profile, the table contains its mass (second column), the quality of its display in the subspace (third column), its inertia in permills of the total inertia (fourth column), its coordinates in each dimension (fifth and eight columns), the (relative) contribution of the principal axes to the point's inertia (sixth and ninth columns), and the (absolute) contribution of the point to the inertia of the axes in permills of the principal inertia (seventh and tenth columns).*

Name	Mass	Qlt	Inr	K=1	Cor	Ctr	K=2	Cor	Ctr
no.preposition	89	597	256	310	597	47	-6	0	0
preposition	161	597	140	-170	597	26	3	0	0
eraClassical	89	657	121	221	652	24	20	5	1
eraEarly	55	379	31	32	32	0	105	347	17
eraLate	106	605	134	-202	585	24	-38	20	4
complGoal	174	589	36	78	523	6	-28	66	4
complSource	76	589	82	-177	523	13	63	66	8
a.animate	48	709	162	363	700	35	41	9	2
a.non.animate	202	709	38	-86	700	8	-10	9	1

CHAPTER 8

Latin Computational Linguistics

8.1 A New Field

The term 'method' refers to a systematic procedure for reaching a goal. In other words, method is the way we do things. In this book I have proposed the use of computational and quantitative methods to study the Latin language. Based on this methodological choice, I define the field of Latin Computational Linguistics as the linguistic field dealing with data from the Latin language and employing computational methods. The originality of this approach is made evident by the new perspective it offers on *how* to tackle traditional issues in Latin Linguistics, as well as on *what* we can investigate, paving the way to new questions in this field.

Computational Linguistics and quantitative Corpus Linguistics offer valuable resources and techniques for doing what Latin linguists have always done, but more efficiently, more systematically, and with better coverage. What is more, these methods allow them to perform tasks they could not have even conceived before.

For example, annotated corpora enable researchers to carry out extensive studies based on large amounts of richly analysed data, overcoming the obstacles typical of small-scale analyses. So, corpora allow us to answer questions like "what is the distribution of preverbal subjects in Augustan poets?". Rather than collecting a sample of texts by Augustan poets and performing the analysis from scratch, I propose to use large corpora that have been independently annotated according to publicly available guidelines, and possibly further enriched with computational tools; this provides the community with a basis for systematic and replicable investigations.

Moreover, the availability of large corpora challenges traditional approaches to text data, because the best way to make sense of large datasets is to employ specific, advanced statistical techniques, going beyond the simple inspection of raw frequencies. This view on historical data makes it possible to adopt new strategies and tackle research questions that could not be asked with traditional methods. As I have shown in the study on preverbs (chapter 6), detecting diachronic trends and patterns in the data, for example, is best achieved with a quantitative approach that measures the significance and the role played by different factors in a linguistic phenomenon. This means that we can effectively explore questions such as "Is the difference between

 | DOI: 10.1163/9789004260122_009

the preference of Caesar for construction A over construction B significant or not?", "Is this correlated with the length of sentences?", "Do the data highlight a diachronic trend?".

8.2 New Resources and New Methods

This work makes a number of important contributions. One contribution is a new lexical resource for the study of Latin verbs, namely the valency lexicon described in chapter 3. This lexicon is the first corpus-based one for Latin. As such, it is fundamentally original with respect to previous Latin valency lexicons (such as Happ 1976), for what concerns its content, the flexible access to its content, its possible uses, and the definition of valency it relies on. Valency information in Latin dictionaries and thesauri is usually incomplete (especially for common verbs), because lexicographers lacked the tools for systematically recording and summarizing valency patterns in all Latin texts, and the users could anyway not make sense of huge amounts of data that had not been selected and filtered.

The approach I followed is radically different. I used two syntactically annotated corpora, built with computational techniques and covering around 150,000 word occurrences. Even if I did not use a complete corpus of Latin because it does not exist in a usable format yet, I was still not limited by space issues when I designed the lexicon, and the methodology I adopted can be applied to a much larger corpus, as soon as it becomes accessible. The availability of the data and the way I processed them has made a huge difference to the end result. The lexicon contains frequency information on verbal arguments occurring in the two Latin treebanks. In addition to valency patterns, it includes information on verbal morphology, as well as morphological and lexical features of the arguments. Following the approach taken in lexical acquisition research in Computational Linguistics, I give a corpus-based definition of valency patterns, which contrasts with the example-based approach followed in traditional Latin dictionaries. Valency patterns are all the sequences of verbal arguments lexically realized in the treebanks (so for example they do not contain omitted arguments); as such, their definition relies on the syntactic annotation of the treebanks and does not rely on subjective selection.

The crucial frequency information contained in the valency lexicon allows for further corpus-based synchronic and diachronic investigations on verbal argument structure which account for language usage. An example of that is given by the case study on Latin preverbs reported on in chapter 6. It is the first study on Latin preverbs which at the same time is quantitative and uses processed data from freely available annotated corpora. This study has allowed me to demonstrate the potential of statistical techniques for diachronic linguistics. The results confirm quantitatively that the argument structure of Latin prefixed verbs is a complex phenomenon, where a number of different morphological, lexical, and semantic factors interact with diachronic variables, showing a very rich picture.

The multivariate techniques I have employed are a very good way to detect and quantify variation, and thus identify patterns in highly complex linguistic data. Following a view shared by several scholars in different frameworks (see e.g. Milroy 1993; Denison 2003; Lightfoot 2006), I consider variation as the key for language change. Thanks to statistical techniques which are able to highlight variation, I have detected a general diachronic trend which corroborates a partial tendency towards the use of prepositional phrases with prefixed verbs, while the bare-case construction occurred already in the Classical era. This change can be connected with a lexicalization process and partially framed within the shift that took place from the satellite-framed group (Latin) to the verb-framed one (Romance languages), according to Talmy's typology of space. The statistical analyses also show that for some authors in the corpora there is so little data evidence that it is not possible to give reliable estimations. This result offers an empirical answer to the question of what should be included in a corpus in order to achieve reliable results; by quantifying the level of confidence of the estimates, these techniques are able to accurately identify possible gaps in the composition of the corpus.

The study on preverbs has also given me the chance to suggest a further methodological innovation for Latin Linguistics, which provides solid empirical grounds to the linguistic interpretation. This is a common procedure in empirical research, where the phases of collection of the data (corpus), analysis (annotation), and interpretation (quantitative studies) are kept distinct. Computational methods help with the first two phases, providing annotated data. Quantitative methods contribute to the third phase, where the complexity of the phenomenon studied is best handled by specific techniques (such as multivariate statistics) that account simultaneously for the contribution of different factors; this is not possible with simpler approaches based on percentages, for instance. In addition, this approach is an innovation with respect to the traditional practice where the researcher is in charge of all phases from collecting the example material to interpreting the results in light of certain linguistic theories.

8.2.1 *Computational Models and Latin*

This work does not only contribute to advances in Latin Linguistics: it also aims at inspiring computational linguists. Building on the valency lexicon, I have proposed a computational model for investigating the lexical-semantic properties of Latin verbal arguments (in terms of selectional preferences) through two approaches: one based on an external ontology, and one based on distributional measures. The former approach relies on the relations of synonymy and hyperonymy as defined in Latin WordNet, while the latter measures the similarity between two words in terms of the syntactic and lexical contexts they share. This research is an example of automatic semantic processing of Latin, which is a computationally less-resourced language. It also provides an example of how to overcome similar difficulties shared by other dead and/or less-resourced languages.

Since there are no semantically annotated corpora for Latin that are of sufficiently large size, my system exploits both existing resources for Latin (treebanks and Latin WordNet) and computational models developed for English (Alishahi, 2008). In this process, I tailored Alishahi's model to the features of the Latin corpora used. This adaptation was challenging because it required solutions to several problems, among which the small size and the low coverage of the resources available were the most severe ones. Moreover, the evaluation phase gave me the chance to compare the performance of the supervised system which relies on WordNet with the unsupervised one based on a distributional measure of similarity calculated on a much larger, automatically parsed corpus. The results show that the former system performs better, which suggests that the supervised procedures seem to be currently the best choice, given the less-resourced status of Latin. However, more research is necessary to investigate whether other distributional models, paired with large corpora, can provide better results: this would pave the way for an unsupervised approach to Latin computational semantics.

8.3 Expanding the Field

The research reported on here covers a range of linguistic topics, each of which can be further developed as the field of Latin Computational Linguistics expands. First, the method for extracting the valency lexicon is fully automatic, hence it can be adapted to other Latin treebanks, both existing ones (such as the PROIEL treebank) and future ones. Furthermore, for the same reason the lexicon can of course be extended as the input treebanks grow in size. Additionally, more information could be included in the lexicon, such as verb senses, the distinction between optional and obligatory arguments of verbs, or valency frame alternations. This could be achieved by drawing upon previous research in Computational Linguistics, where these tasks have been tackled by a number of supervised and unsupervised systems (McCarthy, 2001; Korhonen and Briscoe, 2004; Vlachos et al., 2009).

Second, the selectional preference acquisition system can be improved by including a Word Sense Disambiguation module that assigns different weights to the different word senses contributing to the definition of semantic properties, depending on their frequency. In addition, for the evaluation I performed a comparison between the WordNet version of the system and the distributional one. This comparison could be further developed in order to find the best distributional model for selectional preferences of Latin verbs. This result would help the performance of the system and, at the same time, provide new insights on the semantics of Latin verbs and on their syntax-semantics interface.

Third, the results I have obtained on Latin spatial preverbs have a number of possible future developments. The methodology I have proposed, based on an empirical approach which relies on multivariate statistics, can take into account other important variables potentially affecting the realization of verbal arguments of prefixed verbs. In addition, the range of authors analysed could be increased thanks to the availability of new annotated corpora. In particular, if this reduced the unique associations between chronological eras and genres, it would be possible to assign the trend I have detected to stylistic and diachronic effects.

8.4 A New Paradigm

Innovations in linguistics are usually thought of in terms of new theories, applications of new theories to old data, or analyses of new, hitherto ignored data. Instead, the original contribution of this book lies in its innovative *view* on the field of Historical Linguistics, and Latin Linguistics in particular. This new view is grounded on computational methods and exploits existing collections of Latin texts, aiming at showing how new resources can be built from these collections and how they can be quantitatively analysed. I strongly believe that this approach can enrich the conclusions offered by tradition and help reach further goals in research.

The methodological contribution of this book is intrinsically cross-disciplinary, because it defines Latin Computational Linguistics from the combination of computational methods and Latin data. This approach obviously requires a great deal of technical expertise, while at the same time demanding solid understanding of the theoretical issues involved. Ideally, such work should be carried out by researchers with a non superficial command of both fields, although this might sometimes be difficult to achieve in practice. In lieu of the widespread availability of such cross-disciplinary background, I propose that both historical linguists and computational linguists have a responsibility to acquaint themselves with each other's fields and together explore how the study of linguistic phenomena can be furthered. I also hope that computational and historical linguists alike will be inspired by this work and seek to establish fruitful collaborations in the future. Finally, I have demonstrated that Computational Linguistics has more to offer to historical linguists than a set of tools: it provides a wide selection of flexible models and techniques that in themselves can provide new insights into historical linguistic processes. As such, this constitutes a new perspective in the study of linguistic phenomena, in the spirit of the proposals set forth in Geeraerts (2006).

My work will hopefully have illustrated what can be achieved when traditional barriers between subdisciplines are transcended. I strongly believe that this is an unavoidable step in the digital era. Latin Linguistics, as the other humanistic disciplines, has already started to be affected by the enormous changes in society caused by the new technologies and media, and this process will only continue. The availability of huge amounts of data has already changed our access to information and our view on it (see, for example, Mayer-Schönberger and Cukier (2013)), and quantitative methods are essential to handle these data; moreover, collaboration permeates so many aspects of our work, and digital means facilitate it even further. Historical data are no exception, and I believe that research in Latin Linguistics can only progress through such an approach. Far from taking over each other's roles, Historical and Computational Linguistics can enter into a truly productive symbiosis.

Bibliography

Alishahi, A. (2008). *A probabilistic model of early argument structure acquisition*. Ph. D. thesis, Department of Computer Science, University of Toronto.

Allen, A. (1981). The development of prefixal and parasynthetic verbs in Latin and Romance. *Romance Philology XXXV*(1), 79–88.

Attardi, G. (2006). Experiments with a multilanguage non-projective Dependency Parser. In *Proceedings of the Tenth Conference on Computational Natural Language Learning (CoNLL-X). New York City*, pp. 166–170. Association for Computational Linguistics.

Baayen, R.H. (2008). *Analyzing Linguistic Data*. Cambridge: Cambridge University Press.

Baker, C., C. Fillmore, and J. Lowe (1998). The Berkeley FrameNet project. In *Proceedings of COLING-ACL 1998. Montreal.*

Bamman, D. and G. Crane (2006). The design and use of a Latin dependency treebank. In J. Hajič and J. Nivre (Eds.), *Proceedings of the Fifth International Workshop on Treebanks and Linguistic Theories (TLT 2006). Prague*, pp. 67–78. ÚFAL MFF UK.

Bamman, D. and G. Crane (2007). The Latin Dependency Treebank in a cultural heritage digital library. In *Proceedings of the Workshop on Language Technology for Cultural Heritage Data (LaTeCH 2007). Prague*, pp. 33–40.

Bamman, D. and G. Crane (2008). Building a dynamic lexicon from a digital library. In *Proceedings of the 8th ACM/IEEE-CS Joint Conference on Digital Libraries (JCDL 2008). Pittsburgh.*

Barðdal, J. (2009). The Development of Case in Germanic. In J. Barðdal and S.L. Chelliah (Eds.), *The Role of Semantic, Pragmatic and Discourse Factors in the Development of Case*, pp. 123–159. Amsterdam: John Benjamins.

Barðdal, J., T. Smitherman, V. Bjarnadóttir, S. Danesi, G.B. Jenset, and B. McGillivray (2012). Reconstructing constructional semantics: the dative subject construction in Old Norse-Icelandic, Latin, Ancient Greek, Old Russian and Old Lithuanian. *Studies in Language 36*(3), 511–547.

Bayerische Akademie der Wissenschaften (2002). Thesaurus Linguae Latinae (CD-ROM). http://www.thesaurus.badw.de/english/index.htm.

Bennett, C.E. (1914). *Syntax of early Latin*, Volume II—The Cases. Boston: Allyn and Bacon.

Benveniste, E. (1949). Le système sublogique des prépositions en latin. *Travaux du Cercle Linguistique de Copenhague V. Recherches structurales*, 177–184.

Benzécri, J.-P. (1973). *L'Analyse des Données*, Volume 1. Dunod.

Bilisoly, R. (2008). *Practical text mining with Perl*. Wiley.

Bloomfield, L. (1933). *Language*. New York: Holt.

 | DOI: 10.1163/9789004260122_010

Booij, G. and A. van Kemenade (2003). Preverbs: an introduction. In Booij, Geert and van Marle, Jaap (Ed.), *Yearbook of Morphology*, pp. 1–11. Dordrecht: Kluwer Academic Publishers.

Bortolussi, B. (2005). Le double accusatif aver le verbes préfixés en *circum-* et *trans-*. In C. Moussy (Ed.), *La composition et la préverbation en latin*, pp. 277–292. Presses de l'Université Paris-Sorbonne.

Brachet, J.P. (2000). *Recherches sur les préverbes* de- *et* ex- *du latin*. Bruxelles: Latomus. Revue d'études Latines.

Brachet, J.-P. (2005). Préverbes en *intro* en cours de constitution chez Plaute et Térence. In C. Moussy (Ed.), *La composition et la préverbation en latin*, pp. 309–320. Presses de l'Université Paris-Sorbonne.

Brinton, L.J. and E.C. Traugott (2005). *Lexicalization and language change*. Cambridge: Cambridge University Press.

Brucale, L. (2011, September). Manner of motion verbs in Latin. abstract.

Brucale, L., C. Iacobini, and E. Mocciaro (2011, September). Typological change in the expression of motion events from Latin to Romance languages. abstract.

Buchholz, S. and E. Marsi (2006). CoNLL-X shared task on multilingual dependency parsing. In *Proceedings of the X CoNLL Shared Task*, pp. 149–164.

Busa, R. (1974–1980). *Index Thomisticus: sancti Thomae Aquinatis operum omnium indices et concordantiae, in quibus verborum omnium et singulorum formae et lemmata cum suis frequentiis et contextibus variis modis referuntur quaeque / consociata plurium opera atque electronico IBM automato usus digessit Robertus Busa SJ.* Stuttgart – Bad Cannstatt: Frommann – Holzboog.

Carvalho, P. d. (1998). La grammaire de la préverbation ou: préverbation et "ergativité". In B. García-Hernández (Ed.), *Estudios de Lingüística latina. Actas del IX Coloquio Internacional de Lingüística Latina. Universidad Autonóma de Madrid, 1997*, pp. 273–289. Ediciones Clásicas.

Castiglioni, L. and S. Mariotti (1993). *IL vocabolario della lingua latina*. Loescher.

Centre Traditio Litterarum Occidentalium (2010). Library of Latin Texts (CLCLT-6).

CETEDOC (1999). Bibliotecha Teubneriana Latina. CD-ROM.

Cohen, J. (1988). *Statistical power analysis for the behavioral sciences* (2th ed.). Hillsdale, NJ: Lawrence Erlbaum.

Coleman, R. (1991). Latin prepositional syntax in Indo-European perspective. In R. Coleman (Ed.), *New Studies in Latin Linguistics. Selected papers from the 4th International Colloquium on Latin Linguistics. Cambridge, 1987*, Cambridge, UK, pp. 323–338. John Benjamins.

Covington, M.A. (1990). A dependency parser for variable-word-order languages. Technical report, Artificial Intelligence Programs, University of Georgia. AI-1990-01.

Craig, C. and K. Hale (1988). Relational preverbs in some languages of the Americas: typological and historical perspectives. *Language 64*(2), 312–344.

Crane, G. (1991). Generating and parsing Classical Greek. *Literary and Linguistic Computing* 6(4), 243–245.

Crocco Galèas, G. and C. Iacobini (1992). Parasintesi e doppio stadio derivativo nella formazione verbale del latino. *Archivio Glottologico Italiano* 77, 167–199.

Croft, W. (2000). *Explaining language change: An evolutionary approach.* London: Longman.

Cruse, A. (2011). *Meaning in Language.* Oxford Textbooks in linguistics. Oxford: Oxford University Press.

Cuzzolin, P. (1995). A proposito di *sub vos placo* e della grammaticalizzazione delle adposizioni. *Archivio Glottologico Italiano* 80, 122–143.

Cuzzolin, P., I. Putzu, and P. Ramat (2006). The Indo-European Adverb in diachronic and typological perspective. *Indogermanische Forschungen* 111, 1–38.

De Vivo, A. (1994). Lingua e comico in Plauto. *Bollettino di studi latini* 24(2), 417–431.

Denison, D. (2003). Log(ist)ic and simplistic S-curves. In R. Hickey (Ed.), *Motives for language change*, pp. 54–70. Cambridge: Cambridge University Press.

Dufresne, M., F. Dupuis, and M. Tremblay (2003). Preverbs and particles in Old French. In Booij, Geert and van Marle, Jaap (Ed.), *Yearbook of Morphology*, pp. 33–59. Dordrecht: Kluwer Academic Publishers.

Durante, M. (1981). *Dal latino all'italiano moderno. Saggio di storia linguistica e culturale.* Bologna: Zanichelli.

Echarte Cossío, M.J. (1998). Preposiciones y casos en latín: propuesta de un sistema conjuncto. In B. García-Hernández (Ed.), *Estudios de Lingüística latina. Actas del IX Coloquio Internacional de Lingüística latina. Universidad Autonóma de Madrid, 1997*, pp. 309–323. Ediciones Clásicas.

Ernout, A. and F. Thomas (1972). *Syntaxe latine.* Paris: Klincksieck.

Evert, S. (2006). How Random is a Corpus? The Library Metaphor. *Zeitschrift für Anglistik und Amerikanistik* 54(2), 177–190.

Faraway, J.J. (2006). *Extending the linear model with R.* Boca Raton, FL: Chapman & Hall/CRC.

Firth, J.R. (1957). *Studies in Linguistic Analysis*, Chapter A synopsis of linguistic theory 1930–1955, pp. 1–32. Oxford: Philological Society.

Fischer, I. (1971). Encore sur le caractère de la langue de Plaute. *Studclas* 13, 59–78.

Forcellini, E. (1940). *Lexicon totius latinitatis* (fifth ed.). Padova: Typis Seminarii.

Fruyt, M. (1998). La grammaticalisation en latin. In B. García-Hernández (Ed.), *Estudios de Lingüística latina. Actas del IX Coloquio Internacional de Lingüística latina., Universidad Autonóma de Madrid, 1997*, pp. 877–889. Ediciones Clásicas.

García-Hernández, B. (2005). L'antonymie aspectuelle des préverbes allatifs et ablatifs. In C. Moussy (Ed.), *La composition et la préverbation en latin*, pp. 229–241. Presses de l'Université Paris-Sorbonne.

Geeraerts, D. (2006). Methodology in cognitive linguistics. In G. Kristiansen, M. Achard,

R. Dirven, and F.J. Ruiz de Mendoza Ibáñez (Eds.), *Cognitive linguistics: Current applications and future perspectives*, pp. 21–50. Berlin: Mouton de Gruyter.

Gelman, A., Y.-S. Su, M. Yajima, J. Hill, M.G. Pittau, J. Kerman, and T. Zheng (2009). *arm: Data Analysis Using Regression and Multilevel/Hierarchical Models*. R package version 1.2-9.

Giacomelli, R. (1993). *Storia della lingua latina*. Roma: Jouvence.

Goldberg, A. (2006). *Constructions at Work: The Nature of Generalization in Language*. Oxford: Oxford University Press.

Goldberg, A.E. (1995). *Constructions: a construction grammar approach to argument structure*. The University of Chicago Press.

Gorard, S. (2003). *Quantitative methods in social science*. New York/London: Continuum.

Greenacre, M. (2007). *Correspondence Analysis in practice* (2th ed.). Boca Raton, FL: Chapman & Hall/CRC.

Greenacre, M. and O. Nenadic (2009). *ca: Simple, Multiple and Joint Correspondence Analysis*. R package version 0.3-2.

Hajič, J., J. Panevova, Z. Uresova, and A. Bemova (1999). Annotations at analytical level: Instructions for annotators (English translation by Z. Kirschner). Technical report, UFAL MFF UK, Prague.

Hajič, J., J. Panevová, Z. Urešová, A. Bémová, V. Kolárová-Rezníckova, and P. Pajas (2003). PDT-VALLEX: Creating a large coverage valency lexicon for treebank annotation. In J. Nivre and E. Hinrichs (Eds.), *Proceedings of the Second Workshop on Treebanks and Linguistic Theories (TLT 2003). Växjö*, Volume 9, pp. 57–68. Växjö University Press.

Halácsy, P., A. Kornai, and C. Oravecz (2007). HunPos, an open source trigram tagger. In *Proceedings of the ACL 2007 Demo and Poster Sessions*, pp. 209–212.

Happ, H. (1976). *Grundfragen einer Dependenz-Grammatik des Lateinischen. Goettingen*. Vandenhoeck & Ruprecht.

Haug, D.T.T. and M.L. Jøndal (2008). Creating a parallel treebank of the old Indo-European Bible translations. In *Proceedings of Language Technologies for Cultural Heritage Workshop (LREC 2008). Marrakech*, pp. 27–34.

Haverling, G. (2000). *On SCO- verbs, prefixes and semantic functions*. Number 64 in Studia Graeca et Latina Gothoburgensia. Göteborg: Acta Universitatis Gothoburgensis.

Heine, B., U. Claudi, and F. Hünnemeyer (1991). *Grammaticalization. A conceptual framework*. Chicago/London: The University of Chicago Press.

Herbst, T., D. Heath, I.F. Roe, and D. Götz (2004). *A valency Dictionary of English. A corpus-based analysis of the Complementation Patterns of English Verbs, Nouns and Adjectives*. Berlin/New York: Mouton de Gruyter.

Hewson, J. and V. Bubenik (2006). *From case to adposition*. Amsterdam/Philadelphia: John Benjamins.

Hinton, P.R. (2004). *Statistics explained*. Routledge.

Hofmann, J.B.H. (1980). *La lingua d'uso latina* (Italian ed.). Bologna: Pàtron. Translated by Licinio Ricottilli.

Iacobini, C. (2005). I verbi italiani come base di derivazione prefissale. In *La formazione delle parole. Atti del XXXVII Congresso internazionale di studi della Società di linguistica italiana (SLI). L'Aquila, 25–27 settembre 2003*, Roma, pp. 289–307. Bulzoni.

Iacobini, C. and F. Masini (2007). Verb-particle constructions and prefixed verbs in Italian: typology, diachrony and semantics. In G. Booij, B. Fradin, A. Ralli, and S. Scalise (Eds.), *On-line Proceedings of the Fifth Mediterranean Morphology Meeting (MMM5)*, pp. 157–184. Università degli Studi di Bologna.

Ikegami, Y. (1987). Source vs Goal: A Case of Linguistic Dissymmetry. In R. Dirven and G. Radden (Eds.), *Concepts of Case*, pp. 122–146. Tübingen: Günter Narr Verlag.

Imbert, C. (2008). *Systems dynamics and functional motivations in Path coding. A typological description of Homeric Greek and Old English*. Ph. D. thesis, CNRS / University of Lyon 2.

Jackendoff, R. (1990). *Semantic structures*. Cambridge, MA: MIT Press.

Jacobson, R. (1966). Linguistica e poetica. In L. Heilmann and L. Grassi (Eds.), *Saggi di linguistica generale* (Italian translation ed.)., pp. 181–218. Milano: Feltrinelli.

Janssen, H.H. (1988). *La lingua poetica latina* (Italian ed.)., Chapter Le caratteristiche della lingua poetica romana, pp. 67–130. Bologna: Patron. Translated by Aldo Lunelli.

Jenset, G.B. (2010). *A Corpus-based Study on the Evolution of* There*: Statistical Analysis and Cognitive Interpretation*. Ph. D. thesis, University of Bergen.

Kilgarriff, A., P. Rychly, P. Smrz, and D. Tugwell (2004). The Sketch Engine. In G. Williams and S. Vessier (Eds.), *Proceedings of the eleventh Euralex International Congress*, Lorient, pp. 105–116. Université de Bretagne-Sud.

Kingsbury, P. and M. Palmer (2002). From Treebank to Propbank. In *Proceedings of the Third International Conference on Language Resources and Evaluation (LREC 2002)*, Las Palmas, Canary Islands.

Koch, U. (1993). The enhancement of a dependency parser for Latin. Technical Report AI-1993-03, Artificial Intelligence Programs, University of Georgia.

Korhonen, A. (2002). *Subcategorization acquisition*. Ph. D. thesis, University of Cambridge, Cambridge, UK.

Korhonen, A. and T. Briscoe (2004, May 2–May 7). Extended lexical-semantic classification of English verbs. In D. Moldovan and R. Girju (Eds.), *HLT-NAACL 2004: Workshop on Computational Lexical Semantics*, Boston, Massachusetts, USA, pp. 38–45. Association for Computational Linguistics.

Korhonen, A., Y. Krymolowski, and T. Briscoe (2006). A large subcategorization lexicon for Natural Language Processing Applications. In *Proceedings of the Fifth International Conference on Language Resources and Evaluation (LREC 2006). Genoa.*

Koster, C.H.A. (1991). Affix grammars for natural languages. In *Attribute Grammars,*

Applications and Systems, International Summer School SAGA. Prague, Volume 545 of *Lecture Notes in Computer Science*.

Koster, C.H.A. (2005). Constructing a parser for Latin. In *Computational Linguistics and Intelligent Text Processing*, Lecture Notes in Computer Science, Berlin/Heidelberg, pp. 48–59. Springer.

Krauwer, S. (1998). ELSNET and ELRA: A common past and a common future. *ELRA Newsletter 3*(2), 4–5.

Krauwer, S. (2003). The Basic Language Resource Kit (BLARK) as the First Milestone for the Language Resources Roadmap. In *Proceedings of the 2003 International Workshop Speech and Computer (SPECOM 2003)*, pp. 8–15. Moscow State Linguistic University.

Lakusta, L. and B. Landau (2005). Starting at the end: the importance of goals in spatial language. *Cognition 96*, 1–33.

Lehmann, C. (1983). Latin preverbs and cases. In H. Pinkster (Ed.), *New studies in Latin Linguistics: selected papers from the International Colloquium on Latin Linguistics, 1981*, Amsterdam/Philadelphia, pp. 144–165. John Benjamins.

Lenci, A. (2008). Distributional semantics in linguistic and cognitive research. A foreword. *Italian Journal of Linguistics 20*, 1–31.

Lenci, A., B. McGillivray, S. Montemagni, and V. Pirrelli (2008). Unsupervised acquisition of verb subcategorization frames from shallow-parsed corpora. In *Proceedings of the 6th Language Resources and Evaluation Conference (LREC 2008). Marrakech*, pp. 3000–3006. European Language Resources Association.

Lenci, A., S. Montemagni, and V. Pirrelli (2005). *Testo e computer. Elementi di linguistica computazionale*. Roma: Carocci.

Leumann, M., A. Szantyr, W. Otto, and J.B. Hofmann (1965). *Lateinische Grammatik*. Munich: Beck.

Levin, B. (1993). *English Verb Classes and Alternations*. The University of Chicago Press.

Levin, B. and M. Rappaport Hovav (2005). *Argument Realization*. Cambridge: Cambridge University Press.

Lewis, C.T. and C. Short (1879). *A Latin Dictionary, Founded on Andrews' edition of Freund's Latin dictionary revised, enlarged, and in great part rewritten by Charlton T. Lewis, Ph.D. and Charles Short, LL.D.* Oxford: Clarendon Press. url: http://www.lib.uchicago.edu/efts/PERSEUS/Reference/lewisandshort.html.

Li, H. and N. Abe (1998). Generalizing case frames using a thesaurus and the MDL principle. *Computational Linguistics 24*(2), 217–244.

Lightfoot, D. (2006). *How new languages emerge*. Cambridge: Cambridge University Press.

Löfstedt, E. (1956). *Syntactica* (2nd ed.). Lund.

Longrée, D. (2005). Verbes préfixés et concurrences syntaxiques chez Tacite. In C. Moussy (Ed.), *La composition et la préverbation en latin*, pp. 293–307. Presses de l'Université Paris-Sorbonne.

López Moreda, S. (1998). Interferencias semántico-sintácticas entre preverbios y preposiciones. In B. García-Hernández (Ed.), *Estudios de Lingüística latina. Actas del IX Coloquio Internacional de Lingüística latina. Universidad Autonóma de Madrid, 1997*, pp. 953–969. Ediciones Clásicas.

Luraghi, S. (1998). Omission of the direct object in Classical Latin. *Indogermanische Forschungen 102*, 239–257.

Luraghi, S. (2010). The rise (and possible downfall) of configurationality. In S. Luraghi and V. Bubenik (Eds.), *Continuum Companion to Historical Linguistics*, pp. 212–229. London/New York: Continuum.

MacDonell, A.A. (1953). *A Vedic grammar for students*. Bombay/Calcutta/Madras: Oxford University.

Marcus, M., B. Santorini, and M.A. Marcinkiewicz (1993). Building a large annotated corpus of English: The Penn Treebank. *Computational Linguistics 19*(2), 313–330.

Masini, F. (2005). Multi-word expressions between syntax and the lexicon: the case of Italian verb-particle constructions. *SKY journal of linguistics 18*, 145–173.

MathWorks Inc., T. (2004). Matlab [7.0].

Mayer-Schönberger, V. and K. Cukier (2013). *Big Data*. London: John Murray.

Mayrhofer, M. (1980). *Zur Gestaltung des etymologischen Wörterbuchs einer "Großcorpus-Sprache"*. Wien: Österr. Akademie der Wissenschaften. Phil-Hist. Klasse.

McCarthy, D. (2001). *Lexical acquisition at the syntax-semantics interface: diathesis alternations, subcategorization frames and selectional preferences*. Ph. D. thesis, University of Sussex.

McEnery, T. and A. Wilson (2001). *Corpus linguistics. An introduction*. Edinburgh: Edinburgh University Press.

McGillivray, B. (2012). Latin preverbs and verb argument structure: new insights from new methods. In J. Barðdal, M. Cennamo, and E. van Gelderen (Eds.), *Argument Structure: the Naples/Capri Papers*, Studies in Language Companion Series. John Benjamins.

McGillivray, B. and A. Kilgarriff (2013). Tools for historical corpus research, and a corpus of Latin. In P. Bennett, M. Durrell, S. Scheible, and R.J. Whitt (Eds.), *New Methods in Historical Corpus Linguistics*, Volume 3 of *Corpus Linguistics and Interdisciplinary Perspectives on Language*, Tübingen. Narr.

McGillivray, B. and M. Passarotti (2012). Accessing and using a corpus-driven latin valency lexicon. In *Proceedings of The 16th International Colloquium on Latin Linguistics*, Uppsala.

McGillivray, B., M. Passarotti, and P. Ruffolo (2009). The *Index Thomisticus* Treebank Project: Annotation, Parsing and Valency Lexicon. *TAL 50*(2), 103–127.

Meillet, A. and J. Vendryes (1963). *Traité de grammaire comparée des langues classiques*. Paris: Librairie Ancienne Honoré Champion.

Meini, L. and B. McGillivray (2010). Between semantics and syntax: spatial verbs and prepositions in Latin. In *Proceedings of the Space in Language Conference, Pisa October 8–10 2009*, Pisa.

Mellado Rodríguez, J. (2001). Determinación sintáctica y determinación semántica: diferencias y repercusión en algunas proposiciones latinas. In C. Moussy (Ed.), *De lingua latina novae quaestiones. Actes du Xè Colloque International de Linguistique Latine. Paris-Sèvres, 1999*, pp. 459–472. Peeters.

Mel'čuk, I. (1988). *Dependency Syntax: Theory and Practice*. Albany: State University of New York Press.

Miller, G.A., R. Beckwith, C. Fellbaum, D. Gross, and K.J. Miller (1990). Introduction to WordNet: an on-line lexical database. *International Journal of Lexicography 3*(4), 235–244.

Milroy, J. (1993). On the social origins of language change. In C. Jones (Ed.), *Historical linguistics: Problems and perspectives*, pp. 215–236. London: Longman.

Minozzi, S. (2009). The Latin WordNet Project. In P. Anreiter and M. Kienpointner (Eds.), *Proceedings of the 15th International Colloquium on Latin Linguistics (ICLL)*, Innsbrucker Beitraege zur Sprachwissenschaft, Innsbruck.

Mosteller, F. (1968). Association and estimation in contingency tables. *Journal of the American Statistical Association 321*(63), 1–28.

Moussy, C. (Ed.) (2005). *La composition et la préverbation en latin*. Presses de l'Université Paris-Sorbonne.

Oniga, R. (2005). Composition et préverbation en latin: problèmes de typologie. In C. Moussy (Ed.), *La composition et la préverbation en latin*, pp. 211–227. Presses de l'Université Paris-Sorbonne.

Passarotti, M. (2007a). LEMLAT. Uno strumento per la lemmatizzazione morfologica automatica del latino. In F. Citti and T. Del Vecchio (Eds.), *From Manuscript to Digital Text. Problems of Interpretation and Markup. Proceedings of the Colloquium (Bologna, June 12th 2003). Roma*, pp. 107–128.

Passarotti, M. (2007b). Verso il Lessico Tomistico Biculturale. La treebank dell'*Index Thomisticus*. In R. Petrilli and D. Femia (Eds.), *Il filo del discorso. Intrecci testuali, articolazioni linguistiche, composizioni logiche. Atti del XIII Congresso Nazionale della Società di Filosofia del Linguaggio. Viterbo*, pp. 187–205.

Passarotti, M. (2010). Leaving Behind the Less-Resourced Status. The Case of Latin through the Experience of the Index Thomisticus Treebank. In *Proceedings of the 7th SaLTMiL Workshop on Creation and Use of Basic Lexical Resources for Less-Resourced Languages", LREC 2010, La Valletta, Malta, 23 May 2010*, pp. 27–32.

Passarotti, M. (2013). When Praguian Functionalism Meets Latin. From Analytical to Tectogrammatical Annotation of Latin Syntax. In *Proceedings of the International Conference on Linguistics and Classical Languages (LCL), 17–19 February 2011, University of Roma Tre, Roma, Italy*.

Passarotti, M. and F. Dell'Orletta (2010). Improvements in Parsing the *Index Thomisti-*

cus Treebank. Revision, Combination and a Feature Model for Medieval Latin. In *Proceedings of the Seventh International Conference on Language Resources and Evaluation (LREC 2010). May 19–21, 2010, La Valletta, Malta*, pp. 1964–1971. European Language Resources Association (ELRA).

Passarotti, M., B. McGillivray, and D. Bamman (2012). A treebank-based Study on Latin Word Order. In *Proceedings of The 16th International Colloquium on Latin Linguistics*, Uppsala.

Passarotti, M. and P. Ruffolo (2009). Parsing the *Index Thomisticus Treebank*. Some preliminary results. In P. Anreiter and M. Kienpointner (Eds.), *Proceedings of the 15th International Colloquium on Latin Linguistics*, Innsbrucker Beiträge zur Sprachwissenschaft, Innsbruck.

Pinkster, H. (1990). *Latin Syntax and Semantics*. London: Routledge.

Pinkster, H. (2010). The use of the dative with Latin compounds. *STUF 63*, 32–43.

Piotrowski, M. (2012). *Natural Language Processing for Historical Texts*. Synthesis Lectures on Human Language Technologies. Morgan & Claypool Publishers.

Poccetti, P., D. Poli, and C. Santini (1999). *Una storia della lingua latina*. Roma: Carocci.

R Development Core Team (2008). *R: A Language and Environment for Statistical Computing*. Vienna: R Foundation for Statistical Computing. ISBN 3-900051-07-0.

Rasinger, S.M. (2008). *Quantitative research in linguistics*. London/New York: Continuum.

Resnik, P. (1997). Selectional preference and sense disambiguation. In *Proceedings of the ACL SIGLEX Workshop on Tagging Text with Lexical Semantics: Why What and How?*, Washington, pp. 79–86.

Richens, T. (2008). Anomalies in the WordNet Verb Hierarchy. In *Proceedings of the 22nd International Conference on Computational Linguistics* (*Coling 2008*), pp. 729–736.

Rohlfs, G. (1970). *Grammatica storica della lingua italiana e dei suoi dialetti* (Italian ed.). Giulio Einaudi. translated by Temistocle Franceschi and Maria Caciagli Fancelli.

Romagno, D. (2004). Ancora su preverbazione e sistemi verbali: il caso dei preverbi greci. *Archivio Glottologico Italiano 89*, 165–180.

Rosén, H. (1999). *Latine loqui. Trends and directions in the crystallization of Classical Latin*. München: Fink.

Rousseau, A. (Ed.) (1995). *Les Préverbes dans les langues d'Europe: introduction à l'étude de la préverbation*, Lille. Presses Universitaires du Septentrion.

Sahlgren, M. (2008). The distributional hypothesis. *Rivista di Linguistica 20*(1), 33–53.

Salvi, G. and L. Vanelli (1992). *Grammatica essenziale di riferimento della lingua italiana*. Istituto Geografico De Agostini. Le Monnier.

Schmid, G. (1994). TreeTagger—a language independent part-of-speech tagger. Available at http://www.ims.uni-stuttgart.de/Tools/DecisionTreeTagger.html.

Schmid, H. (1995). Improvements in Part-of-Speech Tagging with an Application to German. In *Proceedings of the ACL SIGDAT-Workshop*, pp. 47–50.

Schulte im Walde, S. (2003). *Experiments on the automatic induction of German semantic verb classes*. Ph. D. thesis, Institut für Maschinelle Sprachverarbeitung, Universität Stuttgart.

Schwegler, A. (1990). *Analyticity and Syntheticity: A Diachronic Perspective with Special Reference to Romance Languages*. Berlin: Mouton de Gruyter.

Sgall, P., E. Hajicová, and J. Panevová (1986). *The Meaning of the Sentence in its Semantic and Pragmatic Aspects*. D. Reidel, Dordrecht, NL.

Simone, R. (1997). Esistono verbi sintagmatici in italiano? In T. De Mauro and V. Lo Cascio (Eds.), *Lessico e grammatica. Teorie linguistiche e applicazioni lessicografiche*, pp. 155–170. Roma: Bulzoni.

Simone, R. (2008). I verbi sintagmatici come costruzione e come categoria. In M. Cini (Ed.), *I verbi sintagmatici in italiano e nelle varietà dialettali. Stato dell'arte e prospettive di ricerca. Atti delle giornate di studio Torino, 19–20 febbraio 2007*, Frankfurt am Main. Peter Lang.

Sinha, C. and T. Kuteva (1995). Distributed spatial semantics. *Nordic Journal of Linguistics 18*, 167–199.

Slobin, D.I. (2004). The many ways to search for a frog: linguistic typology and the expression of motion events. In S. Strömqvist and L. Verhoeven (Eds.), *Relating events in narrative*, Volume 2. Typological and contextual perspective, pp. 219–257. Mahwah, NJ: Lawrence Erlbaum Associates.

Stefanowitsch, A. and A. Rohde (2004). The goal bias in the encoding of motion events. In K.-U. Panther and G. Radden (Eds.), *Motivation in Grammar*, pp. 249–268. Berlin/New York: Mouton de Gruyter.

Stolova, N.I. (2008). From satellite-framed Latin to verb-framed Romance: Late Latin as an intermediate stage. In R. Wright (Ed.), *Latin vulgaire–latin tardif VIII: actes du VIIIe Colloque international sur le latin vulgaire et tardif, Oxford, 6–9 septembre 2006*, Hildesheim/New York, pp. 253–262. Olms-Weidmann.

Sweetser, E. (1988). Grammaticalization and semantic bleaching. In S. Axmaker, A. Jaisser, and H. Singmaster (Eds.), *Grammaticalization, Proceedings of the fourteenth annual meeting of the Berkeley Linguistics Society, 13–15 February 1988*, Berkeley, pp. 389–405. Berkeley Linguistic Society.

Talmy, L. (1991). Path to realization: a typology of event conflation. In *Proceedings of the 17th Annaul Meeting of the Berkeley Linguistics Society*, Volume 17, Berkeley, CA, pp. 480–591. Berkeley Linguistic Society.

Talmy, L. (2000). *Toward a cognitive semantics*, Volume II. Bradford Books.

Tekavčić, P. (1972). *Grammatica storica dell'italiano*, Volume II Morfosintassi; III Lessico. Bologna: Il Mulino.

Tesnière, L. (1959). *Éléments de syntaxe structurale*. Paris: Klincksieck.

Tognini-Bonelli, E. (2001). *Corpus Linguistics at work*. Amsterdam/Philadelphia: John Benjamins.

Traina, A. (1999). *Forma e suono da Plauto a Pascoli*. Bologna: Pàtron.

Traina, A. and T. Bertotti (1993). *Sintassi normativa della lingua latina*. Cappelli.

Tukey, J.W. (1977). *Exploratory Data Analysis*. Reading, MA: Addison-Wesley.

Untermann, J. (1983). Indogermanische Restsprachen als Gegenstand der Indogermanistik. In E. Vineis (Ed.), *Le lingue indoeuropee di frammentaria attestazione. Die indogermanischen Restsprachen. Atti del convegno della Societa italiana di glottologia e della Indogermanische Gesellschaft. Udine, 22–24 settembre 1981*, Pisa, pp. 11–28. Società Italiana di Glottologia: Giardini.

Väänänen, V. (1971). *Introduzione al latino volgare*. Bologna: Pàtron.

Vicario, F. (1997). *I verbi analitici in friulano*. Milano: Franco Angeli.

Vincent, N. (1997). Synthetic and analytic structures. In M. Maiden and Parry (Eds.), *Dialects of Italy*. London: Routledge.

Vincent, N. (1999). The evolution of c-structure: prepositions and PPs from Indo-European to Romance. *Linguistics 37*, 1111–1154.

Viti, C. (2008). From space words to transitive markers: the case of ancient Greek en 'in'. *Transactions of the Philological Society 106*(3), 375–413.

Vlachos, A., A. Korhonen, and Z. Ghahramani (2009). Unsupervised and Constrained Dirichlet Process Mixture Models for Verb Clustering. In *Proceedings of the EACL workshop on Geometrical Models of Natural Language Semantics*, Athens, pp. 74–82.

Wälchli, B. (2000). A typology of displacement (with special reference to Latvian). *Sprachtypologie und Universalienforschung 54*(3), 298–323.

Wu, Z. and M. Palmer (1994). Verb semantics and lexical selection. In *Proceedings of the 32nd Annual Meeting of the Association for Computational Linguistics*, pp. 133–138.

Index

 | DOI: 10.1163/9789004260122_011

www.ingramcontent.com/pod-product-compliance
Lightning Source LLC
LaVergne TN
LVHW010642300926
849161LV00005B/1019
9789004260115